Media Laws and Ethics

Understanding Legal Framework and Ethical Considerations

Media Laws and Ethics

Understanding Legal Framework and Ethical Considerations

Dr. Saima Pervez
Assistant Professor, Delhi Metropolitan Education,
Noida

The Readers Paradise
New Delhi - 110002

Media Laws and Ethics

Understanding Legal Framework and Ethical Considerations

Dr. Saima Pervez

Ist edition in India

ISBN - 978-93-5977-174-8

Published by

THE READERS PARADISE

103, 4787/23, Ansari Road, Daryaganj,
New Delhi - 110002
Phone - 011-23246222, 9811197091, 9312220441
e-mail : thereadersparadisesales@gmail.com
Website - www.thereadersparadise.com

Price - Rs. 1695.00
Pages - 246 | paper - 80gsm | Size - 7.5x9.5

Typesetting by
Sanya Computers, Bhajanpura, Delhi

Cover Design by
Shri Sai Printographers, Mukherjee Nagar, Delhi - 110009

Printed in India
Trident Enterprises, Noida

Preface

In the realm of information dissemination and public discourse, the media plays a pivotal role, shaping perceptions, influencing societal norms, and holding power accountable. Within this context, media laws and ethics operate as a delicate balance, ensuring the fundamental right to freedom of expression while protecting individual rights, maintaining public order, and upholding ethical standards. Understanding this intricate framework is crucial for media professionals, legal practitioners, and informed citizens alike.

Law and ethics, though often intertwined, represent distinct spheres of guidance. Law, embodied in a system of statutes and regulations, establishes enforceable rules of conduct that govern society. It defines offenses, establishes penalties, and provides mechanisms for dispute resolution. Ethics, on the other hand, encompasses a set of moral principles and values that guide individual behavior. It reflects societal norms, professional standards, and personal conscience. In the context of media, laws provide the legal framework within which media organizations and professionals operate, defining their rights and responsibilities. Ethical principles, on the other hand, serve as a moral compass, guiding decision-making and ensuring responsible journalism practices.

The Indian Constitution, the supreme law of the land, stands as a beacon of freedom and justice. Article 19(1)(a) enshrines freedom of speech and expression as a fundamental right, extending this protection to the press. This right empowers the media to function independently, inform the public without undue government interference, and hold power accountable. However, this right is not absolute. Article 19(2) outlines reasonable restrictions that can be imposed in the interest of public order, morality, decency, or to protect the reputation or rights of others. These restrictions are further defined and elaborated in various laws, including the Press Council Act, 1978; the Indian Penal Code, 1860; the Information Technology Act, 2000; and the Cable Television Networks (Regulation) Act, 1995.

Defamation, sedition, and contempt of court are three legal concepts that often arise in the context of media coverage. Defamation involves making false statements that damage an individual's reputation. Media professionals must exercise due diligence to ensure the accuracy of their reporting and avoid making defamatory statements. Sedition, a more serious offense, involves inciting violence or disaffection against the government. Media professionals must be mindful of their language and avoid using rhetoric that could be construed as seditious. Contempt of court refers to any act that interferes with the administration of justice. Media professionals must respect the court proceedings and avoid publishing anything that could prejudice a fair trial or undermine the authority of the court.

Beyond the general principles of criminal law, specific media laws and regulations provide additional guidance for media operations. These laws aim to promote responsible journalism, protect individual rights, and maintain public order. The Press Council Act, 1978, establishes the Press Council of India, a quasi-judicial body that oversees the press and promotes ethical standards. The Information Technology Act, 2000, regulates online content and intermediaries, addressing issues such as cybercrime, obscenity, and hate speech. The Cable Television Networks (Regulation) Act, 1995, regulates the content and operation of cable television networks.

Intellectual property rights (IPR) are crucial for safeguarding creativity and innovation in the media industry. Copyright protects original works of authorship, such as literary and artistic creations, while trademarks protect distinctive signs used to identify goods or services. Media organizations must be aware of IPR laws and ensure that they do not infringe upon the rights of others. This includes obtaining proper licenses for using copyrighted material and respecting trademarks to avoid infringement lawsuits.

To ensure compliance with media laws and regulations, various regulatory bodies play a crucial role. These bodies include the Press Council of India, the Ministry of Information and Broadcasting, and the Central Board of Film Certification. These bodies issue guidelines and regulations, monitor media content, and take action against violations. They also provide a mechanism for redressal for individuals or organizations aggrieved by media coverage.

The interplay of media laws and ethics in India is a dynamic and evolving field, constantly adapting to new technologies, societal changes, and legal developments. Understanding this framework is essential for media professionals to operate responsibly, for legal practitioners to provide sound counsel, and for informed citizens to engage critically with the media landscape. By upholding ethical principles, adhering to legal boun daries, and adapting to the changing media environment, we can ensure that the media fulfills.

—Author

Contents

Introduction

Significance of Media Laws and Ethics

The role of the media in the 21st century is tremendously significant. A day without social media is not acceptable for a majority of people. Social media has become a part of life for people of all ages and different backgrounds. From providing information to entertaining people, the media has an immense power to shape the minds of the viewers, which constitutes a major population of the society.

Media law determines what can be published and be broadcasted. Censorship, privacy, intellectual property, defamation tort, etc, come under media law; it is a combination of multiple laws and ethics which is an important element for the media industry and journalism. The law draws a line on how the journalists must work, how the companies and organizations must operate, and what is to be published.

In India, there was no such restriction on media until the British Government started constraining the newspapers. In 1780, James Augustus Hicky started Hicky's Bengal Gazette, the first newspaper in India. In 1872, it was seized as it questioned the functioning of the government. The Company introduced the Gagging Act for the license to run or own a printing press. They strictly refrained their workers from maintaining a connection with the press. After attaining Independence, more rules and regulations have been enacted and the old ones amended for the new formed territory.

The Constitution of India does not have a provision specifically for freedom of media. But Article 19 (1) (A), which grants the freedom of speech and expression, is a provision for mass media. Article 19 (2) of the Constitution also imposes certain 'reasonable' restrictions to the freedom of media. Media has no special right that is deprived of the commoners. The editors and journalists of the agencies are after all citizens of the country and are utilizing their right to expression through a medium.

The Ministry of Electronics and Information Technology has announced the Information Technology (Intermediary Guidelines and Digital Media Ethics Code) Rules, 2021. These new rules deal with the provisions of social media, over-the-top (OTT) platforms, and digital news. The rules seek to provide conformity of law and a problem-solving mechanism for users of social media platforms, messaging applications, streaming services, and digital news publishers. The Government is doing it so as to control hate speech which spreads through the platforms and threatens national security. Recently, the Foundation for Independent Journalism, the publisher of social media platform 'The Wire', filed a petition regarding the Information Technology Rules. The petition pleaded the IT Rules as being 'ultra vires' of the IT Act, 2000 as they set up a classification of 'publishers of news and current affairs content' as a section of 'digital media'.

The Press Council is an authority created by the Press Council Act of 1978. It is the apex authority for the regulation of print media in India. They define and determine the standards of media. They resolve complaints and cases regarding the press for violating ethics and freedom of the press. An editor or a journalist of an agency can complain to the PCI about any professional misconduct or violation of journalistic ethics by another editor or journalist. But their power is restricted on the print media and has no power to enforce the rules and regulations on electronic radio, ie, television, radio, social media, etc.

Media ethics is a subsection of applied ethics that deals with ethical principles and media standards. Being ethical does not mean being passive, but being dynamic. They criticize the government society constructively to make them better. Journalists, reporters, and news providing agencies are accountable not only to their convictions but also to their viewers and readers. They have a responsibility that is binding via contract to the media and their organization. They have a social responsibility to the public regarding the authenticity of the content they provide. The content providers have a responsibility to comply with the legal system of their nation along with respecting the international public by respecting the universal laws.

The main objective of journalism is to provide news and information to society on matters of public interest in a just, accurate, unbiased, appropriate manner. Publicizing wrong, inaccurate, misleading content should be avoided. Newspapers must not publish any defamatory or libelous content against any person or organization unless, after proper research and checking, have sufficient reason to believe that it is fact and that publication of the content will be for the public good. Intruding or invading the privacy of an individual is not acceptable unless it is outweighed by genuine public interest. The private life, even of a public figure is intimate. Exposing and/or invading their privacy is not acceptable unless there are proper reasons to believe that it is a fact. Regarding communal disputes and riots, provocative and rousing headlines should be avoided. Headlines must justify the content printed under it and headlines containing claims should either identify the source or at least carry quotation marks. While reporting issues that involve crimes like rape, abduction, or sexual assault on children, that raise doubts regarding the chastity, character, and privacy of women, the names, photographs, or the victims or other particulars leading to their identity should not be published. As publicizing those details serves no legitimate purpose, it may bring social exclusion to the victim and social embarrassment to their relations, family, friends, community, religious order, or the institution to which they belong.

Global Perspective on Media Laws and Ethics

Media, often referred to as the "Fourth Estate," plays a pivotal role in democratic societies worldwide. It serves as a watchdog, holding those in power accountable, and acts as a conduit for information dissemination. However, the responsible exercise of this power necessitates a framework of laws and ethical guidelines. The global perspective on media laws and ethics is a dynamic and multifaceted subject, reflecting diverse cultural, political, and legal contexts.

Media Laws: A Varied Landscape

Media laws differ significantly from one country to another, reflecting the unique sociopolitical environments in which they operate. These laws encompass a wide range of aspects, including freedom of speech, defamation, privacy, copyright, and national security. While some nations prioritize robust protections for press freedom, others may impose restrictions to varying degrees, often balancing the need for a free press with concerns over national security and public order.

- Press Freedom and Freedom of Expression: Countries such as the United States enshrine a strong protection for freedom of expression in their constitutions. The First Amendment of the U.S. Constitution, for example, guarantees the right to freedom of speech and of the press. This allows journalists to operate with a considerable degree of independence and report on matters of public interest without fear of government interference.
- Defamation and Libel Laws: Defamation laws vary widely across the globe. In some countries, a strict liability approach is taken, making it easier for individuals or organizations to sue for defamation. In others, a stronger emphasis is placed on proving actual malice or false statements made with knowledge of their falsity or with reckless disregard for the truth.
- Privacy Laws: Media laws also address the delicate balance between the public's right to know and an individual's right to privacy. This is especially relevant in cases involving the publication of private information, images, or footage without consent.
- Copyright and Intellectual Property: Intellectual property laws safeguard the rights of creators and publishers. They regulate the use and reproduction of copyrighted material, ensuring that media organizations and journalists adhere to legal standards when utilizing third-party content.
- National Security and Classified Information: Governments often enact laws to protect national security interests, regulating the dissemination of classified or

sensitive information. Balancing the need for transparency with the imperative to safeguard national security is a continual challenge in this area.

Ethical Considerations in Media: Universal Principles

In addition to legal frameworks, media practitioners are guided by ethical principles that transcend national borders. These principles are rooted in the pursuit of truth, accuracy, fairness, and the public's right to know. Key ethical considerations include:

- Accuracy and Truthfulness: Upholding accuracy in reporting is a fundamental ethical duty for journalists. Verifying information and providing context ensures that the public is well-informed.
- Fairness and Impartiality: Journalists are expected to present a balanced view of events, giving all relevant parties an opportunity to provide their perspective.
- Independence and Objectivity: Maintaining independence from political, commercial, or ideological influences is crucial to ensure that reporting remains unbiased and free from undue influence.
- Avoiding Harm and Sensationalism: Ethical journalism prioritizes the well-being of individuals and communities. This means exercising caution when reporting on sensitive or potentially harmful topics.
- Respecting Privacy and Dignity: Journalists must be mindful of individuals' rights to privacy, treating subjects with respect and dignity, and obtaining consent when appropriate.

Global Challenges and Emerging Trends

While there are universal principles that underpin media ethics, the evolving digital landscape and the rise of social media platforms have brought about new challenges. Issues such as misinformation, disinformation, online harassment, and the proliferation of user-generated content have sparked debates about how to adapt existing ethical guidelines to the digital age.

1

Concept of Law and Ethics

Understanding Law and Ethics

Law

Law is a set of rules that are created and are enforceable by social or governmental institutions to regulate behavior, with its precise definition a matter of longstanding debate. It has been variously described as a science and as the art of justice. State-enforced laws can be made by a group legislature or by a single legislator, resulting in statutes; by the executive through decrees and regulations; or established by judges through precedent, usually in common law jurisdictions. Private individuals may create legally binding contracts, including arbitration agreements that adopt alternative ways of resolving disputes to standard court litigation. The creation of laws themselves may be influenced by a constitution, written or tacit, and the rights encoded therein. The law shapes politics, economics, history and society in various ways and also serves as a mediator of relations between people.

Legal systems vary between jurisdictions, with their differences analysed in comparative law. In civil law jurisdictions, a legislature or other central body codifies and consolidates the law. In common law systems, judges may make binding case law through precedent, although on occasion this may be overturned by a higher court or the legislature. Historically, religious law has influenced secular matters and is, as of the 21st century, still in use in some religious communities. Sharia law based on Islamic principles is used as the primary legal system in several countries, including Iran and Saudi Arabia.

The scope of law can be divided into two domains: public law concerns government and society, including constitutional law, administrative law, and criminal law; while private law deals with legal disputes between parties in areas such as contracts, property, torts, delicts and commercial law. This distinction is stronger in civil law countries, particularly those with a separate system of administrative courts; by contrast, the public-private law divide is less pronounced in common law jurisdictions.

Law provides a source of scholarly inquiry into legal history, philosophy, economic analysis and sociology. Law also raises important and complex issues concerning equality, fairness, and justice.

Philosophy of Law

The philosophy of law is commonly known as jurisprudence. Normative jurisprudence asks "what should law be?", while analytic jurisprudence asks "what is law?"

Analytical Jurisprudence

There have been several attempts to produce "a universally acceptable definition of law". In 1972, Baron Hampstead suggested that no such definition could be produced. McCoubrey and White said that the question "what is law?" has no simple answer. Glanville Williams said that the meaning of the word "law" depends on the context in which that word is used. He said that, for example, "early customary law" and "municipal law" were contexts where the word "law" had two different and irreconcilable meanings. Thurman Arnold said that it is obvious that it is impossible to define the word "law" and that it is also equally obvious that the struggle to define that word should not ever be abandoned. It is possible to take the view that there is no need to define the word "law" (e.g. "let's forget about generalities and get down to cases").

One definition is that law is a system of rules and guidelines which are enforced through social institutions to govern behaviour. In *The Concept of Law,* H. L. A. Hart argued that law is a "system of rules"; John Austin said law was "the command of a sovereign, backed by the threat of a sanction"; Ronald Dworkin describes law as an "interpretive concept" to achieve justice in his text titled *Law's Empire*; and Joseph Raz argues law is an "authority" to mediate people's interests. Oliver Wendell Holmes defined law as "the prophecies of what the courts will do in fact, and nothing more pretentious." In his *Treatise on Law,* Thomas Aquinas argues that law is a rational ordering of things, which concern the common good, that is promulgated by whoever is charged with the care of the community. This definition has both positivist and naturalist elements.

Connection to Morality and Justice

Definitions of law often raise the question of the extent to which law incorporates morality. John Austin's utilitarian answer was that law is "commands, backed by threat of sanctions, from a sovereign, to whom people have a habit of obedience". Natural lawyers, on the other hand, such as Jean-Jacques Rousseau, argue that law reflects essentially moral and unchangeable laws of nature. The concept of "natural law" emerged in ancient Greek philosophy concurrently and in connection with the notion of justice, and re-entered the mainstream of Western culture through the writings of Thomas Aquinas, notably his *Treatise on Law.*

Hugo Grotius, the founder of a purely rationalistic system of natural law, argued that law arises from both a social impulse—as Aristotle had indicated—and reason. Immanuel Kant believed a moral imperative requires laws "be chosen as though they should hold as universal laws of nature". Jeremy Bentham and his student Austin, following David Hume, believed that this conflated the "is" and what "ought to be" problem. Bentham and Austin argued for law's positivism; that real law is entirely separate from "morality". Kant was also criticised by Friedrich Nietzsche, who rejected the principle of equality, and believed that law emanates from the will to power, and cannot be labeled as "moral" or "immoral".

In 1934, the Austrian philosopher Hans Kelsen continued the positivist tradition in his book the *Pure Theory of Law*. Kelsen believed that although law is separate from morality, it is endowed with "normativity", meaning we ought to obey it. While laws are positive "is" statements (e.g. the fine for reversing on a highway *is* •500); law tells us what we "should" do. Thus, each legal system can be hypothesised to have a basic norm (*Grundnorm*) instructing us to obey. Kelsen's major opponent, Carl Schmitt, rejected both positivism and the idea of the rule of law because he did not accept the primacy of abstract normative principles over concrete political positions and decisions. Therefore, Schmitt advocated a jurisprudence of the exception (state of emergency), which denied that legal norms could encompass all of the political experience.

Later in the 20th century, H. L. A. Hart attacked Austin for his simplifications and Kelsen for his fictions in *The Concept of Law*. Hart argued law is a system of rules, divided into primary (rules of conduct) and secondary ones (rules addressed to officials to administer primary rules). Secondary rules are further divided into rules of adjudication (to resolve legal disputes), rules of change (allowing laws to be varied) and the rule of recognition (allowing laws to be identified as valid). Two of Hart's students continued the debate: In his book *Law's Empire*, Ronald Dworkin attacked Hart and the positivists for their refusal to treat law as a moral issue. Dworkin argues that law is an "interpretive concept" that requires judges to find the best fitting and most just solution to a legal dispute, given their Anglo-American constitutional traditions. Joseph Raz, on the other hand, defended the positivist outlook and criticised Hart's "soft social thesis" approach in *The Authority of Law*. Raz argues that law is authority, identifiable purely through social sources and without reference to moral reasoning. In his view, any categorisation of rules beyond their role as authoritative instruments in mediation are best left to sociology, rather than jurisprudence.

History

The history of law links closely to the development of civilization. Ancient Egyptian law, dating as far back as 3000 BC, was based on the concept of Ma'at and characterised by tradition, rhetorical speech, social equality and impartiality. By the 22nd century BC, the ancient Sumerian ruler Ur-Nammu had formulated the first law code, which consisted of casuistic statements ("if ... then ..."). Around 1760 BC, King Hammurabi further developed Babylonian law, by codifying and inscribing it in stone. Hammurabi placed several copies of his law code throughout the kingdom of Babylon as stelae, for the entire public to see; this became known as the Codex Hammurabi. The most intact copy of these stelae was discovered in the 19th century by British Assyriologists, and has since been fully transliterated and translated into various languages, including English, Italian, German, and French.

The Old Testament dates back to 1280 BC and takes the form of moral imperatives as recommendations for a good society. The small Greek city-state, ancient Athens, from about the 8th century BC was the first society to be based on broad inclusion of its citizenry, excluding women and enslaved people. However, Athens had no legal science or single word for "law", relying instead on the three-way distinction between divine law (*thémis*), human decree (*nomos*) and custom (*díkç*). Yet Ancient Greek law contained major constitutional innovations in the development of democracy.

Roman law was heavily influenced by Greek philosophy, but its detailed rules were developed by professional jurists and were highly sophisticated. Over the centuries between the rise and decline of the Roman Empire, law was adapted to cope with the changing social situations and underwent major codification under Theodosius II and Justinian I. Although codes were replaced by custom and case law during the Early Middle Ages, Roman law was rediscovered around the 11th century when medieval legal scholars began to research Roman codes and adapt their concepts to the canon law, giving birth to the *jus commune*. Latin legal maxims (called brocards) were compiled for guidance. In medieval England, royal courts developed a body of precedent which later became the common law. A Europe-wide Law Merchant was formed so that merchants could trade with common standards of practice rather than with the many splintered facets of local laws. The Law Merchant, a precursor to modern commercial law, emphasised the freedom to contract and alienability of property. As nationalism grew in the 18th and 19th centuries, the Law Merchant was incorporated into countries' local law under new civil codes. The Napoleonic and German Codes became the most influential. In contrast to English common law, which consists of enormous tomes of case law, codes in small books are easy to export and easy for judges to apply. However, today there are signs that civil and common law are converging. EU law is codified in treaties, but develops through *de facto* precedent laid down by the European Court of Justice.

Ancient India and China represent distinct traditions of law, and have historically had independent schools of legal theory and practice. The *Arthashastra*, probably compiled around 100 AD (although it contains older material), and the *Manusmriti* (c. 100–300 AD) were foundational treatises in India, and comprise texts considered authoritative legal guidance. Manu's central philosophy was tolerance and pluralism, and was cited across Southeast Asia. During the Muslim conquests in the Indian subcontinent, sharia was established by the Muslim sultanates and empires, most notably Mughal Empire's Fatawa-e-Alamgiri, compiled by emperor Aurangzeb and various scholars of Islam. In India, the Hindu legal tradition, along with Islamic law, were both supplanted by common law when India became part of the British Empire. Malaysia, Brunei, Singapore and Hong Kong also adopted the common law system. The eastern Asia legal tradition reflects a unique blend of secular and religious influences. Japan was the first country to begin modernising its legal system along western lines, by importing parts of the French, but mostly the German Civil Code. This partly reflected Germany's status as a rising power in the late 19th century.

Similarly, traditional Chinese law gave way to westernisation towards the final years of the Qing Dynasty in the form of six private law codes based mainly on the Japanese model of German law. Today Taiwanese law retains the closest affinity to the codifications from that period, because of the split between Chiang Kai-shek's nationalists, who fled there, and Mao Zedong's communists who won control of the mainland in 1949. The current legal infrastructure in the People's Republic of China was heavily influenced by Soviet Socialist law, which essentially prioritises administrative law at the expense of private law rights. Due to rapid industrialisation, today China is undergoing a process of reform, at least in terms of economic, if not social and political, rights. A new contract code in 1999 represented a move away from administrative domination. Furthermore, after negotiations lasting fifteen years, in 2001 China joined the World Trade Organization.

Legal Systems

In general, legal systems can be split between civil law and common law systems. Modern scholars argue that the significance of this distinction has progressively declined. The numerous legal transplants, typical of modern law, result in the sharing of many features traditionally considered typical of either common law or civil law. The third type of legal system is religious law, based on scriptures. The specific system that a country is ruled by is often determined by its history, connections with other countries, or its adherence to international standards. The sources that jurisdictions adopt as authoritatively binding are the defining features of any legal system.

Civil Law

Civil law is the legal system used in most countries around the world today. In civil law the sources recognised as authoritative are, primarily, legislation—especially codifications in constitutions or statutes passed by government—and custom. Codifications date back millennia, with one early example being the Babylonian *Codex Hammurabi*. Modern civil law systems essentially derive from legal codes issued by Byzantine Emperor Justinian I in the 6th century, which were rediscovered by 11th century Italy. Roman law in the days of the Roman Republic and Empire was heavily procedural, and lacked a professional legal class. Instead a lay magistrate, *iudex*, was chosen to adjudicate. Decisions were not published in any systematic way, so any case law that developed was disguised and almost unrecognised. Each case was to be decided afresh from the laws of the State, which mirrors the (theoretical) unimportance of judges' decisions for future cases in civil law systems today. From 529 to 534 AD the Byzantine Emperor Justinian I codified and consolidated Roman law up until that point, so that what remained was one-twentieth of the mass of legal texts from before. This became known as the *Corpus Juris Civilis*. As one legal historian wrote, "Justinian consciously looked back to the golden age of Roman law and aimed to restore it to the peak it had reached three centuries before." The Justinian Code remained in force in the East until the fall of the Byzantine Empire. Western Europe, meanwhile, relied on a mix of the Theodosian Code and Germanic customary law until the Justinian Code was rediscovered in the 11th century, which scholars at the University of Bologna used to interpret their own laws. Civil law codifications based closely on Roman law, alongside some influences from religious laws such as canon law, continued to spread throughout Europe until the Enlightenment. Then, in the 19th century, both France, with the *Code Civil*, and Germany, with the *Bürgerliches Gesetzbuch*, modernised their legal codes. Both these codes heavily influenced not only the law systems of the countries in continental Europe, but also the Japanese and Korean legal traditions. Today, countries that have civil law systems range from Russia and Turkey to most of Central and Latin America.

Anarchist and Socialist Law

Anarchist law primarily deals with how anarchism is implemented upon a society, the framework based on decentralized organizations and mutual aid, with representation through a form of direct democracy. Laws being based upon their need. A large portion of anarchist ideologies such as anarcho-syndicalism and anarcho-communism primarily focuses on decentralized worker unions, cooperatives and syndicates as the main instrument of society.

Socialist law is the legal systems in communist states such as the former Soviet Union and the People's Republic of China. Academic opinion is divided on whether it is a separate system from civil law, given major deviations based on Marxist–Leninist ideology, such as subordinating the judiciary to the executive ruling party.

Common Law and Equity

In common law legal systems, decisions by courts are explicitly acknowledged as "law" on equal footing with legislative statutes and executive regulations. The "doctrine of precedent", or *stare decisis* (Latin for "to stand by decisions") means that decisions by higher courts bind lower courts to assure that similar cases reach similar results. In contrast, in civil law systems, legislative statutes are typically more detailed, and judicial decisions are shorter and less detailed, because the adjudicator is only writing to decide the single case, rather than to set out reasoning that will guide future courts.

Common law originated from England and has been inherited by almost every country once tied to the British Empire (except Malta, Scotland, the U.S. state of Louisiana, and the Canadian province of Quebec). In medieval England during the Norman conquest, the law varied shire-to-shire based on disparate tribal customs. The concept of a "common law" developed during the reign of Henry II during the late 12th century, when Henry appointed judges that had authority to create an institutionalised and unified system of law common to the country. The next major step in the evolution of the common law came when King John was forced by his barons to sign a document limiting his authority to pass laws. This "great charter" or *Magna Carta* of 1215 also required that the King's entourage of judges hold their courts and judgments at "a certain place" rather than dispensing autocratic justice in unpredictable places about the country. A concentrated and elite group of judges acquired a dominant role in law-making under this system, and compared to its European counterparts the English judiciary became highly centralised. In 1297, for instance, while the highest court in France had fifty-one judges, the English Court of Common Pleas had five. This powerful and tight-knit judiciary gave rise to a systematised process of developing common law.

As time went on, many felt that the common law was overly systematised and inflexible, and increasing numbers of citizens petitioned the King to override the common law. On the King's behalf, the Lord Chancellor started giving judgments to do what was equitable in a case. From the time of Sir Thomas More, the first lawyer to be appointed as Lord Chancellor, a systematic body of equity grew up alongside the rigid common law, and developed its own Court of Chancery. At first, equity was often criticised as erratic. Over time, courts of equity developed solid principles, especially under Lord Eldon. In the 19th century in England, and in 1937 in the U.S., the two systems were merged.

In developing the common law, academic writings have always played an important part, both to collect overarching principles from dispersed case law, and to argue for change. William Blackstone, from around 1760, was the first scholar to collect, describe, and teach the common law. But merely in describing, scholars who sought explanations and underlying structures slowly changed the way the law actually worked.

Religious Law

Religious law is explicitly based on religious precepts. Examples include the Jewish Halakha and Islamic Sharia—both of which translate as the "path to follow". Christian canon law also survives in some church communities. Often the implication of religion for law is unalterability, because the word of God cannot be amended or legislated against by judges or governments. Nonetheless, most religious jurisdictions rely on further human elaboration to provide for thorough and detailed legal systems. For instance, the Quran has some law, and it acts as a source of further law through interpretation, *Qiyas* (reasoning by analogy), *Ijma* (consensus) and precedent. This is mainly contained in a body of law and jurisprudence known as Sharia and Fiqh respectively. Another example is the Torah or Old Testament, in the Pentateuch or Five Books of Moses. This contains the basic code of Jewish law, which some Israeli communities choose to use. The Halakha is a code of Jewish law that summarizes some of the Talmud's interpretations.

A number of countries are sharia jurisdictions. Israeli law allows litigants to use religious laws only if they choose. Canon law is only in use by members of the Catholic Church, the Eastern Orthodox Church and the Anglican Communion.

Canon Law

Canon law is a set of ordinances and regulations made by ecclesiastical authority, for the government of a Christian organisation or church and its members. It is the internal ecclesiastical law governing the Catholic Church, the Eastern Orthodox Church, the Oriental

Orthodox Churches, and the individual national churches within the Anglican Communion. The way that such church law is legislated, interpreted and at times adjudicated varies widely among these three bodies of churches. In all three traditions, a canon was originally a rule adopted by a church council; these canons formed the foundation of canon law.

The Catholic Church has the oldest continuously functioning legal system in the western world, predating the evolution of modern European civil law and common law systems. The 1983 Code of Canon Law governs the Latin Church *sui juris*. The Eastern Catholic Churches, which developed different disciplines and practices, are governed by the *Code of Canons of the Eastern Churches*. The canon law of the Catholic Church influenced the common law during the medieval period through its preservation of Roman law doctrine such as the presumption of innocence.

Sharia Law

Until the 18th century, Sharia law was practiced throughout the Muslim world in a non-codified form, with the Ottoman Empire's Mecelle code in the 19th century being a first attempt at codifying elements of Sharia law. Since the mid-1940s, efforts have been made, in country after country, to bring Sharia law more into line with modern conditions and conceptions. In modern times, the legal systems of many Muslim countries draw upon both civil and common law traditions as well as Islamic law and custom. The constitutions of certain Muslim states, such as Egypt and Afghanistan, recognise Islam as the religion of the state, obliging legislature to adhere to Sharia. Saudi Arabia recognises the Quran as its constitution, and is governed on the basis of Islamic law. Iran has also witnessed a reiteration of Islamic law into its legal system after 1979. During the last few decades, one of the fundamental features of the movement of Islamic resurgence has been the call to restore the Sharia, which has generated a vast amount of literature and affected world politics.

Legal Methods

There are distinguished methods of legal reasoning (applying the law) and methods of interpreting (construing) the law. The former are legal syllogism, which holds sway in civil law legal systems, analogy, which is present in common law legal systems, especially in the US, and argumentative theories that occur in both systems. The latter are different rules (directives) of legal interpretation such as directives of linguistic interpretation, teleological interpretation or systemic interpretation as well as more specific rules, for instance, golden rule or mischief rule. There are also many other arguments and cannons of interpretation which altogether make statutory interpretation possible.

Law professor and former United States Attorney General Edward H. Levi noted that the "basic pattern of legal reasoning is reasoning by example"—that is, reasoning by comparing outcomes in cases resolving similar legal questions. In a U.S. Supreme Court case regarding procedural efforts taken by a debt collection company to avoid errors, Justice Sotomayor cautioned that "legal reasoning is not a mechanical or strictly linear process".

Jurimetrics is the formal application of quantitative methods, especially probability and statistics, to legal questions. The use of statistical methods in court cases and law review articles has grown massively in importance in the last few decades.

Legal Institutions

The main institutions of law in industrialised countries are independent courts, representative parliaments, an accountable executive, the military and police, bureaucratic organisation, the legal profession and civil society itself. John Locke, in his *Two Treatises of Government*, and Baron de Montesquieu in *The Spirit of the Laws*, advocated for a separation of powers between the political, legislature and executive bodies. Their principle was that no person should be able to usurp all powers of the state, in contrast to the absolutist theory of Thomas Hobbes' *Leviathan*. Sun Yat-sen's Five Power Constitution for the Republic of China took the separation of powers further by having two additional branches of government—a Control Yuan for auditing oversight and an Examination Yuan to manage the employment of public officials.

Max Weber and others reshaped thinking on the extension of state. Modern military, policing and bureaucratic power over ordinary citizens' daily lives pose special problems for accountability that earlier writers such as Locke or Montesquieu could not have foreseen. The custom and practice of the legal profession is an important part of people's access to justice, whilst civil society is a term used to refer to the social institutions, communities and partnerships that form law's political basis.

Judiciary

A judiciary is a number of judges mediating disputes to determine outcome. Most countries have systems of appeal courts, with an apex court as the ultimate judicial authority. In the United States, this authority is the Supreme Court; in Australia, the High Court; in India, the Supreme Court of India;in the UK, the Supreme Court; in Germany, the *Bundesverfassungsgericht*; and in France, the *Cour de Cassation*. For most European countries the European Court of Justice in Luxembourg can overrule national law, when EU law is relevant. The European Court of Human Rights in Strasbourg allows citizens of the Council of Europe member states to bring cases relating to human rights issues before it.

Some countries allow their highest judicial authority to overrule legislation they determine to be unconstitutional. For example, in *Brown v. Board of Education*, the United States Supreme Court nullified many state statutes that had established racially segregated schools, finding such statutes to be incompatible with the Fourteenth Amendment to the United States Constitution.

A judiciary is theoretically bound by the constitution, just as all other government bodies are. In most countries judges may only interpret the constitution and all other laws. But in common law countries, where matters are not constitutional, the judiciary may also create law under the doctrine of precedent. The UK, Finland and New Zealand assert the ideal of parliamentary sovereignty, whereby the unelected judiciary may not overturn law passed by a democratic legislature.

In communist states, such as China, the courts are often regarded as parts of the executive, or subservient to the legislature; governmental institutions and actors exert thus various forms of influence on the judiciary. In Muslim countries, courts often examine whether state laws adhere to the Sharia: the Supreme Constitutional Court of Egypt may invalidate such laws, and in Iran the Guardian Council ensures the compatibility of the legislation with the "criteria of Islam".

Legislature

Prominent examples of legislatures are the Houses of Parliament in London, the Congress in Washington, D.C., the Bundestag in Berlin, the Duma in Moscow, the Parlamento Italiano in Rome and the *Assemblée nationale* in Paris. By the principle of representative government people vote for politicians to carry out *their* wishes. Although countries like Israel, Greece, Sweden and China are unicameral, most countries are bicameral, meaning they have two separately appointed legislative houses.

In the 'lower house' politicians are elected to represent smaller constituencies. The 'upper house' is usually elected to represent states in a federal system (as in Australia, Germany or the United States) or different voting configuration in a unitary system (as in France). In the UK the upper house is appointed by the government as a house of review. One criticism of bicameral systems with two elected chambers is that the upper and lower houses may simply mirror one another. The traditional justification of bicameralism is that an upper chamber acts as a house of review. This can minimise arbitrariness and injustice in governmental action.

To pass legislation, a majority of the members of a legislature must vote for a bill (proposed law) in each house. Normally there will be several readings and amendments proposed by the different political factions. If a country has an entrenched constitution, a special majority for changes to the constitution may be required, making changes to the law more difficult. A government usually leads the process, which can be formed from Members of Parliament (e.g. the UK or Germany). However, in a presidential system, the government is usually formed by an executive and his or her appointed cabinet officials (e.g. the United States or Brazil).

Executive

The executive in a legal system serves as the centre of political authority of the State. In a parliamentary system, as with Britain, Italy, Germany, India, and Japan, the executive is known as the cabinet, and composed of members of the legislature. The executive is led by the head of government, whose office holds power under the confidence of the legislature. Because popular elections appoint political parties to govern, the leader of a party can change in between elections.

The head of state is apart from the executive, and symbolically enacts laws and acts as representative of the nation. Examples include the President of Germany (appointed by members of federal and state legislatures), the Queen of the United Kingdom (an hereditary office), and the President of Austria (elected by popular vote). The other important model is the presidential system, found in the United States and in Brazil. In presidential systems, the executive acts as both head of state and head of government, and has power to appoint an unelected cabinet. Under a presidential system, the executive branch is separate from the legislature to which it is not accountable.

Although the role of the executive varies from country to country, usually it will propose the majority of legislation, and propose government agenda. In presidential systems, the executive often has the power to veto legislation.

Most executives in both systems are responsible for foreign relations, the military and police, and the bureaucracy. Ministers or other officials head a country's public offices, such as a foreign ministry or defence ministry. The election of a different executive is therefore capable of revolutionising an entire country's approach to government.

Military and Police

While military organisations have existed as long as government itself, the idea of a standing police force is a relatively modern concept.

For example, Medieval England's system of travelling criminal courts, or assizes, used show trials and public executions to instill communities with fear to maintain control. The first modern police were probably those in 17th-century Paris, in the court of Louis XIV, although the Paris Prefecture of Police claim they were the world's first uniformed policemen.

Max Weber famously argued that the state is that which controls the monopoly on the legitimate use of force. The military and police carry out enforcement at the request of the government or the courts. The term failed state refers to states that cannot implement or enforce policies; their police and military no longer control security and order and society moves into anarchy, the absence of government.

Bureaucracy

The etymology of *bureaucracy* derives from the French word for *office* (*bureau*) and the Ancient Greek for word *power* (*kratos*). Like the military and police, a legal system's government servants and bodies that make up its bureaucracy carry out the directives of the executive. One of the earliest references to the concept was made by Baron de Grimm, a German author who lived in France. In 1765, he wrote:

The real spirit of the laws in France is that bureaucracy of which the late Monsieur de Gournay used to complain so greatly; here the offices, clerks, secretaries, inspectors and *intendants* are not appointed to benefit the public interest, indeed the public interest appears to have been established so that offices might exist.

Cynicism over "officialdom" is still common, and the workings of public servants is typically contrasted to private enterprise motivated by profit. In fact private companies, especially large ones, also have bureaucracies. Negative perceptions of "red tape" aside, public services such as schooling, health care, policing or public transport are considered a crucial state function making public bureaucratic action the locus of government power.

Writing in the early 20th century, Max Weber believed that a definitive feature of a developed state had come to be its bureaucratic support. Weber wrote that the typical characteristics of modern bureaucracy are that officials define its mission, the scope of work is bound by rules, and management is composed of career experts who manage top down, communicating through writing and binding public servants' discretion with rules.

Legal Profession

A corollary of the rule of law is the existence of a legal profession sufficiently autonomous to invoke the authority of the independent judiciary; the right to assistance of a barrister in a court proceeding emanates from this corollary—in England the function of barrister or advocate is distinguished from legal counselor. As the European Court of Human Rights has stated, the law should be adequately accessible to everyone and people should be able to foresee how the law affects them.

In order to maintain professionalism, the practice of law is typically overseen by either a government or independent regulating body such as a bar association, bar council or law society. Modern lawyers achieve distinct professional identity through specified legal procedures (e.g. successfully passing a qualifying examination), are required by law to have a special qualification (a legal education earning the student a Bachelor of Laws, a Bachelor of Civil Law, or a Juris Doctor degree. Higher academic degrees may also be pursued. Examples include a Master of Laws, a Master of Legal Studies, a Bar Professional Training Course or a Doctor of Laws.), and are constituted in office by legal forms of appointment (being admitted to the bar). There are few titles of respect to signify famous lawyers, such as Esquire, to indicate barristers of greater dignity, and Doctor of law, to indicate a person who obtained a PhD in Law.

Many Muslim countries have developed similar rules about legal education and the legal profession, but some still allow lawyers with training in traditional Islamic law to practice law before personal status law courts. In China and other developing countries there are not sufficient professionally trained people to staff the existing judicial systems, and, accordingly, formal standards are more relaxed.

Once accredited, a lawyer will often work in a law firm, in a chambers as a sole practitioner, in a government post or in a private corporation as an internal counsel. In addition a lawyer may become a legal researcher who provides on-demand legal research through a library, a commercial service or freelance work. Many people trained in law put their skills to use outside the legal field entirely.

Significant to the practice of law in the common law tradition is the legal research to determine the current state of the law. This usually entails exploring case-law reports, legal periodicals and legislation. Law practice also involves drafting documents such as court pleadings, persuasive briefs, contracts, or wills and trusts. Negotiation and dispute resolution skills (including ADR techniques) are also important to legal practice, depending on the field.

Civil Society

The Classical republican concept of "civil society" dates back to Hobbes and Locke. Locke saw civil society as people who have "a common established law and judicature to appeal to, with authority to decide controversies between them." German philosopher Georg Wilhelm Friedrich Hegel distinguished the "state" from "civil society" (German: *bürgerliche Gesellschaft*) in *Elements of the Philosophy of Right.*

Hegel believed that civil society and the state were polar opposites, within the scheme of his dialectic theory of history. The modern dipole state–civil society was reproduced in the theories of Alexis de Tocqueville and Karl Marx. In post-modern theory, civil society is necessarily a source of law, by being the basis from which people form opinions and lobby for what they believe law should be. As Australian barrister and author Geoffrey Robertson QC wrote of international law, "one of its primary modern sources is found in the responses of ordinary men and women, and of the non-governmental organizations which many of them support, to the human rights abuses they see on the television screen in their living rooms."

Freedom of speech, freedom of association and many other individual rights allow people to gather, discuss, criticise and hold to account their governments, from which the basis of a deliberative democracy is formed. The more people are involved with, concerned by and capable of changing how political power is exercised over their lives, the more acceptable and legitimate the law becomes to the people. The most familiar institutions of civil society include economic markets, profit-oriented firms, families, trade unions, hospitals, universities, schools, charities, debating clubs, non-governmental organisations, neighbourhoods, churches, and religious associations. There is no clear legal definition of the civil society, and of the institutions it includes. Most of the institutions and bodies who try to give a list of institutions (such as the European Economic and Social Committee) exclude the political parties.

Areas of Law

All legal systems deal with the same basic issues, but jurisdictions categorise and identify their legal topics in different ways. A common distinction is that between "public law" (a term related closely to the state, and including constitutional, administrative and criminal law), and "private law" (which covers contract, tort and property). In civil law systems, contract and tort fall under a general law of obligations, while trusts law is dealt with under statutory regimes or international conventions. International, constitutional and administrative law, criminal law, contract, tort, property law and trusts are regarded as the "traditional core subjects", although there are many further disciplines.

International Law

International law can refer to three things: public international law, private international law or conflict of laws and the law of supranational organisations.

- Public international law concerns relationships between sovereign nations. The sources for public international law development are custom, practice and treaties between sovereign nations, such as the Geneva Conventions. Public international law can be formed by international organisations, such as the United Nations (which was established after the failure of the League of Nations to prevent World War II), the International Labour Organisation, the World Trade Organisation (WTO), or the International Monetary Fund. Public international law has a special status as law because there is no international police force, and courts (e.g. the International Court of Justice as the primary UN judicial organ) lack the capacity to penalise disobedience. The prevailing manner of enforcing international law is still essentially "self help"; that is the reaction by states to alleged breaches of international obligations by other states. However, a few bodies, such as the WTO, have effective systems of binding arbitration and dispute resolution backed up by trade sanctions.
- Conflict of laws, or private international law in civil law countries, concerns which jurisdiction a legal dispute between private parties should be heard in and which jurisdiction's law should be applied. Today, businesses are increasingly capable of shifting capital and labour supply chains across borders, as well as trading with overseas businesses, making the question of which country has jurisdiction even more pressing. Increasing numbers of businesses opt for commercial arbitration under the New York Convention 1958.
- European Union law is the first and so far the only example of a supranational law, i.e. an internationally accepted legal system, other than the United Nations and the World Trade Organization. Given the trend of increasing global economic integration, many regional agreements—especially the African Union—seek to follow a similar model. In the EU, sovereign nations have gathered their authority in a system of courts and the European Parliament. These institutions are allowed the ability to enforce legal norms both against or for member states and citizens in a manner which is not possible through public international law. As the European Court of Justice noted in its 1963 Van Gend en Loos decision, European Union law constitutes "a new legal order of international law" for the mutual social and economic benefit of the member states.

Constitutional and Administrative Law

Constitutional and administrative law govern the affairs of the state. Constitutional law concerns both the relationships between the executive, legislature and judiciary and the human rights or civil liberties of individuals against the state. Most jurisdictions, like the United States and France, have a single codified constitution with a bill of rights. A few, like the United Kingdom, have no such document. A "constitution" is simply those laws which constitute the body politic, from statute, case law and convention. A case named *Entick v Carrington* illustrates a constitutional principle deriving from the common law. Entick's house was searched and ransacked by Sheriff Carrington. When Entick complained in court, Sheriff Carrington argued that a warrant from a Government minister, the Earl of Halifax, was valid authority. However, there was no written statutory provision or court authority. The leading judge, Lord Camden, stated:

The great end, for which men entered into society, was to secure their property. That right is preserved sacred and incommunicable in all instances, where it has not been taken away or abridged by some public law for the good of the whole ... If no excuse can be found or produced, the silence of the books is an authority against the defendant, and the plaintiff must have judgment.

The fundamental constitutional principle, inspired by John Locke, holds that the individual can do anything except that which is forbidden by law, and the state may do nothing except that which is authorised by law. Administrative law is the chief method for people to hold state bodies to account. People can sue an agency, local council, public service, or government ministry for judicial review of actions or decisions, to ensure that they comply with the law, and that the government entity observed required procedure. The first specialist administrative court was the *Conseil d'État* set up in 1799, as Napoleon assumed power in France.

A subdiscipline of constitutional law is election law. It deals with rules governing elections. These rules enable the translation of the will of the people into functioning democracies. Election law addresses issues who is entitled to vote, voter registration, ballot access, campaign finance and party funding, redistricting, apportionment, electronic voting and voting machines, accessibility of elections, election systems and formulas, vote counting, election disputes, referendums, and issues such as electoral fraud and electoral silence.

Criminal Law

Criminal law, also known as penal law, pertains to crimes and punishment. It thus regulates the definition of and penalties for offences found to have a sufficiently deleterious social impact but, in itself, makes no moral judgment on an offender nor imposes restrictions on society that physically prevent people from committing a crime in the first place. Investigating, apprehending, charging, and trying suspected offenders is regulated by the law of criminal procedure. The paradigm case of a crime lies in the proof, beyond reasonable doubt, that a person is guilty of two things. First, the accused must commit an act which is deemed by society to be criminal, or *actus reus* (guilty act). Second, the accused must have the requisite malicious intent to do a criminal act, or *mens rea* (guilty mind). However, for so called "strict liability" crimes, an *actus reus* is enough. Criminal systems of the civil law tradition distinguish between intention in the broad sense (*dolus directus* and *dolus eventualis*), and negligence. Negligence does not carry criminal responsibility unless a particular crime provides for its punishment.

Examples of crimes include murder, assault, fraud and theft. In exceptional circumstances defences can apply to specific acts, such as killing in self defence, or pleading insanity. Another example is in the 19th-century English case of *R v Dudley and Stephens*, which tested a defence of "necessity". The *Mignonette*, sailing from Southampton to Sydney, sank. Three crew members and Richard Parker, a 17-year-old cabin boy, were stranded on a raft. They were starving and the cabin boy was close to death. Driven to extreme hunger, the crew killed and ate the cabin boy. The crew survived and were rescued, but put on trial for murder. They argued it was necessary to kill the cabin boy to preserve their own lives. Lord Coleridge, expressing immense disapproval, ruled, "to preserve one's life is generally speaking a duty, but it may be the plainest and the highest duty to sacrifice it." The men were sentenced to hang, but public opinion was overwhelmingly supportive of the crew's right to preserve their own lives. In the end, the Crown commuted their sentences to six months in jail.

Criminal law offences are viewed as offences against not just individual victims, but the community as well. The state, usually with the help of police, takes the lead in prosecution, which is why in common law countries cases are cited as "*The People* v ..." or "*R* (for Rex or Regina) v ...". Also, lay juries are often used to determine the guilt of defendants on points of fact: juries cannot change legal rules. Some developed countries still condone capital punishment for criminal activity, but the normal punishment for a crime will be imprisonment, fines, state supervision (such as probation), or community service. Modern criminal law has been affected considerably by the social sciences, especially with respect to sentencing, legal research, legislation, and rehabilitation. On the international field, 111 countries are members of the International Criminal Court, which was established to try people for crimes against humanity.

Contract Law

Contract law concerns enforceable promises, and can be summed up in the Latin phrase *pacta sunt servanda* (agreements must be kept). In common law jurisdictions, three key elements to the creation of a contract are necessary: offer and acceptance, consideration and the intention to create legal relations. In *Carlill v Carbolic Smoke Ball Company* a medical firm advertised that its new wonder drug, the smokeball, would cure people's flu, and if it did not, the buyers would get £100. Many people sued for their £100 when the drug did not work. Fearing bankruptcy, Carbolic argued the advert was not to be taken as a serious, legally binding offer. It was an invitation to treat, mere puffery, a gimmick. But the Court of Appeal held that to a reasonable man Carbolic had made a serious offer, accentuated by their reassuring statement, "£1000 is deposited". Equally, people had given good consideration for the offer by going to the "distinct inconvenience" of using a faulty product. "Read the advertisement how you will, and twist it about as you will", said Lord

Justice Lindley, "here is a distinct promise expressed in language which is perfectly unmistakable".

Consideration indicates the fact that all parties to a contract have exchanged something of value. Some common law systems, including Australia, are moving away from the idea of consideration as a requirement. The idea of estoppel or *culpa in contrahendo*, can be used to create obligations during pre-contractual negotiations.

Civil law jurisdictions treat contracts differently in a number of respects, with a more interventionist role for the state in both the formation and enforcement of contracts. Compared to common law jurisdictions, civil law systems incorporate more mandatory terms into contracts, allow greater latitude for courts to interpret and revise contract terms and impose a stronger duty of good faith, but are also more likely to enforce penalty clauses and specific performance of contracts. They also do not require consideration for a contract to be binding. In France, an ordinary contract is said to form simply on the basis of a "meeting of the minds" or a "concurrence of wills". Germany has a special approach to contracts, which ties into property law. Their 'abstraction principle' (*Abstraktionsprinzip*) means that the personal obligation of contract forms separately from the title of property being conferred. When contracts are invalidated for some reason (e.g. a car buyer is so drunk that he lacks legal capacity to contract) the contractual obligation to pay can be invalidated separately from the proprietary title of the car. Unjust enrichment law, rather than contract law, is then used to restore title to the rightful owner.

Torts and Delicts

Certain civil wrongs are grouped together as torts under common law systems and delicts under civil law systems. To have acted tortiously, one must have breached a duty to another person, or infringed some pre-existing legal right. A simple example might be unintentionally hitting someone with a cricket ball. Under the law of negligence, the most common form of tort, the injured party could potentially claim compensation for their injuries from the party responsible. The principles of negligence are illustrated by *Donoghue v Stevenson*. A friend of Donoghue ordered an opaque bottle of ginger beer (intended for the consumption of Donoghue) in a café in Paisley. Having consumed half of it, Donoghue poured the remainder into a tumbler. The decomposing remains of a snail floated out. She claimed to have suffered from shock, fell ill with gastroenteritis and sued the manufacturer for carelessly allowing the drink to be contaminated. The House of Lords decided that the manufacturer was liable for Mrs Donoghue's illness. Lord Atkin took a distinctly moral approach and said:

The liability for negligence [...] is no doubt based upon a general public sentiment of moral wrongdoing for which the offender must pay. [...] The rule that you are to love your neighbour becomes in law, you must not injure your neighbour; and the lawyer's question, Who is my neighbour? receives a restricted reply. You must take reasonable care to avoid acts or omissions which you can reasonably foresee would be likely to injure your neighbour.

This became the basis for the four principles of negligence, namely that:

1. Stevenson owed Donoghue a duty of care to provide safe drinks;
2. he breached his duty of care;
3. the harm would not have occurred but for his breach; and
4. his act was the proximate cause of her harm.

Another example of tort might be a neighbour making excessively loud noises with machinery on his property. Under a nuisance claim the noise could be stopped. Torts can also involve intentional acts such as assault, battery or trespass. A better known tort is defamation, which occurs, for example, when a newspaper makes unsupportable allegations that damage a politician's reputation. More infamous are economic torts, which form the basis of labour law in some countries by making trade unions liable for strikes, when statute does not provide immunity.

Property Law

Property law governs ownership and possession. Real property, sometimes called 'real estate', refers to ownership of land and things attached to it. Personal property, refers to everything else; movable objects, such as computers, cars, jewelry or intangible rights, such as stocks and shares. A right *in rem* is a right to a specific piece of property, contrasting to a right *in personam* which allows compensation for a loss, but not a particular thing back. Land law forms the basis for most kinds of property law, and is the most complex. It concerns mortgages, rental agreements, licences, covenants, easements and the statutory systems for land registration. Regulations on the use of personal property fall under intellectual property, company law, trusts and commercial law. An example of a basic case of most property law is *Armory v Delamirie* [1722]. A chimney sweep's boy found a jewel encrusted with precious stones. He took it to a goldsmith to have it valued. The goldsmith's apprentice looked at it, sneakily removed the stones, told the boy it was worth three halfpence and that he would buy it. The boy said he would prefer the jewel back, so the apprentice gave it to him, but without the stones. The boy sued the goldsmith for his apprentice's attempt to cheat him. Lord Chief Justice Pratt ruled that even though the boy could not be said to own the jewel, he should be considered the rightful keeper ("finders keepers") until the original owner is found. In fact the apprentice and the boy both had a right of *possession* in the jewel (a technical concept, meaning evidence that something *could* belong to someone), but the boy's possessory interest was considered better, because it could be shown to be first in time. Possession may be nine-tenths of the law, but not all.

This case is used to support the view of property in common law jurisdictions, that the person who can show the best claim to a piece of property, against any contesting party, is the owner. By contrast, the classic civil law approach to property, propounded by Friedrich Carl von Savigny, is that it is a right good against the world. Obligations, like contracts and torts, are conceptualised as rights good between individuals. The idea of property raises many further philosophical and political issues. Locke argued that our "lives, liberties and estates" are our property because we own our bodies and mix our labour with our surroundings.

Equity and Trusts

Equity is a body of rules that developed in England separately from the "common law". The common law was administered by judges and barristers. The Lord Chancellor on the other hand, as the King's keeper of conscience, could overrule the judge-made law if he thought it equitable to do so. This meant equity came to operate more through principles than rigid rules. Whereas neither the common law nor civil law systems allow people to split the ownership from the control of one piece of property, equity allows this through an arrangement known as a trust. Trustees control property whereas the beneficial, or equitable, ownership of trust property is held by people known as beneficiaries. Trustees owe duties to their beneficiaries to take good care of the entrusted property. In the early case of *Keech v Sandford* [1722], a child had inherited the lease on a market in Romford, London. Mr Sandford was entrusted to look after this property until the child matured. But before then, the lease expired. The landlord had (apparently) told Mr Sandford that he did not want the child to have the renewed lease. Yet the landlord was happy (apparently) to give Mr Sandford the opportunity of the lease instead. Mr Sandford took it. When the child (now Mr Keech) grew up, he sued Mr Sandford for the profit that he had been making by getting the market's lease. Mr Sandford was meant to be trusted, but he put himself in a position of conflict of interest. The Lord Chancellor, Lord King, agreed and ordered Mr Sandford should disgorge his profits. He wrote: "I very well see, if a trustee, on the refusal to renew, might have a lease to himself few trust-estates would be renewed. [...] This may seem very hard, that the trustee is the only person of all mankind who might not have the lease; but it is very proper that the rule should be strictly pursued and not at all relaxed."

Lord King LC was worried that trustees might exploit opportunities to use trust property for themselves instead of looking after it. Business speculators using trusts had just recently caused a stock market crash. Strict duties for trustees made their way into company law and were applied to directors and chief executive officers. Another example of a trustee's duty might be to invest property wisely or sell it. This is especially the case for pension funds, the most important form of trust, where investors are trustees for people's savings until retirement. But trusts can also be set up for charitable purposes, famous examples being the British Museum or the Rockefeller Foundation.

Further Disciplines

Law and society

- Labour law is the study of a tripartite industrial relationship between worker, employer and trade union. This involves collective bargaining regulation, and the right to strike. Individual employment law refers to workplace rights, such as job security, health and safety or a minimum wage.
- Human rights, civil rights and human rights law. These are laid down in codes

such as the Universal Declaration of Human Rights, the European Convention on Human Rights (which founded the European Court of Human Rights) and the U.S. Bill of Rights. The Treaty of Lisbon makes the Charter of Fundamental Rights of the European Union legally binding in all member states except Poland and the United Kingdom.

- Civil procedure and criminal procedure concern the rules that courts must follow as a trial and appeals proceed. Both concern a citizen's right to a fair trial or hearing.
- Evidence law involves which materials are admissible in courts for a case to be built.
- Immigration law and nationality law concern the rights of foreigners to live and work in a nation-state that is not their own and to acquire or lose citizenship. Both also involve the right of asylum and the problem of stateless individuals.
- Family law covers marriage and divorce proceedings, the rights of children and rights to property and money in the event of separation.
- Transactional law is the practice of law concerning business and money.
- Biolaw focuses on the intersection of law and the biosciences.

Law and commerce

- Company law sprang from the law of trusts, on the principle of separating ownership of property and control. The law of the modern company began with the Joint Stock Companies Act 1856, passed in the United Kingdom, which provided investors with a simple registration procedure to gain limited liability under the separate legal personality of the corporation.
- Commercial law covers complex contract and property law. The law of agency, insurance law, bills of exchange, insolvency and bankruptcy law and sales law trace back to the medieval *Lex Mercatoria.* The UK Sale of Goods Act 1979 and the US Uniform Commercial Code are examples of codified common law commercial principles.
- Admiralty law and the sea law lay a basic framework for free trade and commerce across the world's oceans and seas, where outside of a country's zone of control. Shipping companies operate through ordinary principles of commercial law, generalised for a global market. Admiralty law also encompasses specialised issues such as salvage, maritime liens, and injuries to passengers.
- Intellectual property law aims at safeguarding creators and other producers of intellectual goods and services. These are legal rights (copyrights, trademarks, patents, and related rights) which result from intellectual activity in the industrial, literary and artistic fields.

- Space law is a relatively new field dealing with aspects of international law regarding human activities in Earth orbit and outer space. While at first addressing space relations of countries via treaties, increasingly it is addressing areas such as space commercialisation, property, liability, and other issues.

Law and regulation

- Tax law involves regulations that concern value added tax, corporate tax, and income tax.
- Banking law and financial regulation set minimum standards on the amounts of capital banks must hold, and rules about best practice for investment. This is to insure against the risk of economic crises, such as the Wall Street Crash of 1929.
- Regulation deals with the provision of public services and utilities. Water law is one example. Especially since privatisation became popular and took management of services away from public law, private companies doing the jobs previously controlled by government have been bound by varying degrees of social responsibility. Energy, gas, telecomms and water are regulated industries in most OECD countries.
- Competition law, known in the United States as antitrust law, is an evolving field that traces as far back as Roman decrees against price fixing and the English restraint of trade doctrine. Modern competition law derives from the U.S. anti-cartel and anti-monopoly statutes (the Sherman Act and Clayton Act) of the turn of the 20th century. It is used to control businesses who attempt to use their economic influence to distort market prices at the expense of consumer welfare.
- Consumer law could include anything from regulations on unfair contractual terms and clauses to directives on airline baggage insurance.
- Environmental law is increasingly important, especially in light of the Kyoto Protocol and the potential danger of climate change. Environmental protection also serves to penalise polluters within domestic legal systems.
- Aviation law deals with all regulations and technical standards applicable to the safe operation of aircraft, and is an essential part both of pilots' training and pilot's operations. It is framed by national civil aviation acts (or laws), themselves mostly aligned with the recommendations or mandatory standards of the International Civil Aviation Organisation or ICAO.

Ethics

Ethics or moral philosophy is a branch of philosophy that "involves systematizing, defending, and recommending concepts of right and wrong behavior". The field of ethics, along with aesthetics, concerns matters of value; these fields comprise the branch of philosophy called axiology. Ethics seeks to resolve questions of human morality by defining concepts such as good and evil, right and wrong, virtue and vice, justice and crime. As a field of intellectual inquiry, moral philosophy is related to the fields of moral psychology, descriptive ethics, and value theory.

Three major areas of study within ethics recognized today are:

1. Meta-ethics, concerning the theoretical meaning and reference of moral propositions, and how their truth values (if any) can be determined;
2. Normative ethics, concerning the practical means of determining a moral course of action;
3. Applied ethics, concerning what a person is obligated (or permitted) to do in a specific situation or a particular domain of action.

Definition

The English word *ethics* is derived from the Ancient Greek word *çthikós* (èéêüò), meaning "relating to one's character", which itself comes from the root word *êthos* (&èïò) meaning "character, moral nature". This word was transferred into Latin as *ethica* and then into French as *éthique*, from which it was transferred into English.

Rushworth Kidder states that "standard definitions of *ethics* have typically included such phrases as 'the science of the ideal human character' or 'the science of moral duty'". Richard William Paul and Linda Elder define ethics as "a set of concepts and principles that guide us in determining what behavior helps or harms sentient creatures". The *Cambridge Dictionary of Philosophy* states that the word "ethics" is "commonly used interchangeably with 'morality' ... and sometimes it is used more narrowly to mean the moral principles of a particular tradition, group or individual." Paul and Elder state that most people confuse ethics with behaving in accordance with social conventions, religious beliefs, the law, and do not treat ethics as a stand-alone concept.

The word *ethics* in English refers to several things. It can refer to philosophical ethics or moral philosophy—a project that attempts to use reason to answer various kinds of ethical questions. As the English moral philosopher Bernard Williams writes, attempting to explain moral philosophy: "What makes an inquiry a philosophical one is reflective generality and a style of argument that claims to be rationally persuasive." Williams describes the content of this area of inquiry as addressing the very broad question, "how one should live". Ethics can also refer to a common human ability to think about ethical problems that is not particular to philosophy. As bioethicist Larry Churchill has written: "Ethics, understood as the capacity to think critically about moral values and direct our actions in terms of such values, is a generic human capacity."

Meta-ethics

Meta-ethics is the branch of philosophical ethics that asks how we understand, know about, and what we mean when we talk about what is right and what is wrong. An ethical question pertaining to a particular practical situation—such as, "Should I eat this particular piece of chocolate cake?"—cannot be a meta-ethical question (rather, this is an applied ethical question). A meta-ethical question is abstract and relates to a wide range of more specific practical questions. For example, "Is it ever possible to have a secure knowledge of what is right and wrong?" is a meta-ethical question.

Meta-ethics has always accompanied philosophical ethics. For example, Aristotle implies that less precise knowledge is possible in ethics than in other spheres of inquiry, and he regards ethical knowledge as depending upon habit and acculturation in a way that makes it distinctive from other kinds of knowledge. Meta-ethics is also important in G.E. Moore's *Principia Ethica* from 1903. In it he first wrote about what he called *the naturalistic fallacy*. Moore was seen to reject naturalism in ethics, in his open-question argument. This made thinkers look again at second order questions about ethics. Earlier, the Scottish philosopher David Hume had put forward a similar view on the difference between facts and values.

Studies of how we know in ethics divide into cognitivism and non-cognitivism; these, respectively, take descriptive and non-descriptive approaches to moral goodness or value. Non-cognitivism is the view that when we judge something as morally right or wrong, this is neither true nor false. We may, for example, be only expressing our emotional feelings about these things. Cognitivism can then be seen as the claim that when we talk about right and wrong, we are talking about matters of fact.

The ontology of ethics is about value-bearing things or properties, that is, the kind of things or stuff referred to by ethical propositions. Non-descriptivists and non-cognitivists believe that ethics does not need a specific ontology since ethical propositions do not refer. This is known as an anti-realist position. Realists, on the other hand, must explain what kind of entities, properties or states are relevant for ethics, how they have value, and why they guide and motivate our actions.

Moral Skepticism

Moral skepticism (or moral scepticism) is a class of metaethical theories in which all members entail that no one has any moral knowledge. Many moral skeptics also make the stronger, modal claim that moral knowledge is impossible. Moral skepticism is particularly against moral realism which holds the view that there are knowable and objective moral truths.

Some proponents of moral skepticism include Pyrrho, Aenesidemus, Sextus Empiricus, David Hume, Max Stirner, Friedrich Nietzsche, and J.L. Mackie.

Moral skepticism is divided into three sub-classes:

- Moral error theory (or moral nihilism).
- Epistemological moral skepticism.
- Non-cognitivism.

All of these three theories share the same conclusions, which are as follows:

(a) we are never justified in believing that moral claims (claims of the form "state of affairs x is good," "action y is morally obligatory," etc.) are true and, even more so

(b) we never know that any moral claim is true.

However, each method arrives at (a) and (b) by different routes.

Moral error theory holds that we do not know that any moral claim is true because

(i) all moral claims are arguably false, and while none can be definitively proved or denied:

(ii) we have reason to believe that all moral claims are false, and

(iii) since we are not justified in believing any claim we have reason to deny, we are not justified in believing any moral claims.

Epistemological moral skepticism is a subclass of theory, the members of which include Pyrrhonian moral skepticism and dogmatic moral skepticism. All members of epistemological moral skepticism share two things: first, they acknowledge that we are unjustified in believing any moral claim, and second, they are agnostic on whether (i) is true (i.e. on whether all moral claims are false).

- Pyrrhonian moral skepticism holds that the reason we are unjustified in believing any moral claim is that it is irrational for us to believe either that any moral claim is true or that any moral claim is false. Thus, in addition to being agnostic on whether (i) is true, Pyrrhonian moral skepticism denies (ii).
- Dogmatic moral skepticism, on the other hand, *affirms* (ii) and cites (ii)'s truth as the reason we are unjustified in believing any moral claim.

Noncognitivism holds that we can never know that any moral claim is true because moral claims are *incapable* of being true or false (they are not truth-apt). Instead, moral claims are imperatives (e.g. "Don't steal babies!"), expressions of emotion (e.g. "stealing babies: Boo!"), or expressions of "pro-attitudes" ("I do not believe that babies should be stolen.")

Normative Ethics

Normative ethics is the study of ethical action. It is the branch of ethics that investigates the set of questions that arise when considering how one ought to act, morally speaking. Normative ethics is distinct from meta-ethics because normative ethics examines standards for the rightness and wrongness of actions, while meta-ethics studies the meaning of moral language and the metaphysics of moral facts. Normative ethics is also distinct from descriptive ethics, as the latter is an empirical investigation of people's moral beliefs. To put it another way, descriptive ethics would be concerned with determining what proportion of people believe that killing is always wrong, while normative ethics is concerned with whether it is correct to hold such a belief. Hence, normative ethics is sometimes called prescriptive rather than descriptive. However, on certain versions of the meta-ethical view called moral realism, moral facts are both descriptive and prescriptive at the same time.

Traditionally, normative ethics (also known as moral theory) was the study of what makes actions right and wrong. These theories offered an overarching moral principle one could appeal to in resolving difficult moral decisions.

At the turn of the 20th century, moral theories became more complex and were no longer concerned solely with rightness and wrongness, but were interested in many different kinds of moral status. During the middle of the century, the study of normative ethics declined as meta-ethics grew in prominence. This focus on meta-ethics was in part caused by an intense linguistic focus in analytic philosophy and by the popularity of logical positivism.

Virtue Ethics

Virtue ethics describes the character of a moral agent as a driving force for ethical behavior, and it is used to describe the ethics of early Greek philosophers such as Socrates and Aristotle, and ancient Indian philosophers such as Valluvar. Socrates (469–399 BC) was one of the first Greek philosophers to encourage both scholars and the common citizen to turn their attention from the outside world to the condition of humankind. In this view, knowledge bearing on human life was placed highest, while all other knowledge was secondary. Self-knowledge was considered necessary for success and inherently an essential good. A self-aware person will act completely within his capabilities to his pinnacle, while an ignorant person will flounder and encounter difficulty. To Socrates, a person must become aware of every fact (and its context) relevant to his existence, if he wishes to attain self-knowledge. He posited that people will naturally do what is good if they know what is right. Evil or bad actions are the results of ignorance. If a criminal was truly aware of the intellectual and spiritual consequences of his or her actions, he or she would neither commit nor even consider committing those actions. Any person who knows what is truly right will automatically do it, according to Socrates. While he correlated knowledge with virtue, he similarly equated virtue with joy. The truly wise man will know what is right, do what is good, and therefore be happy.

Aristotle (384–323 BC) posited an ethical system that may be termed "virtuous." In Aristotle's view, when a person acts in accordance with virtue this person will do good and be content. Unhappiness and frustration are caused by doing wrong, leading to failed goals and a poor life. Therefore, it is imperative for people to act in accordance with virtue, which is only attainable by the practice of the virtues in order to be content and complete. Happiness was held to be the ultimate goal. All other things, such as civic life or wealth, were only made worthwhile and of benefit when employed in the practice of the virtues. The practice of the virtues is the surest path to happiness. Aristotle asserted that the soul of man had three natures: body (physical/metabolism), animal (emotional/appetite), and rational (mental/conceptual). Physical nature can be assuaged through exercise and care; emotional nature through indulgence of instinct and urges; and mental nature through human reason and developed potential. Rational development was considered the most important, as essential to philosophical self-awareness, and as uniquely human. Moderation was encouraged, with the extremes seen as degraded and immoral. For example, courage is the moderate virtue between the extremes of cowardice and recklessness. Man should not simply live, but live well with conduct governed by virtue. This is regarded as difficult, as virtue denotes doing the right thing, in the right way, at the right time, for the right reason.

Valluvar (before 5th century CE) keeps virtue, or *a_am* (dharma) as he calls it, as the cornerstone throughout the writing of the Kural literature. While religious scriptures generally consider *a_am* as divine in nature, Valluvar describes it as a way of life rather than any spiritual observance, a way of harmonious living that leads to universal happiness. Contrary to what other contemporary works say, Valluvar holds that *a_am* is common for all, irrespective of whether the person is a bearer of palanquin or the rider in it. Valluvar considered justice as a facet of *a_am.* While ancient Greek philosophers such as Plato, Aristotle, and their descendants opined that justice cannot be defined and that it was a divine mystery, Valluvar positively suggested that a divine origin is not required to define the concept of justice. In the words of V. R. Nedunchezhiyan, justice according to Valluvar "dwells in the minds of those who have knowledge of the standard of right and wrong; so too deceit dwells in the minds which breed fraud."

Stoicism

The Stoic philosopher Epictetus posited that the greatest good was contentment and serenity. Peace of mind, or *apatheia*, was of the highest value; self-mastery over one's desires and emotions leads to spiritual peace. The "unconquerable will" is central to this philosophy. The individual's will should be independent and inviolate. Allowing a person to disturb the mental equilibrium is, in essence, offering yourself in slavery. If a person is free to anger you at will, you have no control over your internal world, and therefore no freedom. Freedom from material attachments is also necessary. If a thing breaks, the person should not be upset, but realize it was a thing that could break. Similarly, if someone should die, those close to them should hold to their serenity because the loved one was made of flesh and blood destined to death. Stoic philosophy says to accept things that cannot be changed, resigning oneself to the existence and enduring in a rational fashion. Death is not feared. People do not "lose" their life, but instead "return", for they are returning to God (who initially gave what the person is as a person). Epictetus said difficult problems in life should not be avoided, but rather embraced. They are spiritual exercises needed for the health of the spirit, just as physical exercise is required for the health of the body. He also stated that sex and sexual desire are to be avoided as the greatest threat to the integrity and equilibrium of a man's mind. Abstinence is highly desirable. Epictetus said remaining abstinent in the face of temptation was a victory for which a man could be proud.

Contemporary Virtue Ethics

Modern virtue ethics was popularized during the late 20th century in large part due to a revival of Aristotelianism, and as a response to G.E.M. Anscombe's "Modern Moral Philosophy". Anscombe argues that consequentialist and deontological ethics are only feasible as universal theories if the two schools ground themselves in divine law. As a deeply devoted Christian herself, Anscombe proposed that either those who do not give ethical credence to notions of divine law take up virtue ethics, which does not necessitate universal laws as agents themselves are investigated for virtue or vice and held up to "universal standards", or that those who wish to be utilitarian or consequentialist ground their theories in religious conviction. Alasdair MacIntyre, who wrote the book *After Virtue*, was a key contributor and proponent of modern virtue ethics, although some claim that MacIntyre supports a relativistic account of virtue based on cultural norms, not objective standards. Martha Nussbaum, a contemporary virtue ethicist, objects to MacIntyre's relativism, among that of others, and responds to relativist objections to form an objective account in her work "Non-Relative Virtues: An Aristotelian Approach". However, Nussbaum's accusation of relativism appears to be a misreading. In *Whose Justice, Whose Rationality?*, MacIntyre's ambition of taking a rational path beyond relativism was quite clear when he stated "rival claims made by different traditions [...] are to be evaluated [...] without relativism" (p. 354) because indeed "rational debate between and rational choice among rival traditions is possible" (p. 352). *Complete Conduct Principles for the 21st Century* blended the Eastern virtue ethics and the Western virtue ethics, with some modifications to suit the 21st Century, and formed a part of contemporary virtue ethics. Mortimer J. Adler described Aristotle's Nicomachean Ethics as a "unique book in the Western tradition of moral philosophy, the only ethics that is sound, practical, and undogmatic."

One major trend in contemporary virtue ethics is the Modern Stoicism movement.

Intuitive Ethics

Ethical intuitionism (also called moral intuitionism) is a family of views in moral epistemology (and, on some definitions, metaphysics). At minimum, ethical intuitionism is the thesis that our intuitive awareness of value, or intuitive knowledge of evaluative facts, forms the foundation of our ethical knowledge.

The view is at its core a foundationalism about moral knowledge: it is the view that some moral truths can be known non-inferentially (i.e., known without one needing to infer them from other truths one believes). Such an epistemological view implies that there are moral beliefs with propositional contents; so it implies cognitivism. As such, ethical intuitionism is to be contrasted with coherentist approaches to moral epistemology, such as those that depend on reflective equilibrium.

Throughout the philosophical literature, the term "ethical intuitionism" is frequently used with significant variation in its sense. This article's focus on foundationalism reflects the core commitments of contemporary self-identified ethical intuitionists.

Sufficiently broadly defined, ethical intuitionism can be taken to encompass cognitivist forms of moral sense theory. It is usually furthermore taken as essential to ethical intuitionism that there be self-evident or *a priori* moral knowledge; this counts against considering moral sense theory to be a species of intuitionism.

Ethical intuitionism was first clearly shown in use by the philosopher Francis Hutcheson. Later ethical intuitionists of influence and note include Henry Sidgwick, G.E. Moore, Harold Arthur Prichard, C.S. Lewis and, most influentially, Robert Audi.

Objections to ethical intuitionism include whether or not there are objective moral values (an assumption which the ethical system is based upon) the question of why many disagree over ethics if they are absolute, and whether Occam's razor cancels such a theory out entirely.

Hedonism

Hedonism posits that the principal ethic is maximizing pleasure and minimizing pain. There are several schools of Hedonist thought ranging from those advocating the indulgence of even momentary desires to those teaching a pursuit of spiritual bliss. In their consideration of consequences, they range from those advocating self-gratification regardless of the pain and expense to others, to those stating that the most ethical pursuit maximizes pleasure and happiness for the most people.

Cyrenaic Hedonism

Founded by Aristippus of Cyrene, Cyrenaics supported immediate gratification or pleasure. "Eat, drink and be merry, for tomorrow we die." Even fleeting desires should be indulged, for fear the opportunity should be forever lost. There was little to no concern with the future, the present dominating in the pursuit of immediate pleasure. Cyrenaic hedonism encouraged the pursuit of enjoyment and indulgence without hesitation, believing pleasure to be the only good.

Epicureanism

Epicurean ethics is a hedonist form of virtue ethics. Epicurus "presented a sustained argument that pleasure, correctly understood, will coincide with virtue." He rejected the extremism of the Cyrenaics, believing some pleasures and indulgences to be detrimental to human beings. Epicureans observed that indiscriminate indulgence sometimes resulted in negative consequences. Some experiences were therefore rejected out of hand, and some unpleasant experiences endured in the present to ensure a better life in the future. To Epicurus, the *summum bonum*, or greatest good, was prudence, exercised through moderation and caution. Excessive indulgence can be destructive to pleasure and can even lead to pain. For example, eating one food too often makes a person lose a taste for it. Eating too much food at once leads to discomfort and ill-health. Pain and fear were to be avoided. Living was essentially good, barring pain and illness. Death was not to be feared. Fear was considered the source of most unhappiness. Conquering the fear of death would naturally lead to a happier life. Epicurus reasoned if there were an afterlife and immortality, the fear of death was irrational. If there was no life after death, then the person would not be alive to suffer, fear, or worry; he would be non-existent in death. It is irrational to fret over circumstances that do not exist, such as one's state of death in the absence of an afterlife.

State Consequentialism

State consequentialism, also known as Mohist consequentialism, is an ethical theory that evaluates the moral worth of an action based on how much it contributes to the basic goods of a state. The *Stanford Encyclopedia of Philosophy* describes Mohist consequentialism, dating back to the 5th century BC, as "a remarkably sophisticated version based on a plurality of intrinsic goods taken as constitutive of human welfare". Unlike utilitarianism, which views pleasure as a moral good, "the basic goods in Mohist consequentialist thinking are ... order, material wealth, and increase in population". During Mozi's era, war and famines were common, and population growth was seen as a moral necessity for a harmonious society. The "material wealth" of Mohist consequentialism refers to basic needs like shelter and clothing, and the "order" of Mohist consequentialism refers to Mozi's stance against warfare and violence, which he viewed as pointless and a threat to social stability.

Stanford sinologist David Shepherd Nivison, in *The Cambridge History of Ancient China*, writes that the moral goods of Mohism "are interrelated: more basic wealth, then more reproduction; more people, then more production and wealth ... if people have plenty, they would be good, filial, kind, and so on unproblematically." The Mohists believed that morality is based on "promoting the benefit of all under heaven and eliminating harm to all under heaven". In contrast to Bentham's views, state consequentialism is not utilitarian because it is not hedonistic or individualistic. The importance of outcomes that are good for the community outweighs the importance of individual pleasure and pain.

Consequentialism

Consequentialism refers to moral theories that hold the consequences of a particular action form the basis for any valid moral judgment about that action. Thus, from a consequentialist standpoint, morally right action is one that produces a good outcome, or consequence. This view is often expressed as the aphorism *"The ends justify the means"*.

The term "consequentialism" was coined by G.E.M. Anscombe in her essay "Modern Moral Philosophy" in 1958, to describe what she saw as the central error of certain moral theories, such as those propounded by Mill and Sidgwick. Since then, the term has become common in English-language ethical theory.

The defining feature of consequentialist moral theories is the weight given to the consequences in evaluating the rightness and wrongness of actions. In consequentialist theories, the consequences of an action or rule generally outweigh other considerations. Apart from this basic outline, there is little else that can be unequivocally said about consequentialism as such. However, there are some questions that many consequentialist theories address:

- What sort of consequences count as good consequences?
- Who is the primary beneficiary of moral action?
- How are the consequences judged and who judges them?

One way to divide various consequentialisms is by the many types of consequences that are taken to matter most, that is, which consequences count as good states of affairs. According to utilitarianism, a good action is one that results in an increase and positive effect, and the best action is one that results in that effect for the greatest number. Closely related is eudaimonic consequentialism, according to which a full, flourishing life, which may or may not be the same as enjoying a great deal of pleasure, is the ultimate aim. Similarly, one might adopt an aesthetic consequentialism, in which the ultimate aim is to produce beauty. However, one might fix on non-psychological goods as the relevant effect. Thus, one might pursue an increase in material equality or political liberty instead of something like the more ephemeral "pleasure". Other theories adopt a package of several goods, all to be promoted equally. Whether a particular consequentialist theory focuses on a single good or many, conflicts and tensions between different good states of affairs are to be expected and must be adjudicated.

Utilitarianism

Utilitarianism is an ethical theory that argues the proper course of action is one that maximizes a positive effect, such as "happiness", "welfare", or the ability to live according to personal preferences. Jeremy Bentham and John Stuart Mill are influential proponents of this school of thought. In *A Fragment on Government* Bentham says 'it is the greatest happiness of the greatest number that is the measure of right and wrong' and describes this as a fundamental axiom. In *An Introduction to the Principles of Morals and Legislation* he talks of 'the principle of utility' but later prefers "the greatest happiness principle".

Utilitarianism is the paradigmatic example of a consequentialist moral theory. This form of utilitarianism holds that the morally correct action is the one that produces the best outcome for all people affected by the action. John Stuart Mill, in his exposition of utilitarianism, proposed a hierarchy of pleasures, meaning that the pursuit of certain kinds of pleasure is more highly valued than the pursuit of other pleasures. Other noteworthy proponents of utilitarianism are neuroscientist Sam Harris, author of *The Moral Landscape*, and moral philosopher Peter Singer, author of, amongst other works, *Practical Ethics*.

The major division within utilitarianism is between *act utilitarianism* and *rule utilitarianism*. In act utilitarianism, the principle of utility applies directly to each alternative act in a situation of choice. The right act is the one that brings about the best results (or the least bad results). In rule utilitarianism, the principle of utility determines the validity of rules of conduct (moral principles). A rule like promise-keeping is established by looking at the consequences of a world in which people break promises at will and a world in which promises are binding. Right and wrong are the following or breaking of rules that are sanctioned by their utilitarian value. A proposed "middle ground" between these two types is Two-level utilitarianism, where rules are applied in ordinary circumstances, but with an allowance to choose actions outside of such rules when unusual situations call for it.

Deontology

Deontological ethics or deontology is an approach to ethics that determines goodness or rightness from examining acts, or the rules and duties that the person doing the act strove to fulfill. This is in contrast to consequentialism, in which rightness is based on the consequences of an act, and not the act by itself. Under deontology, an act may be considered right even if it produces a bad consequence, if it follows the *rule* or moral law. According to the deontological view, people have a *duty* to act in ways that are deemed inherently good ("truth-telling" for example), or follow an objectively obligatory rule (as in rule utilitarianism).

Kantianism

Immanuel Kant's theory of ethics is considered deontological for several different reasons. First, Kant argues that to act in the morally right way, people must act from duty (*Pflicht*). Second, Kant argued that it was not the consequences of actions that make them right or wrong but the motives of the person who carries out the action.

Kant's argument that to act in the morally right way one must act purely from duty begins with an argument that the highest good must be both good in itself and good without qualification. Something is "good in itself" when it is intrinsically good, and "good without qualification", when the addition of that thing never makes a situation ethically worse. Kant then argues that those things that are usually thought to be good, such as intelligence, perseverance and pleasure, fail to be either intrinsically good or good without qualification. Pleasure, for example, appears not to be good without qualification, because when people take pleasure in watching someone suffer, this seems to make the situation ethically worse. He concludes that there is only one thing that is truly good:

Nothing in the world—indeed nothing even beyond the world—can possibly be conceived which could be called good without qualification except a *good will.*

Kant then argues that the consequences of an act of willing cannot be used to determine that the person has a good will; good consequences could arise by accident from an action that was motivated by a desire to cause harm to an innocent person, and bad consequences could arise from an action that was well-motivated. Instead, he claims, a person has goodwill when he 'acts out of respect for the moral law'. People 'act out of respect for the moral law' when they act in some way *because* they have a duty to do so. So, the only thing that is truly good in itself is goodwill, and goodwill is only good when the willer chooses to do something because it is that person's duty, i.e. out of "respect" for the law. He defines respect as "the concept of a worth which thwarts my self-love". Kant's three significant formulations of the categorical imperative are:

- Act only according to that maxim by which you can also will that it would become a universal law.
- Act in such a way that you always treat humanity, whether in your own person or in the person of any other, never simply as a means, but always at the same time as an end.
- Every rational being must so act as if he were through his maxim always a legislating member in a universal kingdom of ends.

Kant argued that the only absolutely good thing is a good will, and so the single determining factor of whether an action is morally right is the will, or motive of the person doing it. If they are acting on a bad maxim, e.g. "I will lie", then their action is wrong, even if some good consequences come of it. In his essay, *On a Supposed Right to Lie Because of Philanthropic Concerns*, arguing against the position of Benjamin Constant, *Des réactions politiques*, Kant states that "Hence a lie defined merely as an intentionally untruthful declaration to another man does not require the additional condition that it must do harm to another, as jurists require in their definition (*mendacium est falsiloquium in praeiudicium alterius*). For a lie always harms another; if not some human being, then it nevertheless does harm to humanity in general, inasmuch as it vitiates the very source of right [*Rechtsquelle*] ... All practical principles of right must contain rigorous truth ... This is because such exceptions would destroy the universality on account of which alone they bear the name of principles."

Divine Command Theory

Although not all deontologists are religious, some believe in the 'divine command theory', which is actually a cluster of related theories which essentially state that an action is right if God has decreed that it is right. According to Ralph Cudworth, an English philosopher, William of Ockham, René Descartes, and eighteenth-century Calvinists all accepted various versions of this moral theory, as they all held that moral obligations arise from God's commands.

The Divine Command Theory is a form of deontology because, according to it, the rightness of any action depends upon that action being performed because it is a duty, not because of any good consequences arising from that action. If God commands people not to work on Sabbath, then people act rightly if they do not work on Sabbath *because God has commanded that they do not do so*. If they do not work on Sabbath because they are lazy, then their action is not truly speaking "right", even though the actual physical action performed is the same. If God commands not to covet a neighbor's goods, this theory holds that it would be immoral to do so, even if coveting provides the beneficial outcome of a drive to succeed or do well.

One thing that clearly distinguishes Kantian deontologism from divine command deontology is that Kantianism maintains that man, as a rational being, makes the moral law universal, whereas divine command maintains that God makes the moral law universal.

Discourse Ethics

German philosopher Jürgen Habermas has proposed a theory of discourse ethics that he states is a descendant of Kantian ethics. He proposes that action should be based on communication between those involved, in which their interests and intentions are discussed so they can be understood by all. Rejecting any form of coercion or manipulation, Habermas believes that agreement between the parties is crucial for a moral decision to be reached. Like Kantian ethics, discourse ethics is a cognitive ethical theory, in that it supposes that truth and falsity can be attributed to ethical propositions. It also formulates a rule by which ethical actions can be determined and proposes that ethical actions should be universalizable, in a similar way to Kant's ethics.

Habermas argues that his ethical theory is an improvement on Kant's ethics. He rejects the dualistic framework of Kant's ethics. Kant distinguished between the phenomena world, which can be sensed and experienced by humans, and the noumena, or spiritual world, which is inaccessible to humans. This dichotomy was necessary for Kant because it could explain the autonomy of a human agent: although a human is bound in the phenomenal world, their actions are free in the noumenal world. For Habermas, morality arises from discourse, which is made necessary by their rationality and needs, rather than their freedom.

Pragmatic Ethics

Associated with the pragmatists Charles Sanders Peirce, William James, and especially John Dewey, pragmatic ethics holds that moral correctness evolves similarly to scientific knowledge: socially over the course of many lifetimes. Thus, we should prioritize social reform over attempts to account for consequences, individual virtue or duty (although these may be worthwhile attempts, if social reform is provided for).

Ethics of Care

Care ethics contrasts with more well-known ethical models, such as consequentialist theories (e.g. utilitarianism) and deontological theories (e.g., Kantian ethics) in that it seeks to incorporate traditionally feminized virtues and values that—proponents of care ethics contend—are absent in such traditional models of ethics. These values include the importance of empathetic relationships and compassion. Care-focused feminism is a branch of feminist thought, informed primarily by ethics of care as developed by Carol Gilligan and Nel Noddings. This body of theory is critical of how caring is socially assigned to women, and consequently devalued. They write, "Care-focused feminists regard women's capacity for care as a human strength," that should be taught to and expected of men as well as women. Noddings proposes that ethical caring has the potential to be a more concrete evaluative model of moral dilemma than an ethic of justice. Noddings' care-focused feminism requires practical application of relational ethics, predicated on an ethic of care.

Feminist Matrixial Ethics

The 'metafeminist' theory of the matrixial gaze and the matrixial time-space, coined and developed Bracha L. Ettinger since 1985, articulates a revolutionary philosophical approach that, in "daring to approach", to use Griselda Pollock's description of Ettinger's ethical turn, "the prenatal with the pre-maternal encounter", violence toward women at war, and the Shoah, has philosophically established the rights of each female subject over her own reproductive body, and offered a language to relate to human experiences which escape the phallic domain.

The matrixial sphere is a psychic and symbolic dimension that the 'phallic' language and regulations cannot control. In Ettinger's model, the relations between self and other are of neither assimilation nor rejection but 'coemergence'. In her conversation with Emmanuel Levinas, 1991, Ettinger prooses that the source of human Ethics is feminine-maternal and feminine-pre-maternal matrixial encounter-event. Sexuality and maternality coexist and are not in contradiction (the contradiction established by Sigmund Freud and Jacques Lacan), and the feminine is not an absolute alterity (the alterity established by Jacques Lacan and Emmanuel Levinas).

With the 'originary response-ability', 'wit(h)nessing', 'borderlinking', 'communicaring', 'com-passion', 'seduction into life' and other processes invested by affects that occur in the Ettingerian matrixial time-space, the feminine is presented as the source of humanized Ethics in all genders. Compassion and Seduction into life occurs earlier than the primary seduction which passes through enigmatic signals from the maternal sexuality according to Jean Laplanche, since it is active in 'coemergence' in 'withnessing' for any born subject, earlier to its birth. Ettinger suggests to Emanuel Levinas in their conversations in 1991, that the feminine understood via the matrixial perspective is the heart and the source of Ethics.

At the beginning of life, an originary 'fascinance' felt by the infant is related to the passage from response-ability to responsibility, from com-passion to compassion, and from wit(h)nessing to witnessing operated and transmitted by the m/Other. The 'differentiation in jointness' that is at the heart of the matrixial borderspace has deep implications in the relational field and for the ethics of care. The matrixial theory that proposes new ways to rethink sexual difference through the fluidity of boundaries informs aesthetics and ethics of compassion, carrying and non-abandonment in 'subjectivity as encounter-event'. It has become significant in Psychoanalysis and in transgender studies.

Role Ethics

Role ethics is an ethical theory based on family roles. Unlike virtue ethics, role ethics is not individualistic. Morality is derived from a person's relationship with their community. Confucian ethics is an example of role ethics though this is not straightforwardly uncontested. Confucian roles center around the concept of filial piety or *xiao*, a respect for family members. According to Roger T. Ames and Henry Rosemont, "Confucian normativity is defined by living one's family roles to maximum effect." Morality is determined through a person's fulfillment of a role, such as that of a parent or a child. Confucian roles are not rational, and originate through the *xin*, or human emotions.

Anarchist Ethics

Anarchist ethics is an ethical theory based on the studies of anarchist thinkers. The biggest contributor to anarchist ethics is Peter Kropotkin.

Starting from the premise that the goal of ethical philosophy should be to help humans adapt and thrive in evolutionary terms, Kropotkin's ethical framework uses biology and anthropology as a basis – in order to scientifically establish what will best enable a given social order to thrive biologically and socially – and advocates certain behavioural practices to enhance humanity's capacity for freedom and well-being, namely practices which emphasise solidarity, equality, and justice.

Kropotkin argues that ethics itself is evolutionary, and is inherited as a sort of a social instinct through cultural history, and by so, he rejects any religious and transcendental explanation of morality. The origin of ethical feeling in both animals and humans can be found, he claims, in the natural fact of "sociality" (mutualistic symbiosis), which humans can then combine with the instinct for justice (i.e. equality) and then with the practice of reason to construct a non-supernatural and anarchistic system of ethics. Kropotkin suggests that the principle of equality at the core of anarchism is the same as the Golden rule:

This principle of treating others as one wishes to be treated oneself, what is it but the very same principle as equality, the fundamental principle of anarchism? And how can any one manage to believe himself an anarchist unless he practices it? We do not wish to be ruled. And by this very fact, do we not declare that we ourselves wish to rule nobody? We do not wish to be deceived, we wish always to be told nothing but the truth. And by this very fact, do we not declare that we ourselves do not wish to deceive anybody, that we promise to always tell the truth, nothing but the truth, the whole truth? We do not wish to have the fruits of our labor stolen from us. And by that very fact, do we not declare that we respect the fruits of others' labor? By what right indeed can we demand that we should be treated in one fashion, reserving it to ourselves to treat others in a fashion entirely different? Our sense of equality revolts at such an idea.

Postmodern Ethics

Antihumanists such as Louis Althusser, Michel Foucault and structuralists such as Roland Barthes challenged the possibilities of individual agency and the coherence of the notion of the 'individual' itself. This was on the basis that personal identity was, in the most part, a social construction. As critical theory developed in the later 20th century, post-structuralism sought to problematize human relationships to knowledge and 'objective' reality. Jacques Derrida argued that access to meaning and the 'real' was always deferred, and sought to demonstrate via recourse to the linguistic realm that "there is no outside-text/non-text" ("*il n'y a pas de hors-texte*" is often mistranslated as "there is nothing outside the text"); at the same time, Jean Baudrillard theorised that signs and symbols or simulacra mask reality (and eventually the absence of reality itself), particularly in the consumer world.

Post-structuralism and postmodernism argue that ethics must study the complex and relational conditions of actions. A simple alignment of ideas of right and particular acts is not possible. There will always be an ethical remainder that cannot be taken into account or often even recognized. Such theorists find narrative (or, following Nietzsche and Foucault, genealogy) to be a helpful tool for understanding ethics because narrative is always about particular lived experiences in all their complexity rather than the assignment of an idea or norm to separate and individual actions.

Zygmunt Bauman says postmodernity is best described as modernity without illusion, the illusion being the belief that humanity can be repaired by some ethic principle. Postmodernity can be seen in this light as accepting the messy nature of humanity as unchangeable. In this postmodern world, the means to act collectively and globally to solve large-scale problems have been all but discredited, dismantled or lost. Problems can be handled only locally and each on its own. All problem-handling means building a mini-order at the expense of order elsewhere, and at the cost of rising global disorder as well as depleting the shrinking supplies of resources which make ordering possible. He considers Emmanuel Levinas's ethics as postmodern. Unlike the modern ethical philosophy which leaves the Other on the outside of the self as an ambivalent presence, Levinas's philosophy readmits her as a neighbor and as a crucial character in the process through which the moral self comes into its own.

David Couzens Hoy states that Emmanuel Levinas's writings on the face of the Other and Derrida's meditations on the relevance of death to ethics are signs of the "ethical turn" in Continental philosophy that occurred in the 1980s and 1990s. Hoy describes post-critique ethics as the "obligations that present themselves as necessarily to be fulfilled but are neither forced on one or are enforceable".

Hoy's post-critique model uses the term *ethical resistance*. Examples of this would be an individual's resistance to consumerism in a retreat to a simpler but perhaps harder lifestyle, or an individual's resistance to a terminal illness. Hoy describes Levinas's account as "not the attempt to use power against itself, or to mobilize sectors of the population to exert their political power; the ethical resistance is instead the resistance of the powerless".

Hoy concludes that

- The ethical resistance of the powerless others to our capacity to exert power over them is therefore what imposes unenforceable obligations on us. The obligations are unenforceable precisely because of the other's lack of power. That actions are at once obligatory and at the same time unenforceable is what put them in the category of the ethical. Obligations that were enforced would, by the virtue of the force behind them, not be freely undertaken and would not be in the realm of the ethical.

Applied Ethics

Applied ethics is a discipline of philosophy that attempts to apply ethical theory to real-life situations. The discipline has many specialized fields, such as engineering ethics, bioethics, geoethics, public service ethics and business ethics.

Specific Questions

Applied ethics is used in some aspects of determining public policy, as well as by individuals facing difficult decisions. The sort of questions addressed by applied ethics include: "Is getting an abortion immoral?"; "Is euthanasia immoral?"; "Is affirmative action right or wrong?"; "What are human rights, and how do we determine them?"; "Do animals have rights as well?"; and "Do individuals have the right of self-determination?"

A more specific question could be: "If someone else can make better out of his/her life than I can, is it then moral to sacrifice myself for them if needed?" Without these questions, there is no clear fulcrum on which to balance law, politics, and the practice of arbitration—in fact, no common assumptions of all participants—so the ability to formulate the questions are prior to rights balancing. But not all questions studied in applied ethics concern public policy. For example, making ethical judgments regarding questions such as, "Is lying always wrong?" and, "If not, when is it permissible?" is prior to any etiquette.

People, in general, are more comfortable with dichotomies (two opposites). However, in ethics, the issues are most often multifaceted and the best-proposed actions address many different areas concurrently. In ethical decisions, the answer is almost never a "yes or no" or a "right or wrong" statement. Many buttons are pushed so that the overall condition is improved and not to the benefit of any particular faction.

And it has not only been shown that people consider the character of the moral agent (i.e. a principle implied in virtue ethics), the deed of the action (i.e. a principle implied in deontology), and the consequences of the action (i.e. a principle implied in utilitarianism) when formulating moral judgments, but moreover that the effect of each of these three components depends on the value of each component.

Particular Fields of Application

Bioethics

Bioethics is the study of controversial ethics brought about by advances in biology and medicine. Bioethicists are concerned with the ethical questions that arise in the relationships among life sciences, biotechnology, medicine, politics, law, and philosophy. It also includes the study of the more commonplace questions of values ("the ethics of the ordinary") that arise in primary care and other branches of medicine.

Bioethics also needs to address emerging biotechnologies that affect basic biology and future humans. These developments include cloning, gene therapy, human genetic engineering, astroethics and life in space, and manipulation of basic biology through altered DNA, RNA and proteins, e.g. "three parent baby, where baby is born from genetically modified embryos, would have DNA from a mother, a father and from a female donor.

Correspondingly, new bioethics also need to address life at its core. For example, biotic ethics value organic gene/protein life itself and seek to propagate it. With such life-centered principles, ethics may secure a cosmological future for life.

Business Ethics

Business ethics (also corporate ethics) is a form of applied ethics or professional ethics that examines ethical principles and moral or ethical problems that arise in a business environment, including fields like medical ethics. Business ethics represents the practices that any individual or group exhibits within an organization that can negatively or positively affect the businesses core values. It applies to all aspects of business conduct and is relevant to the conduct of individuals and entire organizations.

Business ethics has both normative and descriptive dimensions. As a corporate practice and a career specialization, the field is primarily normative. Academics attempting to understand business behavior employ descriptive methods. The range and quantity of business ethical issues reflect the interaction of profit-maximizing behavior with non-economic concerns. Interest in business ethics accelerated dramatically during the 1980s and 1990s, both within major corporations and within academia. For example, today most major corporations promote their commitment to non-economic values under headings such as ethics codes and social responsibility charters.

Adam Smith said, "People of the same trade seldom meet together, even for merriment and diversion, but the conversation ends in a conspiracy against the public, or in some contrivance to raise prices." Governments use laws and regulations to point business behavior in what they perceive to be beneficial directions. Ethics implicitly regulates areas and details of behavior that lie beyond governmental control. The emergence of large corporations with limited relationships and sensitivity to the communities in which they operate accelerated the development of formal ethics regimes. Business ethics also relates to unethical activities of interorganizational relationships, such as strategic alliances, buyer-supplier relationships, or joint ventures. Such unethical practices include, for instance, opportunistic behaviors, contract violations, and deceitful practices.

Machine Ethics

In *Moral Machines: Teaching Robots Right from Wrong*, Wendell Wallach and Colin Allen conclude that issues in machine ethics will likely drive advancement in understanding of human ethics by forcing us to address gaps in modern normative theory and by providing a platform for experimental investigation. The effort to actually program a machine or artificial agent to behave as though instilled with a sense of ethics requires new specificity in our normative theories, especially regarding aspects customarily considered common-sense. For example, machines, unlike humans, can support a wide selection of learning algorithms, and controversy has arisen over the relative ethical merits of these options. This may reopen classic debates of normative ethics framed in new (highly technical) terms.

Military Ethics

Military ethics is concerned with questions regarding the application of force and the ethos of the soldier and is often understood as applied professional ethics. Just war theory is generally seen to set the background terms of military ethics. However, individual countries and traditions have different fields of attention.

Military ethics involves multiple subareas, including the following among others:

1. what, if any, should be the laws of war?
2. justification for the initiation of military force.
3. decisions about who may be targeted in warfare.
4. decisions on choice of weaponry, and what collateral effects such weaponry may have.
5. standards for handling military prisoners.
6. methods of dealing with violations of the laws of war.

Political Ethics

Political ethics (also known as political morality or public ethics) is the practice of making moral judgements about political action and political agents.

Public Sector Ethics

Public sector ethics is a set of principles that guide public officials in their service to their constituents, including their decision-making on behalf of their constituents. Fundamental to the concept of public sector ethics is the notion that decisions and actions are based on what best serves the public's interests, as opposed to the official's personal interests (including financial interests) or self-serving political interests.

Publication Ethics

Publication ethics is the set of principles that guide the writing and publishing process for all professional publications. To follow these principles, authors must verify that the publication does not contain plagiarism or publication bias. As a way to avoid misconduct in research these principles can also apply to experiments that are referenced or analyzed in publications by ensuring the data is recorded honestly and accurately.

Plagiarism is the failure to give credit to another author's work or ideas, when it is used in the publication. It is the obligation of the editor of the journal to ensure the article does not contain any plagiarism before it is published. If a publication that has already been published is proven to contain plagiarism, the editor of the journal can retract the article. Another critical publication ethics issue pertains to citation plagiarism when researchers copy and paste citation entries from other published works without reading the original source.

Publication bias occurs when the publication is one-sided or "prejudiced against results". In best practice, an author should try to include information from all parties involved, or affected by the topic. If an author is prejudiced against certain results, than it can "lead to erroneous conclusions being drawn".

Misconduct in research can occur when an experimenter falsifies results. Falsely recorded information occurs when the researcher "fakes" information or data, which was not used when conducting the actual experiment. By faking the data, the researcher can alter the results from the experiment to better fit the hypothesis they originally predicted. When conducting medical research, it is important to honor the healthcare rights of a patient by protecting their anonymity in the publication. *Respect for autonomy* is the principle that decision-making should allow individuals to be autonomous; they should be able to make decisions that apply to their own lives. This means that individuals should have control of their lives. *Justice* is the principle that decision-makers must focus on actions that are fair to those affected. Ethical decisions need to be consistent with the ethical theory. There are cases where the management has made decisions that seem to be unfair to the employees, shareholders, and other stakeholders. Such decisions are unethical.

Relational Ethics

Relational ethics is related to an ethics of care. They are used in qualitative research, especially ethnography and autoethnography. Researchers who employ relational ethics value and respect the connection between themselves and the people they study, and "...between researchers and the communities in which they live and work". (Ellis, 2007, p. 4). Relational ethics also help researchers understand difficult issues such as conducting research on intimate others that have died and developing friendships with their participants. Relational ethics in close personal relationships form a central concept of contextual therapy.

Ethics of Nanotechnologies

Ethics of nanotechnology is the study of the ethical issues emerging from advances in nanotechnology.

Ethics of Quantification

Ethics of quantification is the study of the ethical issues associated to different forms of visible or invisible forms of quantification.

Animal Ethics

Animal ethics is a term used in academia to describe human-animal relationships and how animals ought to be treated. The subject matter includes animal rights, animal welfare, animal law, speciesism, animal cognition, wildlife conservation, the moral status of nonhuman animals, the concept of nonhuman personhood, human exceptionalism, the history of animal use, and theories of justice.

Ethics of Technology

Ethics of technology is a sub-field of ethics addressing the ethical questions specific to the Technology Age. Some prominent works of philosopher Hans Jonas are devoted to ethics of technology. The subject has also been explored, following the work of Mario Bunge, under the term technoethics.

Moral Psychology

Moral psychology is a field of study that began as an issue in philosophy and that is now properly considered part of the discipline of psychology. Some use the term "moral psychology" relatively narrowly to refer to the study of moral development. However, others tend to use the term more broadly to include any topics at the intersection of ethics and psychology (and philosophy of mind). Such topics are ones that involve the mind and are relevant to moral issues. Some of the main topics of the field are moral responsibility, moral development, moral character (especially as related to virtue ethics), altruism, psychological egoism, moral luck, and moral disagreement.

Evolutionary Ethics

Evolutionary ethics concerns approaches to ethics (morality) based on the role of evolution in shaping human psychology and behavior. Such approaches may be based in scientific fields such as evolutionary psychology or sociobiology, with a focus on understanding and explaining observed ethical preferences and choices.

Descriptive Ethics

Descriptive ethics is on the less philosophical end of the spectrum since it seeks to gather particular information about how people live and draw general conclusions based on observed patterns. Abstract and theoretical questions that are more clearly philosophical—such as, "Is ethical knowledge possible?"—are not central to descriptive ethics. Descriptive ethics offers a value-free approach to ethics, which defines it as a social science rather than a humanities discipline. Its examination of ethics does not start with a preconceived theory but rather investigates observations of actual choices made by moral agents in practice. Some philosophers rely on descriptive ethics and choices made and unchallenged by a society or culture to derive categories, which typically vary by context. This can lead to situational ethics and situated ethics. These philosophers often view aesthetics, etiquette, and arbitration as more fundamental, percolating "bottom up" to imply the existence of, rather than explicitly prescribe, theories of value or of conduct. The study of descriptive ethics may include examinations of the following:

- Ethical codes applied by various groups. Some consider aesthetics itself the basis of ethics—and a personal moral core developed through art and storytelling as very influential in one's later ethical choices.
- Informal theories of etiquette that tend to be less rigorous and more situational.

Some consider etiquette a simple negative ethics, i.e., where can one evade an uncomfortable truth without doing wrong? One notable advocate of this view is Judith Martin ("Miss Manners"). According to this view, ethics is more a summary of common sense social decisions.

- Practices in arbitration and law, e.g., the claim that ethics itself is a matter of balancing "right versus right", i.e., putting priorities on two things that are both right, but that must be traded off carefully in each situation.
- Observed choices made by ordinary people, without expert aid or advice, who vote, buy, and decide what is worth valuing. This is a major concern within disciplines such as political science and economics.

Legal and Ethical Frameworks in India and Rest of the World

Legal and Ethical Frameworks in India

Legal and ethical frameworks form the cornerstone of any functioning society, providing a structured system of rules and moral guidelines that govern individual and collective behavior. In India, a diverse and culturally rich nation, these frameworks play a pivotal role in shaping interactions, institutions, and the overall functioning of the society.

Legal Frameworks in India:

- **Constitutional Foundations:** The Constitution of India, adopted in 1950, serves as the supreme legal framework, providing the foundation for the country's legal system. It enshrines fundamental rights, directive principles of state policy, and the separation of powers between the executive, legislature, and judiciary.
- **Pluralistic Legal System:** India maintains a pluralistic legal system, drawing from a combination of common law, customary law, and religious personal laws. This diversity reflects the complex social fabric of the country.
- **Civil and Criminal Law:** India's legal system encompasses both civil and criminal law. Civil law addresses private disputes between individuals or entities, while criminal law deals with offenses against the state. This dual approach ensures a balanced administration of justice.

Ethical Frameworks in India:

- **Cultural and Philosophical Roots:** India's ethical frameworks are deeply rooted in its cultural, philosophical, and religious traditions. Concepts such as dharma (duty), ahimsa (non-violence), and satya (truth) play a central role in guiding moral conduct.
- **Professional Codes of Ethics:** Various professions in India, including law, medicine, and journalism, adhere to specific codes of ethics. These codes outline professional responsibilities, standards of conduct, and obligations to clients or patients.

- **Universal Ethical Principles:** While Indian ethics may draw from diverse religious and philosophical traditions, there are universal ethical principles, such as honesty, integrity, and respect for human dignity, that transcend cultural boundaries.

Intersection of Legal and Ethical Frameworks in India:

- **Overlapping Principles:** Legal and ethical frameworks in India often share common principles, such as the protection of individual rights and the prohibition of fraud or harm. This overlap reinforces the importance of adhering to ethical imperatives in legal practice.
- **Ethics in Professional Practice:** Professionals in India, including lawyers, doctors, and journalists, are guided not only by legal requirements but also by ethical duties. For example, legal practitioners have an obligation to uphold the integrity of the legal system and provide zealous advocacy for their clients.

Balancing Rights and Responsibilities in India:

- **Individual Autonomy and Collective Welfare:** India's legal and ethical frameworks seek to strike a balance between respecting individual autonomy and safeguarding the common good. This is evident in areas such as healthcare, where patients' right to informed consent must be weighed against public health imperatives.
- **Cultural Diversity and Universal Rights:** India's pluralistic society presents a unique challenge in balancing cultural relativism with universal ethical norms. Striking a balance between respecting diverse cultural practices and upholding fundamental human rights is a continuous endeavor.

Challenges and Controversies in India:

- **Emerging Technologies and Ethical Dilemmas:** India, like many countries, grapples with ethical questions arising from rapid technological advancements. Issues related to data privacy, artificial intelligence, and genetic engineering pose new challenges for both legal and ethical frameworks.
- **Access to Justice and Human Rights:** Ensuring equal access to justice and protecting human rights for all citizens, regardless of socioeconomic status or background, remains a critical area of focus in India's legal and ethical landscape.

Rest of the World

The Foundation of Legal Frameworks:

- **Definition and Purpose:** Legal frameworks consist of a system of laws, regulations, and established norms that guide conduct within a society. They are enforced by governmental authorities and serve multiple purposes, including maintaining order, protecting rights, and promoting justice.

- **Sources of Law:** Legal systems draw from various sources, including written laws (statutes), common law precedents, constitutional provisions, and international treaties. These sources provide a basis for adjudicating disputes and ensuring consistency in legal decision-making.
- **Civil and Criminal Law:** Legal frameworks encompass both civil law, which deals with private disputes between individuals or entities, and criminal law, which addresses offenses against the state. These two branches of law serve distinct but complementary roles in maintaining social order.

The Ethical Imperative:

- **Definition and Significance:** Ethical frameworks are sets of moral principles and values that guide human behavior. They are informed by cultural norms, philosophical theories, religious beliefs, and societal expectations. Ethics provide a moral compass for individuals and organizations, influencing decision-making and conduct.
- **Universal Ethical Principles:** While ethical norms may vary across cultures and belief systems, there are universal principles such as honesty, integrity, respect for autonomy, and the avoidance of harm that underpin ethical frameworks worldwide.
- **Professional Codes of Ethics:** Many professions, including medicine, law, and journalism, have established codes of ethics that provide specific guidelines for practitioners. These codes serve to maintain professional standards, protect the interests of clients or patients, and uphold public trust.

Intersection of Legal and Ethical Frameworks:

- **Overlapping Principles:** Legal and ethical frameworks often share common principles, such as the prohibition of fraud or the protection of individual rights. In such cases, legal requirements may align with ethical imperatives, reinforcing the importance of adherence.
- **Ethical Duties in Legal Practice:** Professionals within the legal system, including lawyers and judges, have ethical duties that go beyond mere compliance with the law. These duties may include confidentiality, zealous advocacy, and impartiality, which serve to uphold the integrity of the legal profession.

Balancing Rights and Responsibilities:

- **Individual Autonomy and the Common Good:** Legal and ethical frameworks seek to strike a balance between respecting individual autonomy and safeguarding the collective welfare. This tension is evident in areas such as healthcare, where patients' right to informed consent must be weighed against public health imperatives.

- **Ethics in Business and Corporate Governance:** In the corporate world, legal compliance is the minimum standard, but ethical conduct is increasingly recognized as vital for long-term success and sustainability. Ethical business practices encompass areas such as fair competition, environmental responsibility, and stakeholder engagement.

Challenges and Controversies:

- **Emerging Technologies and Ethical Dilemmas:** Rapid technological advancements, including artificial intelligence, genetic engineering, and autonomous systems, pose new ethical questions that legal frameworks may struggle to address adequately.
- **Cultural Relativism vs. Universal Ethics:** Debates persist over whether ethical principles are culturally relative or universally applicable. Striking a balance between respecting diverse cultural norms and upholding fundamental human rights remains a complex challenge.

Interplay between Law and Ethics in Media

In the ever-evolving landscape of media, the delicate dance between law and ethics takes center stage, shaping the content we consume, the narratives we encounter, and the societal norms we collectively uphold. This interplay is not a mere intellectual exercise but a dynamic force that influences public discourse, shapes political landscapes, and defines cultural boundaries. This stage embarks on a comprehensive exploration of the intricate relationship between law and ethics in the realm of media, shedding light on how these two domains intersect, converge, and occasionally conflict. As we delve into this multifaceted interplay, we embark on a journey that unravels the complexities, challenges, and critical importance of this dynamic relationship. The Foundations of Media Law and Ethics:

- **Defining Media Law:** Media law encompasses the legal frameworks and regulations that govern the creation, distribution, and consumption of media content. It includes areas such as freedom of expression, defamation, copyright, privacy, and national security.
- **Ethics as the Moral Compass:** Media ethics, on the other hand, serves as the moral compass that guides the behavior and conduct of media practitioners. Rooted in universal principles of truth, fairness, and responsibility, ethical considerations play a pivotal role in shaping journalistic practices.

Balancing Freedom of Expression and Legal Boundaries:

- **Freedom of Expression: A Cornerstone of Democracy:** Freedom of expression is a fundamental right that underpins democratic societies. It empowers individuals and media organizations to voice opinions, report news, and contribute to public discourse without fear of censorship or reprisal.
- **Defining the Limits:** However, this freedom is not without bounds. Legal

constraints exist to prevent the dissemination of false information, hate speech, incitement to violence, and other forms of expression that may harm individuals or threaten national security.

Libel, Defamation, and the Law:

- **Protecting Reputation:** Libel and defamation laws provide individuals with recourse against false statements that harm their reputation. These laws strike a balance between protecting an individual's reputation and safeguarding freedom of expression.
- **Public Figures and the Higher Standard:** When it comes to public figures, such as politicians or celebrities, the threshold for proving defamation is often higher. They must demonstrate that false statements were made with "actual malice" or with knowledge of their falsity.

Privacy in the Age of Digital Media:

- **The Right to Privacy:** Privacy laws safeguard an individual's right to be free from intrusion into their personal affairs. In the digital age, where information can be disseminated globally in an instant, protecting privacy has become an increasingly complex challenge.
- **Balancing Public Interest and Private Lives:** Media professionals must navigate the delicate balance between the public's right to know and an individual's right to privacy. This is particularly pertinent in cases involving public figures or sensitive personal information.

The Responsibility of Gatekeepers: Journalism Ethics in Practice:

- **Truth and Accuracy: The Journalistic Imperatives:** Journalists bear the responsibility of reporting truthfully and accurately. Verifying information, providing context, and correcting errors are essential components of ethical journalism.
- **Fairness and Impartiality:** Journalists are tasked with presenting a balanced view of events, allowing all relevant parties an opportunity to provide their perspective. Avoiding bias and presenting information objectively are core ethical principles.

Challenges in the Digital Age:

- **Misinformation and Disinformation:** The digital era has brought about a proliferation of misinformation and disinformation. Media organizations grapple with the ethical duty to combat false information while upholding principles of free speech.
- **Ethics in New Media:** The rise of social media platforms and citizen journalism has challenged traditional notions of media ethics. Issues such as user-generated content, online harassment, and the rapid spread of information require new ethical considerations.

2

The Constitution of India

Historical Evolution and Relevance of the Indian Constitution

Historical Evolution in Indian Constitution

The Indian constitution visited several historical Evolution in different layers. Here is a list of all the layers of historical Evolution in the Indian Constitution:

- Regulating Act of 1773
- Pitts Act of 1784
- Charter Act of 1813
- Charter Act of 1833
- Charter act of 1853
- Government of India Act of 1858
- Indian Council Act of 1861
- Indian Council Act of 1892
- Morley Minto Reforms of 1909
- Montague-Chelmsford Reforms of 1919
- Government of India Act of 1935
- Indian Independence Act of 1935

Detailed Overview of Reforms in Each Act

Indian Constitution Regulating Act 1773. It started with Warren Hastings, the governor of Bengal, re-appointed as the governor-general of Bengal. 4 members were selected for the executive council to take necessary decisions. In 1774, the supreme court of Calcutta was established as the most superior court of India. There were reforms like the prohibition of officials from engaging in private trade.

Indian Constitution Pitts Act 1784

It separated commercial and political functions with responsibilities like the board of control managing the political affairs and politics, whereas the court of directors handled the commercial output. Governor councils were getting prepared in Madras and Bombay to speed up the structure process for an independent nation.

Indian Constitution Charter Act 1813

The Indian Constitution Charter Act 1813 brought a change in the industrial capital of India. The British East India Company refrained from its monopoly over the trade market of India. However, the trade sector of Tea and Opium was still there with the British company.

Indian Constitution Charter Act 1833

This act brought the redesignation of the Governor-general of Bengal to the Governor-general of India with the first appointment of Lord William Bentinck. The Indian Constitution Charter Act 1833 brought the removal of legislative powers of Bombay and Madras presidencies.

Indian Constitution Charter Act 1853

This brought the separation between the legislative and executive power of the governor-general. It also brought the formation of a six-membered central legislative council. Four out of these six were granted the responsibility by the provisional government of Madras, Agra, Bombay, and Bengal.

Indian Constitution Government of India Act 1858

The 1857 revolution snatched the control and possession of India from the hands of the East India Company, and it fell into the hands of the British Crown without any middleman like the East India Company. It resulted in the appointment of the Secretary of State. There were 15 members of a council appointed to assist the Secretary of State. This act also abolished the board of control and the court of directors.

Indian Constitution Indian Council Act 1861

Three Indians were appointed in the legislative council to represent Indians in the Viceroy council. There were provisions formed to allow the entry of Indians as non-officials in the Viceroy Council. The Madras and Bombay presidencies restored their legislative powers. This act also brought the recognition of the portfolio system.

Indian Constitution Indian Council Act 1892

The Indian Constitution Indian Council Act 1892 brought a significant change with nominations or indirect elections. Legislative councils were granted more power with the budget discussion and executive questioning.

Morley Minto Reforms 1909

It introduced direct elections in India. The Central legislative council transformed into the Imperial legislative council. This act reduced the count of legislative councils to 16, which were 60 before this reform. The Morley Minto Reforms provided the acceptance of a communal electorate.

Montague-Chelmsford Reforms 1919

The Montague-Chelmsford reforms brought the separation between central and provisional subjects. It proposed and implemented the nomination of ministers from the elected members of the legislative council. This act made it mandatory that the Viceroy's executive council should have three members of Indian origin. India's first public service commission was formed due to this act and provided the right to vote, which almost 10% of the population acquired at that time.

Indian Constitution Government of India Act 1935

This act proposed the idea of an All India Federation consisting of members from British India and princely states. Division of subjects into provincial and central took place. Centre was offered the charge of federal subjects, and Provincial was offered the charge of provincial subjects. A new federal court was established with the abolishment of the Indian Council. The financial institution RBI was introduced with the implementation of this law.

Indian Constitution Indian Independence Act 1947

The day 15 August 1947 is India's Independence Day. It was declared independent with the sovereign title. The nominal heads status was given to the Viceroy and the governor. The constituent assembly of India was assigned the powers of legislation and execution.

Constitution of India and its Relevance

A Constitution is an important document in modern democracies. The constitution of India mentions the laws that govern the country. A constitution recognizes and protects a nation's value and gives the foundation to build the government and laws. A constitution gives a fundamental structure for the country and community.

It lays down rules for the citizens and the government. In a way that the government officials exercising power could be held accountable to the people they serve. It safeguards against tyranny and abuse of power by the government. It prevents despotic governments (which is not bound by any higher law or constitution). It determines the relation between citizens and the government and protects and provides basic rights to all the citizens.

It helps in separating and distributing power or authority among the institutions of government. It provides a check and restrain to the institutions of government. It defines power and duties of the executive, legislative and judiciary branches of the government and ensures no branch of government exercises excessive power and maintains rule of law to maintain order and stability. The federal structure of government given in the constitution clearly defines the distribution of power and responsibility for promotion of unity of the country while recognizes the differences.

The constitution ensures equality of all its citizens and prohibits discrimination based on religion, race, caste, gender etc. Equality is critical in promoting social justice and preventing marginalization of certain groups in the society. The constitution celebrates the diversity of India and provides a pluralistic society where people of different cultures, language and religion can coexist harmoniously.

The constitution also works as a social instrument as it provides a basic framework for socio-economic development. It ensures that the marginalized groups receive sense of inclusivity, equality and justice. The Directive Principle of State Policy also motivates the government to create laws.

They serve as an instrument for protecting the environment, uphold the labor rights, promote free access of education to children etc. for equal opportunities, social welfare and promotion of education and public health. Though they are non justiciable and are not enforceable in courts, they are important as they serve as a guide for policymaking for the government.

It also provides legal formwork for economic development as the protection of property rights, regulation of commerce etc.

The independent judiciary of India establishes Supreme Court as the highest judicial authority. The judiciary is the guardian of the constitution and ensures its principles are upheld at all times.

The constitution guarantees fundamental rights to all the citizens irrespective of the class, caste, sex, age, color of skin etc. such as the right to equality, freedom of speech and expression, right to life and personal liberty. The constitution also grants people the right to vote and freedom to express their criticism of those in power. It also serves the purpose of guaranteeing the fundamental human rights of citizens essential to ensure that government does not function in a way that compromises interest of the citizens of country. The constitution ensures that citizens have power to participate in governance of the country.

Constitution also makes sure that there is political stability and keeps the community's sovereignty intact. To make sure that it is strong and is vulnerable to the attacks of external powers. It is also seen that the countries that do not have a rigid constitution their political community is likely to crumble. Therefore, the constitution of India is relevant because it serves as the bedrock of the nation, protecting citizens and their rights, ensuring social justice and celebrating diversity while striving for unity. Though it was influenced by many different pre existing constitutions of countries with many different ideologies it did not just copy from those.

Each article included in the constitution was firstly debated and after many such deliberations when most or all of the constituent assembly members agreed the principle was written in the constitution of our country as an article. But this was not it, the constitution of India is a dynamic and a living document that still adapts to changing times by amendments while upholding its core values and principles at all times to make it useful to the situations and evolutions in the society.

Fundamental Rights and Freedom of Speech and Expression

Fundamental Rights

The Fundamental Rights in India enshrined in part III (Article 12-35) of the Constitution of India guarantee civil liberties such that all Indians can lead their lives in peace and harmony as citizens of India. These rights are known as "fundamental" as they are the most essential for all-round development i.e., material, intellectual, moral and spiritual and protected by fundamental law of the land i.e. constitution. If the rights provided by Constitution especially the Fundamental rights are violated the Supreme Court and the High Courts can issue writs under Articles 32 and 226 of the Constitution, respectively, directing the State Machinery for enforcement of the fundamental rights.

These include individual rights common to most liberal democracies, such as equality before law, freedom of speech and expression, freedom of association and peaceful assembly, freedom to practice religion and the right to constitutional remedies for the protection of civil rights by means of writs such as habeas corpus. Violations of these rights result in punishments as prescribed in the Indian Penal Code, subject to discretion of the judiciary. The Fundamental Rights are defined as basic human freedoms where every Indian citizen has the right to enjoy for a proper and harmonious development of personality and life. These rights apply universally to all citizens of India, irrespective of their race, place of birth, religion, caste or gender. They are enforceable by the courts, subject to certain restrictions. The Rights have their origins in many sources, including England's Bill of Rights, the United States Bill of Rights and France's Declaration of the Rights of Man.

The six fundamental rights are:

1. Right to equality (Article 14–18)
2. Right to freedom (Article 19–22)
3. Right against exploitation (Article 23–24)

4. Right to freedom of religion (Article 25–28)
5. Cultural and educational rights (Article 29–30)
6. Right to constitutional remedies (Article 32-35)

Rights literally mean those freedoms which are essential for personal good as well as the good of the community. The rights guaranteed under the Constitution of India are fundamental as they have been incorporated into the *Fundamental Law of the Land* and are enforceable in a court of law. However, this does not mean that they are absolute or immune from Constitutional amendment.

Fundamental rights for Indians have also been aimed at overturning the inequalities of pre-independence social practices. Specifically, they have also been used to abolish untouchability and hence prohibit discrimination on the grounds of religion, race, caste, sex, or place of birth. They also forbid trafficking of human beings and forced labour. They also protect cultural and educational rights of ethnic and religious minorities by allowing them to preserve their languages and also establish and administer their own education institutions. When the Constitution of India came into force it basically gave seven fundamental rights to its citizens. However, Right to Property was removed as a Fundamental Right through 44th Constitutional Amendment in 1978. In 2009, Right to Education Act was added. Every child between the age of 6 to 14 years is entitled to free education.

In the case of *Kesavananda Bharati v. State of Kerala* (1973)[1], it was held by the Apex Court that Fundamental Rights can be amended by the Parliament, however, such amendment should not contravene the basic structure of the Constitution.

Origins

The first demand for fundamental rights came in the form of the "Constitution of India Bill, in 1895. Also popularly known as the Swaraj Bill 1895, it was written during the emergence of Indian nationalism and increasingly vocal demands by Indians for self-government. It talked about freedom of speech, right to privacy, right to franchise, etc.

In the following period attempts were made from quarters asking the British government to grants rights for Indians. These demand were made in resolution by the INc between 1917 and 1919 in several reports and bills

In 1919, the Rowlatt Act gave extensive powers to the British government and allowed indefinite arrest and detention of individuals, warrantless searches and seizures, restrictions on public gatherings, and intensive censorship of media and publications. The public opposition to this act eventually led to mass campaigns of non-violent civil disobedience throughout the country demanding guaranteed civil freedoms, and limitations on government power. Indians, who were seeking independence and their own government, were particularly influenced by the independence of Ireland and the development of the Irish constitution. Also, the directive principles of state policy in Irish constitution were looked upon by the people of India as an inspiration for independent India's government to comprehensively tackle complex social and economic challenges across a vast, diverse nation and population.

In 1928, the Nehru Commission composing of representatives of Indian political parties proposed constitutional reforms for India that apart from calling for dominion status for India and elections under universal suffrage, would guarantee rights deemed fundamental, representation for religious and ethnic minorities, and limit the powers of the government. In 1931, the Indian National Congress (the largest Indian political party of the time) adopted resolutions committing itself to the defence of fundamental civil rights, as well as socio-economic rights such as the minimum wage and the abolition of untouchability and serfdom. Committing themselves to socialism in 1936, the Congress leaders took examples from the Constitution of the Soviet Union, which inspired the fundamental duties of citizens as a means of collective patriotic responsibility for national interests and challenges.

When India obtained independence on 15 August 1947, the task of developing a constitution for the nation was undertaken by the Constituent Assembly of India, composed of elected representatives under the presidency of Rajendra Prasad. While members of Congress constituted a large majority, Congress leaders appointed persons from diverse political backgrounds to positions of responsibility for developing the constitution and national laws. Notably, B. R. Ambedkar became the chairperson of the Drafting Committee, while Jawaharlal Nehru and Sardar Vallabhbhai Patel became chairpersons of committees and sub-committees responsible for different subjects. A notable development during that period having significant effect on the Indian constitution took place on 10 December 1948 when the United Nations General Assembly adopted the Universal Declaration of Human Rights and called upon all member states to adopt these rights in their respective constitutions.

The fundamental rights were included in the First Draft Constitution (February 1948), the Second Draft Constitution (17 October 1948) and final Third Draft Constitution (26 November 1949), prepared by the Drafting Committee.

Significance and Characteristics

The fundamental rights were included in the constitution because they were considered essential for the development of the personality of every individual and to preserve human dignity. The writers of the constitution regarded democracy of no avail if civil liberties, like freedom of speech and religion, were not recognised and protected by the State. According to them, "democracy" is, in essence, a government by opinion and therefore, the means of formulating public opinion should be secured to the people of a democratic nation. For this purpose, the constitution guaranteed to all the citizens of India the freedom of speech and expression and various other freedoms in the form of the fundamental rights.

All people, irrespective of race, religion, caste or gender, have been given the right to petition the Supreme Court or the High Courts for the enforcement of their fundamental rights. It is not necessary that the aggrieved party has to be the one to do so. Poverty-stricken people may not have the means to do so and therefore, in the public interest, anyone can commence litigation in the court on their behalf. This is known as "public interest litigation". In some cases, High Court judges have acted suo moto on their own on the basis of newspaper reports.

These fundamental rights help not only in protection but also the prevention of gross violations of human rights. They emphasise on the fundamental unity of India by guaranteeing to all citizens the access and use of the same facilities, irrespective of background. Some fundamental rights apply for persons of any nationality whereas others are available only to the citizens of India. The right to life and personal liberty is available to all people and so is the right to freedom of religion. On the other hand, freedoms of speech and expression, and freedom to reside and settle in any part of the country are reserved for citizens alone, including non-resident Indian citizens. The right to equality in matters of public employment cannot be conferred to overseas citizens of India.

Fundamental rights primarily protect individuals from any arbitrary state actions, but some rights are enforceable against individuals. For instance, the Constitution abolishes untouchability and also prohibits *begar*. These provisions act as a check both on state action as well as the action of private individuals. However, these rights are not absolute or uncontrolled and are subject to reasonable restrictions as necessary for the protection of general welfare. They can also be selectively curtailed. The Supreme Court has ruled that all provisions of the Constitution, including fundamental rights, can be amended, but that Parliament cannot alter the basic structure of the constitution. Since the fundamental rights can be altered only by a constitutional amendment, their inclusion is a check not only on the executive branch but also on the Parliament and state legislatures.

A state of national emergency has an adverse effect on these rights. Under such a state, the rights conferred by Article 19 (freedoms of speech, assembly and movement, etc.) remain suspended. Hence, in such a situation, the legislature may make laws that go against the rights given in Article 19. The President may by order suspend the right to move the court for the enforcement of other rights as well.

Right to Equality

The Right to Equality is one of the chief guarantees of the Constitution. It is embodied in Articles 14–18, which collectively encompass the general principles of equality before law and non-discrimination and Articles 17–18 which collectively encompass further the philosophy of social equality.

Article 14

Article 14 of the Constitution of India provides for equality before the law or equal protection of the laws within the territory of India. It states:

- "The State shall not deny to any person equality before the law or the equal protection of the laws within the territory of India."

Reasonable Classification and Non-Arbitrariness

Article 14 guarantees equality to all persons, including citizens, corporations, and foreigners. Its provisions have come up for discussion in the Supreme Court in a number of cases and the case of Ram Krishna Dalmia vs Justice S R Tendolkar reiterated its meaning and scope as follows. Article 14 permits classification, so long as it is 'reasonable', but forbids class legislation. A classification of groups of people is considered reasonable when:

1. The classification is based upon intelligible differentia that distinguishes persons or things that are grouped from others that are left out of the group, and,
2. The differential has a rational relation with the objective of the act.

In addition, the classification must be non-arbitrary. Supreme Court in E. P. Royappa (1973) provided guidance on arbitrariness of an act:

- "Equality is a dynamic concept with many aspects and dimensions and it cannot be 'cribbed, cabined and confined' within the traditional and doctrinaire limits. From the positivistic point of view, equality is antithetic to arbitrariness. In fact, equality and arbitrariness are sworn enemies... Where an act is arbitrary, it is implicit that it is unequal both according to political logic and constitutional law and is therefore violative of Article 14."

Article 15

Article 15 of the Constitution of India forbids discrimination on grounds only of religion, race, caste, gender, or place of birth. It applies Article 14's general principle of equality in specific situations by forbidding classifications made on protected grounds. While prohibiting discrimination based on prejudice, the Article is also the central issue in a large body of judicial decisions, public debate, and legislation revolving around affirmative action, reservations, and quotas. As of the 103rd Amendment of the Constitution of India, Article 15 .

Background

On 29 November 1948, the Constituent Assembly debated the first version of Article 15 as Article 9 of the revised Draft Constitution, 1948. Draft Article 9 read:

(1) The State shall not discriminate against any citizen on grounds only of religion, race, caste, sex or any of them. In particular, no citizen shall, on grounds only of religion, race, caste, sex or any of them, be subject to any disability, liability, restriction or condition with regard to

(a) Access to shops, public restaurants, hotels and places of public entertainment, or

(b) The use of wells, tanks, roads and places of public resort maintained wholly or partly out of the revenues of the State or dedicated to the use of the general public.

(2) Nothing in this article shall prevent the State from making any special provision for women and children.

Some members of the Assembly wanted additional protected grounds, including a prohibition on discrimination based on family and descent. Other members argued further that gardens, roads, and tramways should be included as places where denial of access is prohibited. However, B. R. Ambedkar, the chairman of the Drafting Committee, clarified that the general nature of the text was sufficient to cover a large variety of spaces not specifically included in the Article. Prof. K.T. Shah, a member of the Assembly, proposed that Clause 2 of the Draft Article be amended to provide for special provisions for 'Scheduled Castes or backward tribes for their advantage, safeguard, or betterment.' However, the proposal was rejected, with Ambedkar arguing that adopting the amendment would perpetuate the segregation of these groups. After debate and amendment, the original text remained largely intact and became Article 15 of the Constitution of India.

Clauses 1-2: Prohibition of Discrimination on Protected Grounds

The first two clauses of Article 15 prohibit discrimination *'on grounds only'* of religion, race, caste, sex, place of birth or any of them. In interpreting the phrase 'on grounds only', the Supreme Court has held that the effect of the statute is relevant, not the motive. The phrase was initially interpreted as meaning that an act or law that was based on any ground in addition to the five protected grounds, it would not be prohibited. For example, in 1989, a Regulation that required air hostesses of the national carrier to retire earlier, or under certain conditions including pregnancy or marriage, was only partially struck down. The Supreme Court held that it was discrimination not just on the basis of sex, but other considerations such as working conditions and employment routes. This was criticised by academics and feminists for failing to take the social role of gender into account. However, in 2007, the Court recognised that discrimination on the basis of sex should include discrimination based on stereotypes associated with sex and struck down a law that prevented women from working in premises where liquor was served. Article 15 has since received broader interpretations, and been used to read down a law that criminalised consensual sexual intercourse between persons of the same sex as discriminatory, and provide protections on the grounds of sexual orientation and gender identity. The Court has also recognised that Article 15 should be interpreted through the lens of intersectionality, taking multiple and intersecting identities into account.

General Prohibition against State Discrimination

Clause 1 of the Article prohibits the State from discriminating against citizens on five protected grounds. Within three years of the adoption of the Constitution, the Supreme Court used Article 15 to invalidate a State law which provided for elections which had separate electorates for members of different religious communities. Similarly, courts have found discrimination on the basis of religion under Article 15 in the context of special provisions for Muslims, and reservation of a State legislature seat for one religious community.

The Supreme Court has held that the Article 15 prohibition on race discrimination should be read along with the International Convention on the Elimination of All Forms of Racial Discrimination. The provision was used to direct the Union to set up a committee to address racial discrimination against people from North-East India. Some courts have connected race to protections for Scheduled Tribes. Courts have on occasion struck down discriminatory legislation on the basis of race such as in the case of a law which required members of a particular community to report daily to the police. Courts have also struck down discriminatory legislation on the basis of caste, as in the case of a notification which exempted all Harijan and Muslim residents from a compulsory levy in a locality.

Similarly, the Article has been used to invalidate sex discrimination by legislation, such as prohibitions on proprietresses holding property or working in premises where liquor was served. The Supreme Court has interpreted 'sex' as including both 'sexual orientation' and 'gender identity' which has extended the protection of Article 15 to Gay, Lesbian, Bisexual and Transgender persons.

Like the other protected grounds, 'place of birth' has also been a source of some ambiguity. In 1955, the Supreme Court distinguished between 'place of birth' and 'residence', holding that discrimination on the basis of 'residence' was not prohibited outright by Article 15. In that ruling, the Court upheld a State Medical College's decision to require a capitation fee from students residing outside the region on the grounds that the decision discriminated on the basis of *residence* or domicile and not on 'place of birth'. The Court diluted that decision in Pradeep Jain v. Union of India, holding that residence requirements (while not prohibited outright by Article 15(1)) were inconsistent with the idea of national unity and integration, and limited residence-based reservations to not more than seventy percent of total seats at the MBBS level.

For much of its history, Article 15 did not prohibit indirect discrimination. For example, in 1951, the Madras High Court held that the Evacuation Property Ordinance, 1949 did not violate clause (1), though most individuals affected by the ordinance were Muslim, as the operation of the ordinance was not restricted to Muslims alone on the ground of religion. However, in 2021, the Supreme Court in Lt. Col. Nitisha v. Union of India invalidated a facially neutral criteria for the grant of Permanent Commissions to women on the grounds that it was indirectly discriminatory.

Horizontal Prohibition of Denial of Access

Unlike Clause 1 which is addressed to the State, Clause 2 creates a broader prohibition on disability, liability, restriction, or condition with regard to accessing various public spaces and commercial establishments. Sub-clause (a) uses the word 'shop' broadly, to mean premises where goods are sold in any capacity, and including everything from hairdressing saloons to educational institutions. Therefore, there cannot be shops, public restaurants, or spaces of public entertainment which are reserved on the basis of any of the protected grounds. Some scholarship argues that the definition of 'shop' in sub-clause (a) should extend to all private economic market transactions, including exclusionary covenants for the lease of property. Sub-clause (b) relates to the use of wells, bathing ghats, roads and places of public resort maintained wholly or partly out of State funds or dedicated to the use of the general public. Accordingly, *private* wells and tanks are not regulated by sub-clause (b), unless they are dedicated to the use of the general public.

Clauses 3-6: Special Provisions for Disadvantaged Groups

Article 15, in Clauses (3-6), allows for positive discrimination in favour of disadvantaged groups. These clauses exist to allow the Indian state's expansive programme of affirmative action.

Women and Children

While Article 15 prohibits discrimination on the grounds of sex, special provisions for women and children are permissible. State institutions created exclusively for women, or special places reserved for women in public transport or places of entertainment do not violate Article 15. However, a 'special provision' does not mean that less favourable treatment may be given to women on a gender-based criterion.

Socially and Educationally Backward Classes

Nothing in this article or in clause (2) of Article 29 shall prevent the State from making any special provision for the advancement of any socially and educationally backward classes of citizens or for the Scheduled Castes and the Scheduled Tribes

Reservations in Educational Institutions

Nothing in this article or in sub-clause (g) of clause (1) of Article 19 shall prevent the State from making any special provision, by law, for the advancement of any socially and educationally backward classes of citizens or for the Scheduled Castes or the Scheduled Tribes insofar as such special provisions relate to their admission to educational institutions including private education institutions, whether aided or unaided by the State, other than the minority educational institutions referred to in clause (1) of Article 30.

Economically Weaker Sections

Clause (6) was inserted by the 103rd Constitutional Amendment in 2019. The provision allows for the State to provide for affirmative action including reservations for economically weaker sections (EWS). Various States have introduced schemes to implement reservations for EWS on the basis of Clause (6). In 2021, the Union government issued a notification to introduce EWS reservation in the medical postgraduate entrance exam. This decision was challenged at the Supreme Court.

Challenge to Constitutionality and Supreme Court decision

Various parties challenged the 103rd Amendment at the Supreme Court. They argued that it violates the basic structure of the Indian Constitution, which in their view does not allow reservations on purely economic criteria. On 7 November 2022, a five-judge bench of the Supreme Court of India held, in Janhit Abhiyan v Union of India, that the 103rd Amendment did not violate the basic structure. Justices Maheshwari, Trivedi, and Pardiwala wrote separate judgments for the majority. Justice Bhat wrote a dissenting opinion on behalf of himself and Chief Justice U.U Lalit, that has been praised in progressive quarters.

Article 16

Article 16 guarantees equality of opportunity in matters of public employment and prevents the State from discriminating against anyone in matters of employment on the grounds only of religion, race, caste, sex, descent, place of birth, place of residence or income. It creates exceptions for the implementation of measures of affirmative action for the benefit of any backward class of citizens in order to ensure adequate representation in public service, as well as reservation of an office of any religious institution for a person professing that particular religion.

Article 17

Article 17 abolishes the practice of untouchability in any form, making it an offense punishable by law. The Protection of Civil Rights Act, 1955 was enacted by Parliament to further this objective.

Article 18

Article 18 prohibits the State from conferring any titles other than military or academic distinctions, and the citizens of India cannot accept titles from a foreign state. Thus, Indian aristocratic titles and title of nobility conferred by the British have been abolished. However, military and academic distinctions can be conferred on the citizens of India. The awards of *Bharat Ratna* and *Padma Vibhushan can be used by the recipient as a title and do not, accordingly, come within the constitutional prohibition". The Supreme Court, on 15 December 1995, upheld the validity of such awards.*

Right to Freedom

The Right to Freedom is covered in Article 19 to 22, with the view of guaranteeing individual rights that were considered vital by the framers of the Constitution, and these Articles also include certain restrictions that may be imposed by the State on individual liberty under specified conditions. Article 19 guarantees six freedoms in the nature of civil rights, which are available only to citizens of India. These include the freedom of speech and expression, freedom of assembly without arms, freedom of association, freedom of movement throughout the territory of our country, freedom to reside and settle in any part of the country of India and the freedom to practice any profession. All these freedoms are subject to reasonable restrictions that may be imposed on them by the State, listed under Article 19 itself. The grounds for imposing these restrictions vary according to the freedom sought to be restricted and include national security, public order, decency and morality, contempt of court, incitement to offences and defamation. The State is also empowered, in the interests of the general public to nationalize any trade, industry or service to the exclusion of the citizens.

The freedoms guaranteed by Article 19 are further sought to be protected by Articles 20–22. The scope of these articles, particularly with respect to the doctrine of due process, was heavily debated by the Constituent Assembly. It was argued, especially by Benegal Narsing Rau, that the incorporation of such a clause would hamper social legislation and cause procedural difficulties in maintaining order, and therefore it ought to be excluded from the Constitution altogether.

The Constituent Assembly in 1948 eventually omitted the phrase "due process" in favor of "procedure established by law". As a result, Article 21, which prevents the encroachment of life or personal liberty by the State except in accordance with the procedure established by law, was, until 1978, construed narrowly as being restricted to executive action. However, in 1978, the Supreme Court in the case of *Maneka Gandhi v. Union of India* extended the protection of Article 21 to legislative action, holding that any law laying down a procedure must be just, fair and reasonable, and effectively reading due process into Article 21.

In the same case, the Supreme Court also ruled that "life" under Article 21 meant more than a mere "animal existence"; it would include the right to live with human dignity and all other aspects which made life "meaningful, complete and worth living". Subsequent judicial interpretation has broadened the scope of Article 21 to include within it a number of rights including those to livelihood, good health, clean environment, water, speedy trial and humanitarian treatment while imprisoned. The right to education at elementary level has been made one of the Fundamental Rights under Article 21A by the 86th Constitutional amendment of 2002.

Article 20 provides protection from conviction for offences in certain respects, including the rights against ex post facto laws, double jeopardy and freedom from self-incrimination. Article 22 provides specific rights to arrested and detained persons, in particular the rights to be informed of the grounds of arrest, consult a lawyer of one's own choice, be produced before a magistrate within 24 hours of the arrest, and the freedom not to be detained beyond that period without an order of the magistrate. The Constitution also authorizes the State to make laws providing for preventive detention, subject to certain other safeguards present in Article 22. The provisions pertaining to preventive detention were discussed with scepticism and misgivings by the Constituent Assembly, and were reluctantly approved after a few amendments in 1949. Article 22 provides that when a person is detained under any law of preventive detention, the State can detain such person without trial for only three months, and any detention for a longer period must be authorised by an Advisory Board. The person being detained also has the right to be informed about the grounds of detention, and be permitted to make a representation against it, at the earliest opportunity.

Right to Information (RTI)

Right to information has been given the status of a fundamental right under Article 19(1) of the Constitution in 2005. Article 19 (1) under which every citizen has freedom of speech and expression and the right to know how the government works, what roles it plays, what its functions are, and so on.

Right against Exploitation

The Right against Exploitation contained in Articles 23–24, lays down certain provisions to prevent exploitation of the weaker sections of the society by individuals or the State. Article 23 prohibits human trafficking, making it an offence punishable by law, and also prohibits forced labour or any act of compelling a person to work without wages where he was legally entitled not to work or to receive remuneration for it. However, it permits the State to impose compulsory service for public purposes, including conscription and community service. The Bonded Labour System (Abolition) Act, 1976, has been enacted by Parliament to give effect to this Article. Article 24 prohibits the employment of children below the age of 14 years in factories, mines and other hazardous jobs. Parliament has enacted the Child Labour (Prohibition and Regulation) Act, 1986, providing regulations for the abolition of, and penalties for employing, child labour, as well as provisions for rehabilitation of former child labourers.

Right to Freedom of Religion

The Right to Freedom of Religion, covered in Articles 25–28, provides religious freedom to all citizens and ensures a secular state in India. According to the Constitution, there is no official State religion, and the State is required to treat all religions equally, impartially and neutrally.

- Article 25 guarantees all persons the freedom of conscience and the right to preach, practice and propagate any religion of their choice. This right is, however, subject to public order, morality and health, and the power of the State to take measures for social welfare and reform. The right to propagate, however, does not include the right to convert another individual, since it would amount to an infringement of the other's right to freedom of conscience.
- Article 26 guarantees all religious denominations and sects, subject to public order, morality and health, to manage their own affairs in matters of religion, set up institutions of their own for charitable or religious purposes, and own, acquire and manage a property in accordance with law. These provisions do not derogate from the State's power to acquire property belonging to a religious denomination. The State is also empowered to regulate any economic, political or other secular activity associated with religious practice.
- Article 27 guarantees that no one can be compelled to pay taxes for the promotion of any particular religion or religious institution.

- Article 28 prohibits religious instruction in a wholly or partially state-funded educational institution, and educational institutions receiving aid from the State cannot compel any of their members to receive religious instruction or attend religious worship without their (or their guardian's) consent.

Right to Life

The Constitution guarantees the right to life and personal liberty, which in turn cites specific provisions in which these rights are applied and enforced:

- Protection with respect to a conviction for offences is guaranteed under the right to life and personal liberty. According to Article 20, no one can be awarded punishment which is more than what the law of the land prescribes at the time of commission of the crime. This legal axiom is based on the principle that no criminal law can be made retrospective, that is, for an act to become an offence, the essential condition is that it should have been an offence legally at the time of committing it. Moreover, no person accused of any offence shall be compelled to be a witness against himself. Compulsion in this article refers to what in law is called duress (injury, beating or unlawful imprisonment to make a person do something that he may not want to do). This article is known as a safeguard against self-incrimination. The other principle enshrined in this article is known as the principle of double jeopardy, that is, no person can be convicted twice for the same offence, which has been derived from Anglo-Saxon law. This principle was first established in the Magna Carta.
- Protection of life and personal liberty is also stated under the right to life and personal liberty. Article 21 declares that no citizen can be denied his life and liberty except by due process of law. This means that a person's life and personal liberty can be disputed only if that person has committed a crime. However, the right to life does not include the right to die and hence, suicide or any attempt thereof, is deemed an offence (attempted suicide being interpreted as a crime has seen many debates. The Supreme Court of India gave a landmark ruling in 1994. The court repealed section 309 of the Indian penal code, under which people attempting suicide could face prosecution and prison terms of up to one year). In 1996, another Supreme Court ruling nullified the earlier one. But with the passage of the Mental Healthcare Bill 2017, attempted suicide has been decriminalised. "Personal liberty" includes all the freedoms which are not included in Article 19 (that is, the six freedoms). The right to travel abroad is also covered under "personal liberty" in Article 21.
- In 2002, through the 86th Amendment Act, Article 21A was incorporated. It made the right to primary education part of the right to freedom, stating that the state would provide free and compulsory education to children from six to fourteen years of age. Six years after an amendment was made in the Indian Constitution, the Union Cabinet cleared the Right to Education Bill in 2008.

- Rights of a person arrested under ordinary circumstances is laid down in the right to life and personal liberty. No one can be arrested without being told the grounds for his arrest. If arrested, the person has the right to defend himself through a lawyer of his choice. Also, an arrested citizen has to be brought before the nearest magistrate within 24 hours. The rights of a person arrested under ordinary circumstances are not available to an enemy alien. They are also not available to persons under any law providing for preventive detention. Under preventive detention, the government can imprison a person for a maximum of three months. It means that if the government feels that a person being at liberty can be a threat to the law and order or to the unity and integrity of the nation, it can detain or arrest that person to prevent him/her from doing this possible harm. After three months, such a case is to be brought before an advisory board for review, unless specific legislation(s) by Parliament regarding preventive detention do(es) not necessitate scrutiny by such an advisory board.

Cultural and Educational Rights

The Cultural and Educational rights, given in Articles 29 and 30, are measures to protect the rights of cultural, linguistic, and religious minorities, by enabling them to conserve their heritage and protecting them against discrimination.

- Article 29 grants any section of citizens having a distinct language, script, or culture of its own, the right to conserve and develop the same, and thus safeguards the rights of minorities by preventing the State from imposing any external culture on them. It also prohibits discrimination against any citizen for admission into any educational institutions maintained or aided by the State, on the grounds only of religion, race, caste, language or any of them. However, this is subject to reservation of a reasonable number of seats by the State for socially and educationally backward classes, as well as reservation of up to, 50 percent of seats in any educational institution run by a minority community for citizens belonging to that community.

- Article 30 confers upon all religious and linguistic minorities the right to set up and administer educational institutions of their choice in order to preserve and develop their own culture, and prohibits the State, while granting aid, from discriminating against any institution on the basis of the fact that it is administered by a religious or cultural minority. The term "minority", while not defined in the Constitution, has been interpreted by the Supreme Court to mean any community which numerically forms less than 50% of the population of the state in which it seeks to avail the right under Article 30. In order to claim the right, it is essential that the educational institution must have been established as well as administered by a religious or linguistic minority. Further, the right under Article 30 can be availed of even if the educational institution established does not confine itself to the teaching of the religion or language of the minority concerned, or a majority of students in that institution do not belong to such a minority. This right is subject to the power of the State to impose reasonable regulations regarding educational standards, conditions of service of employees, fee structure, and the utilization of any aid granted by it.

Right to Constitutional Remedies

Article 32 provides a guaranteed remedy, in the form of a Fundamental Right itself, for enforcement of all the other Fundamental Rights, and the Supreme Court is designated as the protector of these rights by the Constitution. The Supreme Court has been empowered to issue writs, namely *habeas corpus*, *mandamus*, *prohibition*, *certiorari* and *quo warranto*, for the enforcement of the Fundamental Rights, while the High Courts have been empowered under Article 226 – which is not a Fundamental Right in itself – to issue these prerogative writs even in cases not involving the violation of Fundamental Rights. The Supreme Court has the jurisdiction to enforce the Fundamental Rights even against private bodies, and in case of any violation, award compensation as well to the affected individual. Exercise of jurisdiction by the Supreme Court can also be *suo motu* or on the basis of a public interest litigation. This right cannot be suspended, except under the provisions of Article 226, when a state of emergency is declared.

Article 33 of the Indian constitution grants the Parliament the authority to enact legislation aimed at limiting the extension of fundamental rights to particular groups, which may encompass individuals within the Indian Army and intelligence agencies.

Article 34 of the Constitution grants authority to the Parliament to provide indemnification for government servants or individuals who may have taken actions in relation to the maintenance or restoration of order within regions where martial law had been enforced. This constitutional provision essentially empowers the Parliament to absolve these individuals from any legal liability or consequences arising from their actions undertaken in the context of martial law implementation. In essence, it allows for the legal protection and exoneration of those involved in maintaining or restoring order during periods when martial law was in effect.

Article 35 of the Indian Constitution is a provision that gives the Parliament the exclusive power to make laws on certain matters related to the fundamental rights, such as the reservation of public employment, the application of fundamental rights to the armed forces, the restriction of fundamental rights during martial law, and the punishment for violating the fundamental rights. It also states that any law that was in force before the Constitution came into effect on these matters will continue to be valid until amended or repealed by the Parliament. Article 35 also clarifies that the term "law in force" has the same meaning as in Article 372, which deals with the continuance of existing laws and their adaptation. Article 35 was added to the Constitution by the Constituent Assembly to ensure that there is uniformity and consistency in the laws relating to the fundamental rights across the country.

Article 35 should not be confused with Article 35A, which was a separate article that empowered the Jammu and Kashmir (union territory) state's legislature to define "permanent residents" of the state and provide special rights and privileges to them. Article 35A was added to the Constitution through a presidential order in 1954, without any amendment by the Parliament. It was abrogated by another presidential order in 2019, along with Article 370, which granted special status to Jammu and Kashmir.[7] Original constitution (2020) pg no.5 and 33 PDF

Dr B. R. Ambedkar wanted a specific guarantee of fundamental rights expressly incorporated in the constitution so that it could be easily enforced. He drafted this Article 32. B. R. Ambedkar had said,

- "If I was asked to name any particular article in this Constitution as the most important – an article without which this Constitution would be a nullity – I could not refer to any other article except this one (Article 32). It is the very soul of the Constitution and the very heart of it."

During the Constituent Assembly debates in December 1948, Dr. Babasaheb Ambedkar had said that the rights invested with the Supreme Court through this Article could not be taken away unless the Constitution itself is amended and hence it was 'one of the greatest safeguards that can be provided for the safety and security of the individual'. The right to constitutional remedies is present for enforcement of fundamental rights.

Right to Privacy

The right to privacy is protected as an intrinsic part of the right to life and personal liberty under Article 21 and as a part of the freedoms guaranteed by Part III of the Constitution. It protects the inner sphere of the individual from interference from both State and non-State actors and allows individuals to make autonomous life choices. On 24 August 2017, the Supreme Court of India in its Right to Privacy verdict ruled that:

- "Right to Privacy is an integral part of Right to Life and Personal Liberty guaranteed in Article 21 of the Constitution,"

Critical Analysis

The fundamental rights have been revised for many reasons. Political and other groups have demanded that the right to work, the right to economic assistance in case of unemployment, old age, and similar rights be enshrined as constitutional guarantees to address issues of poverty and economic insecurity, though these provisions have been enshrined in the directive principles of state policy. The right to freedom and personal liberty has a number of limiting clauses, and thus has been criticised for failing to check the sanctioning of powers often deemed "excessive". There is also the provision of preventive detention and suspension of fundamental rights in times of emergency. The provisions of acts like the Maintenance of Internal Security Act (MISA), Armed Forces (Special Powers) Act (AFSPA) and the National Security Act (NSA) are a means of countering these fundamental rights, because they sanction excessive powers with the aim of fighting internal and cross-border terrorism and political violence, without safeguards for civil rights. The phrases "security of State", "public order" and "morality" are of wide implication. The meaning of phrases like "reasonable restrictions" and "the interest of public order" have not been explicitly stated in the Constitution, and this ambiguity leads to unnecessary litigation. The freedom to assemble peaceably and without arms is exercised, but in some cases, these meetings are broken up by the police through the use of non-fatal methods.

Freedom of press has not been included in the right to freedom, which is necessary for formulating public opinion and to make freedom of expression more legitimate. Employment of child labour in hazardous job environments has been reduced, but their employment even in non-hazardous jobs, including their prevalent employment as domestic help violates the spirit and ideals of the Constitution. More than 16.5 million children are employed and working in India. India was ranked 88 out of 159 in 2005, according to the degree to which corruption is perceived to exist among public officials and politicians worldwide. In 2014, India had improved marginally to a rank of 85. The right to equality in matters regarding public employment is not conferred upon overseas citizens of India, according to the Citizenship (Amendment) Bill, 2003.

As per Article 19 of Part III of the Constitution, the fundamental rights of people such as freedom of speech and expression, gathering peaceably without arms and forming associations or unions shall not effect the interests of the sovereignty unity and integrity of India. The words sovereignty and integrity are the qualities to be cultivated/emulated by Indian people as urged by the Constitution but not used related to the territory of India. Article 1 of Part 1 of the Indian constitution, defines India (Bharat) as a Union of states. In a nutshell, India "is its people, not its land", as enshrined in the Constitution.

Although speedy trial is a fundamental right, the cases involving violations of fundamental rights take an inordinate amount of time for resolution by the Supreme Court which is against the legal maxim 'justice delayed is justice denied'.

Amendments

Changes to the fundamental rights require a constitutional amendment, which has to be passed by a special majority of both houses of Parliament. This means that an amendment requires the approval of two-thirds of the members present and voting. However, the number of members voting in support of the amendment shall not be less than the absolute majority of the total members of a house – whether the Lok Sabha or Rajya Sabha.

Fundamental Rights and its Issues

Basic Structure Doctrine

While deciding the Golaknath case in February 1967, the Supreme Court ruled that Parliament had no power to curtail the fundamental rights. They were made permanent and sacrosanct, reversing the Supreme Court's earlier decision which had upheld Parliament's power to amend all parts of the Constitution, including Part III related to fundamental rights. Up until the 24th constitutional amendment in 1971, the fundamental rights given to the people were permanent and could not be repealed or diluted by Parliament. The 24th constitutional amendment introduced a new article – Article 13(4) – enabling Parliament to legislate on the subjects of Part III of the constitution using its constituent powers per Article 368 (1). In 1973, a 13 member constitutional bench of the Supreme Court also upheld with majority the validity of the 24th constitutional amendment. However, it ruled that the basic structure of the constitution, which is built on the basic foundation representing the dignity and freedom of the individual, could not be altered, and that it was "of supreme importance" and could not be destroyed by means of amendment(s) to the Constitution. Many constitutional amendments to Part III of the Constitution were made deleting, adding or diluting the fundamental rights before the judgement of Golaknath case (Constitutional amendments 1, 4, 7, and 16) and after the validity of 24th constitutional amendment was upheld by the Supreme Court (Constitutional amendments 25, 42, 44, 50, 77, 81, 85, 86, 93, and 97).

Validity of Article 31B

Articles 31A and Article 31B are added by the first constitutional amendment in 1951. Article 31B says that any acts and regulations included in the Ninth Schedule of the constitution by the Parliament can override the fundamental rights and such laws cannot be repealed or made void by the judiciary on the grounds of violating fundamental rights. Thus fundamental rights given in Part III are not equally applicable in each state /region and can be made different by making additions/deletions to Ninth Schedule by constitutional amendments. In 2007, the Supreme Court ruled that there could not be any blanket immunity from judicial review for the laws inserted in the Ninth Schedule. Apex court also stated it shall examine laws included in the Ninth Schedule after 1973 for any incompatibility with the basic structure doctrine.

Amendment to Article 31C

Section 4 of the 42nd Amendment, had changed Article 31C of the Constitution to accord precedence to the Directive Principles (earlier applicable only to clauses b & c of Article 39) over the fundamental rights of individuals. In Minerva Mills v. Union of India case, the Supreme Court ruled that the amendment to Article 31C was not valid and ultra vires.

Right to Property

The Constitution originally provided for the right to property under Articles 19 and 31. Article 19 guaranteed to all citizens the right to acquire, hold and dispose of property. Article 31 provided that "no person shall be deprived of his property save by authority of law." It also provided that compensation would be paid to a person whose property has been taken for public purposes. The provisions relating to the right to property were changed a number of times. The 44th Amendment of 1978 removed the right to property from the list of fundamental rights. A new provision, Article 300-A, was added to the constitution, which provided that "no person shall be deprived of his property save by authority of law". Thus, if a legislator made a law depriving a person of his property, there would be no obligation on the part of the State to pay anything as compensation. Furthermore, the aggrieved person would also have no right to move the court under Article 32 due to the right to property no longer being a fundamental right, though it would still be a constitutional one. If the government appeared to have acted unfairly, the action could have been challenged in a court of law by aggrieved citizens before the amendment.

The liberalisation of the economy and the government's initiative to set up special economic zones has led to many protests by farmers and have led to calls for the reinstatement of the fundamental right to private property. The Supreme Court had sent a notice to the government questioning why the right should not be brought back, but in 2010, the Court rejected the PIL.

Right to Education

The right to education at elementary level has been made one of the fundamental rights in 2002 under the 86th Amendment of 2002. However this right was brought in to implementation after eight years in 2010. On 2 April 2010, India joined a group of few countries in the world, with a historical law making education a fundamental right of every child coming into force.

The Right of Children to Free and Compulsory Education Act is said to be of direct benefit to children who do not go to school. This Act provides for the appointment of teachers with the requisite entry and academic qualifications.

Former Prime Minister Manmohan Singh announced the implementation of the Act. Children, who had either dropped out of schools or never been to any educational institution, would get elementary education as it would be binding on the part of the local and state governments to ensure that all children in the 6–14 age group get schooling. As per the Act, private educational institutions should reserve 25 percent seats for children from the weaker sections of society. The Union and the state governments had agreed to share the financial burden in the ratio of 55:45, while the Finance Commission gave Rs. 250 billion to the states for implementing the Act. The Union government approved an outlay of Rs. 150 billion for 2010–2011.

The school management committee or the local authority would identify the drop-outs or out-of-school children aged above six and admit them in classes appropriate to their age after giving special training.

Freedom of speech

Freedom of speech is a principle that supports the freedom of an individual or a community to articulate their opinions and ideas without fear of retaliation, censorship, or legal sanction. The right to freedom of expression has been recognised as a human right in the Universal Declaration of Human Rights and international human rights law by the

United Nations. Many countries have constitutional law that protects free speech. Terms like *free speech*, *freedom of speech,* and *freedom of expression* are used interchangeably in political discourse. However, in a legal sense, the freedom of expression includes any activity of seeking, receiving, and imparting information or ideas, regardless of the medium used.

Article 19 of the UDHR states that "everyone shall have the right to hold opinions without interference" and "everyone shall have the right to freedom of expression; this right shall include freedom to seek, receive, and impart information and ideas of all kinds, regardless of frontiers, either orally, in writing or in print, in the form of art, or through any other media of his choice". The version of Article 19 in the ICCPR later amends this by stating that the exercise of these rights carries "special duties and responsibilities" and may "therefore be subject to certain restrictions" when necessary "[f]or respect of the rights or reputation of others" or "[f]or the protection of national security or of public order (ordre public), or of public health or morals".

Freedom of speech and expression, therefore, may not be recognized as being absolute, and common limitations or boundaries to freedom of speech relate to libel, slander, obscenity, pornography, sedition, incitement, fighting words, hate speech, classified information, copyright violation, trade secrets, food labeling, non-disclosure agreements, the right to privacy, dignity, the right to be forgotten, public security, and perjury. Justifications for such include the harm principle, proposed by John Stuart Mill in *On Liberty*, which suggests that "the only purpose for which power can be rightfully exercised over any member of a civilized community, against his will, is to prevent harm to others".

The idea of the "offense principle" is also used to justify speech limitations, describing the restriction on forms of expression deemed offensive to society, considering factors such as extent, duration, motives of the speaker, and ease with which it could be avoided. With the evolution of the digital age, application of freedom of speech becomes more controversial as new means of communication and restrictions arise, for example, the Golden Shield Project, an initiative by Chinese government's Ministry of Public Security that filters potentially unfavourable data from foreign countries.

The Human Rights Measurement Initiative measures the right to opinion and expression for countries around the world, using a survey of in-country human rights experts.

Historical Origins

Freedom of speech and expression has a long history that predates modern international human rights instruments. It is thought that the ancient Athenian democratic principle of free speech may have emerged in the late 6th or early 5th century BC.

Freedom of speech was vindicated by Erasmus and Milton. Edward Coke claimed freedom of speech as "an ancient custom of Parliament" in the 1590s, and it was affirmed in the Protestation of 1621. Restating what is written in the English Declaration of Right,

1689, England's Bill of Rights 1689 legally established the constitutional right of freedom of speech in Parliament, which is still in effect. This so-called parliamentary privilege includes no possible defamation claims meaning Parliamentarians are free to speak up in the House without fear of legal action. This protection extends to written proceedings: for example, written and oral questions, motions and amendments tabled to bills and motions.

One of the world's first freedom of the press acts was introduced in Sweden in 1766 (Swedish Freedom of the Press Act), mainly due to the classical liberal member of parliament and Ostrobothnian priest Anders Chydenius. In a report published in 1776, he wrote:

- No evidence should be needed that a certain freedom of writing and printing is one of the strongest bulwarks of a free organization of the state, as, without it, the estates would not have sufficient information for the drafting of good laws, and those dispensing justice would not be monitored, nor would the subjects know the requirements of the law, the limits of the rights of government, and their responsibilities. Education and ethical conduct would be crushed; coarseness in thought, speech, and manners would prevail, and dimness would darken the entire sky of our freedom in a few years.

Under the leadership of Anders Chydenius, the Caps at the Swedish Riksdag in Gävle on December 2, 1766, passed the adoption of a freedom of the press regulation that stopped censorship and introduced the principle of public access to official records in Sweden. Excluded were defamation of the king's majesty and the Swedish Church.

The Declaration of the Rights of Man and of the Citizen, adopted during the French Revolution in 1789, specifically affirmed freedom of speech as an inalienable right. Adopted in 1791, freedom of speech is a feature of the First Amendment to the United States Constitution. The French Declaration provides for freedom of expression in Article 11, which states that:

- The free communication of ideas and opinions is one of the most precious of the rights of man. Every citizen may, accordingly, speak, write, and print with freedom, but shall be responsible for such abuses of this freedom as shall be defined by law.

Article 19 of the Universal Declaration of Human Rights, adopted in 1948, states that:

- Everyone has the right to freedom of opinion and expression; this right includes freedom to hold opinions without interference and to seek, receive and impart information and ideas through any media and regardless of frontiers.

Today, freedom of speech, or the freedom of expression, is recognised in international and regional human rights law. The right is enshrined in Article 19 of the International Covenant on Civil and Political Rights, Article 10 of the European Convention on Human Rights, Article 13 of the American Convention on Human Rights and Article 9 of the

African Charter on Human and Peoples' Rights. Based on John Milton's arguments, freedom of speech is understood as a multi-faceted right that includes not only the right to express, or disseminate, information and ideas but three further distinct aspects:

1. the right to seek information and ideas;
2. the right to receive information and ideas;
3. the right to impart information and ideas

International, regional and national standards also recognise that freedom of speech, as the freedom of expression, includes any medium, whether orally, in writing, in print, through the internet or art forms. This means that the protection of freedom of speech as a right includes the content and the means of expression.

Relationship to other Rights

The right to freedom of speech and expression is closely related to other rights. It may be limited when conflicting with other rights. The right to freedom of expression is also related to the right to a fair trial and court proceeding which may limit access to the search for information, or determine the opportunity and means in which freedom of expression is manifested within court proceedings. As a general principle freedom of expression may not limit the right to privacy, as well as the honor and reputation of others. However, greater latitude is given when criticism of public figures is involved.

The right to freedom of expression is particularly important for media, which play a special role as the bearer of the general right to freedom of expression for all. However, freedom of the press does not necessarily enable freedom of speech. Judith Lichtenberg has outlined conditions in which freedom of the press may constrain freedom of speech. For example, if all the people who control the various mediums of publication suppress information or stifle the diversity of voices inherent in freedom of speech. This limitation was famously summarised as "Freedom of the press is guaranteed only to those who own one". Lichtenberg argues that freedom of the press is simply a form of property right summed up by the principle "no money, no voice".

As a Negative Right

Freedom of speech is usually seen as a negative right. This means that the government is legally obliged to take no action against the speaker based on the speaker's views, but that no one is obliged to help any speakers publish their views, and no one is required to listen to, agree with, or acknowledge the speaker or the speaker's views.

Democracy in Relation to Social Interaction

Freedom of speech is understood to be fundamental in a democracy. The norms on limiting freedom of expression mean that public debate may not be completely suppressed even in times of emergency. One of the most notable proponents of the link between freedom of speech and democracy is Alexander Meiklejohn. He has argued that the concept of democracy is that of self-government by the people. For such a system to work, an informed electorate is necessary. In order to be appropriately knowledgeable, there must be no constraints on the free flow of information and ideas. According to Meiklejohn, democracy will not be true to its essential ideal if those in power can manipulate the electorate by withholding information and stifling criticism. Meiklejohn acknowledges that the desire to manipulate opinion can stem from the motive of seeking to benefit society. However, he argues, choosing manipulation negates, in its means, the democratic ideal.

Eric Barendt has called this defence of free speech on the grounds of democracy "probably the most attractive and certainly the most fashionable free speech theory in modern Western democracies". Thomas I. Emerson expanded on this defence when he argued that freedom of speech helps to provide a balance between stability and change. Freedom of speech acts as a "safety valve" to let off steam when people might otherwise be bent on revolution. He argues that "The principle of open discussion is a method of achieving a more adaptable and at the same time more stable community, of maintaining the precarious balance between healthy cleavage and necessary consensus". Emerson furthermore maintains that "Opposition serves a vital social function in offsetting or ameliorating (the) normal process of bureaucratic decay".

Research undertaken by the Worldwide Governance Indicators project at the World Bank, indicates that freedom of speech, and the process of accountability that follows it, have a significant impact on the quality of governance of a country. "Voice and Accountability" within a country, defined as "the extent to which a country's citizens are able to participate in selecting their government, as well as freedom of expression, freedom of association, and free media" is one of the six dimensions of governance that the Worldwide Governance Indicators measure for more than 200 countries. Against this backdrop it is important that development agencies create grounds for effective support for a free press in developing countries.

Richard Moon has developed the argument that the value of freedom of speech and freedom of expression lies with social interactions. Moon writes that "by communicating an individual forms relationships and associations with others – family, friends, co-workers, church congregation, and countrymen. By entering into discussion with others an individual participates in the development of knowledge and in the direction of the community".

Limitations

Freedom of speech is not regarded as absolute by some, with most legal systems generally setting limits on the freedom of speech, particularly when freedom of speech conflicts with other rights and protections, such as in the cases of libel, slander, pornography, obscenity, fighting words, and intellectual property.

Some limitations to freedom of speech may occur through legal sanction, and others may occur through social disapprobation. In Saudi Arabia, Journalists are forbidden to write with disrespect or disapproval of the royal family, religion, or the government.

Journalists are also not given any legal protection for their writing in Saudi Arabia. Journalist Jamal Khashoggi was a critic of the Saudi Arabian government. He was killed in 2018 by Saudi Arabian officials for his writing.

Content Viewed as Harmful and Offensive

Some views are illegal to express because they are perceived by some to be harmful to others. This category often includes speech that is both false and potentially dangerous, such as falsely shouting "Fire!" in a theatre and causing a panic. Justifications for limitations to freedom of speech often reference the "harm principle" or the "offence principle".

In *On Liberty* (1859), John Stuart Mill argued that "...there ought to exist the fullest liberty of professing and discussing, as a matter of ethical conviction, any doctrine, however immoral it may be considered". Mill argues that the fullest liberty of expression is required to push arguments to their logical limits, rather than the limits of social embarrassment.

In 1985, Joel Feinberg introduced what is known as the "offence principle". Feinberg wrote, "It is always a good reason in support of a proposed criminal prohibition that it would probably be an effective way of preventing serious offence (as opposed to injury or harm) to persons other than the actor, and that it is probably a necessary means to that end". Hence Feinberg argues that the harm principle sets the bar too high and that some forms of expression can be legitimately prohibited by law because they are very offensive. Nevertheless, as offending someone is less serious than harming someone, the penalties imposed should be higher for causing harm. In contrast, Mill does not support legal penalties unless they are based on the harm principle. Because the degree to which people may take offence varies, or may be the result of unjustified prejudice, Feinberg suggests that several factors need to be taken into account when applying the offence principle, including: the extent, duration and social value of the speech, the ease with which it can be avoided, the motives of the speaker, the number of people offended, the intensity of the offence, and the general interest of the community at large.

Jasper Doomen argued that harm should be defined from the point of view of the individual citizen, not limiting harm to physical harm since nonphysical harm may also be involved; Feinberg's distinction between harm and offence is criticized as largely trivial.

In 1999, Bernard Harcourt wrote of the collapse of the harm principle: "Today the debate is characterized by a cacophony of competing harm arguments without any way to resolve them. There is no longer an argument within the structure of the debate to resolve the competing claims of harm. The original harm principle was never equipped to determine the relative importance of harms".

Interpretations of both the harm and offense limitations to freedom of speech are culturally and politically relative. For instance, in Russia, the harm and offense principles have been used to justify the Russian LGBT propaganda law restricting speech (and action) concerning LGBT issues. Many European countries outlaw speech that might be interpreted as Holocaust denial. These include Austria, Belgium, Canada, the Czech Republic, France,

Germany, Hungary, Israel, Liechtenstein, Lithuania, Luxembourg, Netherlands, Poland, Portugal, Russia, Slovakia, Switzerland and Romania. Armenian genocide denial is also illegal in some countries.

In some countries, blasphemy is a crime. For example, in Austria, defaming Muhammad, the prophet of Islam, is not protected as free speech. In contrast, in France, blasphemy and disparagement of Muhammad are protected under free speech law.

Certain public institutions may also enact policies restricting the freedom of speech, for example, speech codes at state-operated schools.

In the U.S., the standing landmark opinion on political speech is *Brandenburg v. Ohio* (1969), expressly overruling *Whitney v. California*. In *Brandenburg*, the U.S. Supreme Court referred to the right even to speak openly of violent action and revolution in broad terms:

- [Our] decisions have fashioned the principle that the constitutional guarantees of free speech and free press do not allow a State to forbid or proscribe advocacy of the use of force or law violation except where such advocacy is directed to inciting or producing imminent lawless action and is likely to incite or cause such action.

The opinion in *Brandenburg* discarded the previous test of "clear and present danger" and made the right to freedom of (political) speech protections in the United States almost absolute. Hate speech is also protected by the First Amendment in the United States, as decided in *R.A.V. v. City of St. Paul*, (1992) in which the Supreme Court ruled that hate speech is permissible, except in the case of imminent violence.

Time, Place and Manner

Limitations based on time, place, and manner apply to all speech, regardless of the view expressed. They are generally restrictions that are intended to balance other rights or a legitimate government interest. For example, a time, place, and manner restriction might prohibit a noisy political demonstration at a politician's home during the middle of the night, as that impinges upon the rights of the politician's neighbors to quiet enjoyment of their own homes. An otherwise identical activity might be permitted if it happened at a different time (e.g., during the day), at a different place (e.g., at a government building or in another public forum), or in a different manner (e.g., a silent protest). Funeral Protests are a complex issue in the United States. It is a right to Americans to be able to hold a peaceful protest against various policies they deem unreasonable. It is a question of whether or not it is appropriate through the time, place and manner outlook to protest funeral proceedings. Because of recent flare ups of this occurring, legislation has been put to action to limit this. Now, funeral protests are governed and prohibited by law on a state-to-state basis inside the United States.

The Internet and Information Society

Jo Glanville, editor of the *Index on Censorship*, states that "the Internet has been a revolution for censorship as much as for free speech". International, national and regional standards recognise that freedom of speech, as one form of freedom of expression, applies to any medium, including the Internet. The Communications Decency Act (CDA) of 1996 was the first major attempt by the United States Congress to regulate pornographic material on the Internet. In 1997, in the landmark cyberlaw case of *Reno v. ACLU*, the US Supreme Court partially overturned the law. Judge Stewart R. Dalzell, one of the three federal judges who in June 1996 declared parts of the CDA unconstitutional, in his opinion stated the following:

- The Internet is a far more speech-enhancing medium than print, the village green, or the mails. Because it would necessarily affect the Internet itself, the CDA would necessarily reduce the speech available for adults on the medium. This is a constitutionally intolerable result. Some of the dialogue on the Internet surely tests the limits of conventional discourse. Speech on the Internet can be unfiltered, unpolished, and unconventional, even emotionally charged, sexually explicit, and vulgar – in a word, "indecent" in many communities. But we should expect such speech to occur in a medium in which citizens from all walks of life have a voice. We should also protect the autonomy that such a medium confers to ordinary people as well as media magnates.[...] My analysis does not deprive the Government of all means of protecting children from the dangers of Internet communication. The Government can continue to protect children from pornography on the Internet through vigorous enforcement of existing laws criminalising obscenity and child pornography. [...] As we learned at the hearing, there is also a compelling need for public educations about the benefits and dangers of this new medium, and the Government can fill that role as well. In my view, our action today should only mean that Government's permissible supervision of Internet contents stops at the traditional line of unprotected speech. [...] The absence of governmental regulation of Internet content has unquestionably produced a kind of chaos, but as one of the plaintiff's experts put it with such resonance at the hearing: "What achieved success was the very chaos that the Internet is. The strength of the Internet is chaos." Just as the strength of the Internet is chaos, so that strength of our liberty depends upon the chaos and cacophony of the unfettered speech the First Amendment protects.

The World Summit on the Information Society (WSIS) Declaration of Principles adopted in 2003 makes specific reference to the importance of the right to freedom of expression for the "Information Society" in stating:

- We reaffirm, as an essential foundation of the Information society, and as outlined in Article 19 of the Universal Declaration of Human Rights, that everyone has the right to freedom of opinion and expression; that this right includes freedom to hold opinions without interference and to seek, receive and impart information and ideas through any media and regardless of frontiers. Communication is a fundamental social process, a basic human need and the foundation of all social organisation. It is central to the Information Society. Everyone, everywhere should have the opportunity to participate and no one should be excluded from the benefits of the Information Society offers.

According to Bernt Hugenholtz and Lucie Guibault, the public domain is under pressure from the "commodification of information" as information with previously little or no economic value has acquired independent economic value in the information age. This includes factual data, personal data, genetic information and pure ideas. The commodification of information is taking place through intellectual property law, contract law, as well as broadcasting and telecommunications law.

Freedom of Information

Freedom of information is an extension of freedom of speech where the medium of expression is the Internet. Freedom of information may also refer to the right to privacy in the context of the Internet and information technology. As with the right to freedom of expression, the right to privacy is a recognised human right and freedom of information acts as an extension to this right. Freedom of information may also concern censorship in an information technology context, i.e., the ability to access Web content, without censorship or restrictions. Freedom of information is also explicitly protected by acts such as the Freedom of Information and Protection of Privacy Act of Ontario, in Canada. The Access to Information Act gives Canadian citizens, permanent residents, and any person or corporation present in Canada a right to access records of government institutions that are subject to the Act.

Internet Censorship

The concept of freedom of information has emerged in response to state sponsored censorship, monitoring and surveillance of the internet. Internet censorship includes the control or suppression of the publishing or accessing of information on the Internet. The Global Internet Freedom Consortium claims to remove blocks to the "free flow of information" for what they term "closed societies". According to the Reporters without Borders (RWB) "internet enemy list" the following states engage in pervasive internet censorship: Mainland China, Cuba, Iran, Myanmar/Burma, North Korea, Saudi Arabia, Syria, Turkmenistan, Uzbekistan, and Vietnam.

A widely publicized example of internet censorship is the "Great Firewall of China" (in reference both to its role as a network firewall and the ancient Great Wall of China). The system blocks content by preventing IP addresses from being routed through and consists of standard firewall and proxy servers at the internet gateways. The system also selectively engages in DNS poisoning when particular sites are requested. The government does not appear to be systematically examining Internet content, as this appears to be technically impractical. Internet censorship in the People's Republic of China is conducted under a wide variety of laws and administrative regulations, including more than sixty regulations directed at the Internet. Censorship systems are vigorously implemented by provincial branches of state-owned ISPs, business companies, and organizations.

Saudi Arabia's government had been intensifying the scrutiny of social media accounts, under which they were detaining several activists, critics and even normal social media users over few critical tweets. A law professor, Awad Al-Qarni became a victim of Saudi's internet censorship and was facing death sentence. Saudi-controlled media portrayed him as a dangerous preacher due to his Twitter and WhatsApp posts, but dissidents considered him as an important intellectual who maintained strong social media influence.

Relationship with Disinformation

Some legal scholars (such as Tim Wu of Columbia University) have argued that the traditional issues of free speech—that "the main threat to free speech" is the censorship of "suppressive states", and that "ill-informed or malevolent speech" can and should be overcome by "more and better speech" rather than censorship—assumes scarcity of information. This scarcity prevailed during the 20th century, but with the arrival of the internet, information became plentiful, "but the attention of listeners" scarce. Furthermore, in the words of Wu, this "cheap speech" made possible by the internet " ... may be used to attack, harass, and silence as much as it is used to illuminate or debate". The Electronic Frontier Foundation (EFF) has argued that "censorship cannot be the only answer to disinformation online" and that tech companies "have a history of overcorrecting and censoring accurate, useful speech—or, even worse, reinforcing misinformation with their policies."

According to Wu, in the 21st century, the danger is not "suppressive states" that target "speakers directly", but that:

- ...targets listeners or it undermines speakers indirectly. More precisely, emerging techniques of speech control depend on (1) a range of new punishments, like unleashing "troll armies" to abuse the press and other critics, and (2) "flooding" tactics (sometimes called "reverse censorship") that distort or drown out disfavored speech through the creation and dissemination of fake news, the payment of fake commentators, and the deployment of propaganda robots. As journalist Peter Pomerantsev writes, these techniques employ "information ... in weaponized terms, as a tool to confuse, blackmail, demoralize, subvert and paralyze."

History of Dissent and Truth

Before the invention of the printing press, a written work, once created, could only be physically multiplied by highly laborious and error-prone manual copying. No elaborate system of censorship and control over scribes existed, who until the 14th century were restricted to religious institutions, and their works rarely caused wider controversy. In response to the printing press, and the theological heresies it allowed to spread, the Roman Catholic Church moved to impose censorship. Printing allowed for multiple exact copies of a work, leading to a more rapid and widespread circulation of ideas and information. The origins of copyright law in most European countries lie in efforts by the Roman Catholic Church and governments to regulate and control the output of printers.

In 1501, Pope Alexander VI issued a Bill against the unlicensed printing of books. In 1559, Pope Paul IV promulgated the *Index Expurgatorius*, or *List of Prohibited Books*. The *Index Expurgatorius* is the most famous and long-lasting example of "bad books" catalogues issued by the Roman Catholic Church, which presumed to be in authority over private thoughts and opinions, and suppressed views that went against its doctrines. The *Index Expurgatorius* was administered by the Roman Inquisition, but enforced by local government authorities, and went through 300 editions. Amongst others, it banned or censored books written by René Descartes, Giordano Bruno, Galileo Galilei, David Hume, John Locke, Daniel Defoe, Jean-Jacques Rousseau and Voltaire. While governments and church encouraged printing in many ways because it allowed for the dissemination of Bibles and government information, works of dissent and criticism could also circulate rapidly. Consequently, governments established controls over printers across Europe, requiring them to have official licenses to trade and produce books.

The notion that the expression of dissent or subversive views should be tolerated, not censured or punished by law, developed alongside the rise of printing and the press. *Areopagitica*, published in 1644, was John Milton's response to the Parliament of England's re-introduction of government licensing of printers, hence publishers. Church authorities had previously ensured that Milton's essay on the right to divorce was refused a license for publication. In *Areopagitica*, published without a license, Milton made an impassioned plea for freedom of expression and toleration of falsehood, stating:

- Give me the liberty to know, to utter, and to argue freely according to conscience, above all liberties.

Milton's defense of freedom of expression was grounded in a Protestant worldview. He thought that the English people had the mission to work out the truth of the Reformation, which would lead to the enlightenment of all people. Nevertheless, Milton also articulated the main strands of future discussions about freedom of expression. By defining the scope of freedom of expression and "harmful" speech, Milton argued against the principle of pre-censorship and in favor of tolerance for a wide range of views. Freedom of the press ceased being regulated in England in 1695 when the Licensing Order of 1643 was allowed to expire after the introduction of the Bill of Rights 1689 shortly after the Glorious Revolution. The emergence of publications like the *Tatler* (1709) and the *Spectator* (1711) are credited for creating a 'bourgeois public sphere' in England that allowed for a free exchange of ideas and information.

More governments attempted to centralize control as the "menace" of printing spread. The French crown repressed printing and the printer Etienne Dolet was burned at the stake in 1546. In 1557 the British Crown thought to stem the flow of seditious and heretical books by chartering the Stationers' Company. The right to print was limited to the members of that guild. Thirty years later, the Star Chamber was chartered to curtail the "greate enormities and abuses" of "dyvers contentyous and disorderlye persons professinge the arte or mystere of pryntinge or selling of books". The right to print was restricted to two universities and the 21 existing printers in the city of London, which had 53 printing presses.

As the British crown took control of type founding in 1637, printers fled to the Netherlands. Confrontation with authority made printers radical and rebellious, with 800 authors, printers, and book dealers being incarcerated in the Bastille in Paris before it was stormed in 1789.

A succession of English thinkers was at the forefront of early discussion on a right to freedom of expression, among them John Milton (1608–74) and John Locke (1632–1704). Locke established the individual as the unit of value and the bearer of rights to life, liberty, property and the pursuit of happiness. However, Locke's ideas evolved primarily around the concept of the right to seek salvation for one's soul. He was thus primarily concerned with theological matters. Locke neither supported a universal toleration of peoples nor freedom of speech; according to his ideas, some groups, such as atheists, should not be allowed.

By the second half of the 17th century philosophers on the European continent like Baruch Spinoza and Pierre Bayle developed ideas encompassing a more universal aspect freedom of speech and toleration than the early English philosophers. By the 18th century the idea of freedom of speech was being discussed by thinkers all over the Western world, especially by French philosophes like Denis Diderot, Baron d'Holbach and Claude Adrien Helvétius. The idea began to be incorporated in political theory both in theory as well as practice; the first state edict in history proclaiming complete freedom of speech was the one issued 4 December 1770 in Denmark-Norway during the regency of Johann Friedrich Struensee. However Struensee himself imposed some minor limitations to this edict on 7 October 1771, and it was even further limited after the fall of Struensee with legislation introduced in 1773, although censorship was not reintroduced.

John Stuart Mill (1806–1873) argued that without human freedom, there could be no progress in science, law, or politics, which according to Mill, required free discussion of opinion. Mill's *On Liberty*, published in 1859, became a classic defence of the right to freedom of expression. Mill argued that truth drives out falsity, therefore the free expression of ideas, true or false, should not be feared. Truth is not stable or fixed but evolves with time. Mill argued that much of what we once considered true has turned out false. Therefore, views should not be prohibited for their apparent falsity. Mill also argued that free discussion is necessary to prevent the "deep slumber of a decided opinion". Discussion would drive the march of truth, and by considering false views, the basis of true views could be re-affirmed. Furthermore, Mill argued that an opinion only carries intrinsic value to the owner of that opinion, thus silencing the expression of that opinion is an injustice to a basic human right. It is generally held that for Mill, the only instance in which speech can be justifiably suppressed is to prevent harm from a clear and direct threat. Neither economic or moral implications nor the speaker's own well-being would justify suppression of speech. However Mill in *On Liberty* suggests the speech of pimps — instigating clients and sex workers to have sex — should be restricted. This suggests he may be willing to restrict some speech that, while not harming others, undermines their decisional autonomy.

In her 1906 biography of Voltaire, Evelyn Beatrice Hall coined the following sentence to illustrate Voltaire's beliefs: "I disapprove of what you say, but I will defend to the death your right to say it". Hall's quote is frequently cited to describe the principle of freedom of speech. Noam Chomsky stated, "If you believe in freedom of speech, you believe in freedom of speech for views you don't like. Dictators such as Stalin and Hitler, were in favor of freedom of speech for views they liked only. If you're in favor of freedom of speech, that means you're in favor of freedom of speech precisely for views you despise". Lee Bollinger argues that "the free speech principle involves a special act of carving out one area of social interaction for extraordinary self-restraint, the purpose of which is to develop and demonstrate a social capacity to control feelings evoked by a host of social encounters". Bollinger argues that tolerance is a desirable value, if not essential. However, critics argue that society should be concerned by those who directly deny or advocate, for example, genocide.

As chairman of the London-based PEN International, a club which defends freedom of expression and a free press, English author H. G. Wells met with Stalin in 1934 and was hopeful of reform in the Soviet Union. However, during their meeting in Moscow, Wells said, "the free expression of opinion—even of opposition opinion, I do not know if you are prepared yet for that much freedom here".

The 1928 novel *Lady Chatterley's Lover* by D. H. Lawrence was banned for obscenity in several countries, including the United Kingdom, the United States, Australia, Canada, and India. In the late 1950s and early 1960s, it was the subject of landmark court rulings that saw the ban for obscenity overturned. Dominic Sandbrook of *The Telegraph* in the UK wrote, "Now that public obscenity has become commonplace, it is hard to recapture the atmosphere of a society that saw fit to ban books such as *Lady Chatterley's Lover* because it was likely to 'deprave and corrupt' its readers". Fred Kaplan of *The New York Times* stated the overturning of the obscenity laws "set off an explosion of free speech" in the U.S. The 1960s also saw the Free Speech Movement, a massive long-lasting student protest on the campus of the University of California, Berkeley, during the 1964–65 academic year.

In contrast to Anglophone nations, France was a haven for literary freedom. The innate French regard for the mind meant that France was disinclined to punish literary figures for their writing, and prosecutions were rare. While it was prohibited everywhere else, James Joyce's *Ulysses* was published in Paris in 1922. Henry Miller's 1934 novel *Tropic of Cancer* (banned in the U.S. until 1963) and Lawrence's *Lady Chatterley's Lover* were published in France decades before they were available in the respective authors' home countries.

In 1964 comedian Lenny Bruce was arrested in the U.S. due to complaints again about his use of various obscenities. A three-judge panel presided over his widely publicized six-month trial. He was found guilty of obscenity in November 1964. He was sentenced on 21 December 1964, to four months in a workhouse. He was set free on bail during the appeals process and died before the appeal was decided. On 23 December 2003, thirty-seven years after Bruce's death, New York Governor George Pataki granted him a posthumous pardon for his obscenity conviction.

In the United States, the right to freedom of expression has been interpreted to include the right to take and publish photographs of strangers in public areas without their permission or knowledge. This is not the case worldwide.

Offences

In some countries, people are not allowed to talk about certain things such as Lèse-majesté which is an offence against the dignity of a reigning sovereign or against a state. Doing so constitutes an offence. For example, Saudi Arabia is responsible for executing journalist Jamal Khashoggi in 2018. As he entered the Saudi embassy in Turkey, a team of Saudi assassins killed him. Another Saudi writer, Raif Badawi, was arrested in 2012 and lashed.

On 4 March 2022, Russian President Vladimir Putin signed into law a bill introducing prison sentences of up to 15 years for spreading "fake news" about Russia's military operation in Ukraine. As of December 2022, more than 4,000 Russians were prosecuted under "fake news" laws. The 1993 Russian Constitution expressly prohibits censorship in Article 29 of Chapter 2, Rights and Liberties of Man and Citizen.

Freedom of Expression

The Constitution of India provides the right to freedom, given in article 19 with the view of guaranteeing individual rights that were considered vital by the framers of the constitution. The right to freedom in Article 19 guarantees the freedom of speech and expression, as one of its six freedoms.

The law in the current form finds its root in the Hate Speech Law Section 295(A) enacted by the British Administration in India. This act was brought about in the backdrop of a series of murders of Arya Samaj leaders who polemicized against Islam. This started in 1897 with the murder of Pandit Lekhram by a Muslim because he had written a book criticizing Islam. Koenraad Elst argues that "Section 295b was not instituted by Hindu society, but against it. It was imposed by the British on the Hindus in order to shield Islam from criticism". The murder series caught lime-light in December, 1926 after the murder of Swami Shraddhananda for the protection he gave to a family of converts from Islam to Hinduism in addition to writing *Hindu Sangathan, Saviour of the Dying Race* in 1926.

Precedence to this law started even before this as in a case against Arya Samaj preacher Dharm Bir in 1915, ten Muslims were sentenced for rioting, but Dharm Bir was also charged under section 298 for "using offensive phrases and gestures (...) with the deliberate intention of wounding the religious feelings" of another community; and under Section 153, for "wantonly provoking the riot which subsequently occurred" and "a judge was brought in who could assure conviction".

Constitutional Antecedents

The Constitution of India 1950 was drafted by the Constituent Assembly from 1946 to 1950. However, this Constitution drew on a longer history of antecedents documents drafted either as legislation governing British India or aspirational political documents.

The Constitution of India Bill 1895, widely considered to be the first Indian articulation of a constitutional vision, contained the following provision related to freedom of speech and expression - 'Every citizen may express his thoughts by words or writings, and publish them in print without liability to censure, but they shall be answerable to abuses, which they may commit in the exercise of this right, in the cases and in the mode the Parliament shall determine.' Other constitutional antecedent documents too contained provisions on freedom of speech and expression. These included: Commonwealth of India Bill 1925, Nehru Report 1928, and States and Minorities 1945. In most cases, the provisions contained some form of restrictions on freedom of speech and expression.

The Debate in the Constituent Assembly

The Constituent Assembly of India debated on freedom of speech and expression (Article 19(1) of the Draft Constitution,1948) on 1 December 1948, 2 December 1948 and 17 October 1949. The draft article read:

'Subject to the other provisions of this article, all citizens shall have the right – (a) to freedom of speech and expression; ...

Proviso: Nothing in sub-clause (a) of clause (1) of this article shall affect the operation of any existing law, or prevent the State from making any law, relating to libel, slander, defamation, sedition or any other matter which offends against decency or morality or undermines the security of, or tends to overthrow, the State.'

Most members of the Constituent Assembly welcomed the inclusion of the right. However, conflict emerged around the provision in the Article that placed restrictions on the right: while some members opposed the mention of restrictions on the right, others supported it. Members who opposed the restrictions argued that 1. There is no point in having a right to freedom of speech and expression in the presence of restrictions. 2. Putting restrictions on the freedom of speech and expression was a British practice.

Members who supported the restrictions argued that

1. Restrictions were fine as the government was no longer a colonial one.
2. The right to free speech was not absolute anywhere in the world.
3. The law, order and security of the state could not be compromised.

In the end, the Constituent Assembly voted on the Article and included a "Right to freedom of speech and expression" in the Constitution of India, 1950 with restrictions similar to the ones mentioned in the Draft Constitution, 1948.

Constitutional Law

In a landmark judgment of the case *Maneka Gandhi v. Union of India*, the Supreme

Court held that the freedom of speech and expression has no geographical limitation and it carries with it the right of a citizen to gather information and to exchange thought with others not only in India but abroad also.

The constitution of India does not specifically mention the freedom of press. Freedom of press is implied from the Article 19(1)(a) of the Constitution. Thus the press is subject to the restrictions that are provided under the Article 19(2) of the Constitution. Before Independence, there was no constitutional or statutory provision to protect the freedom of press. As observed by the *Privy Council in Channing Arnold v. King Emperor*: "The freedom of the journalist is an ordinary part of the freedom of the subject and to whatever length, the subject in general may go, so also may the journalist, but apart from statute his privilege is no other and no higher. The range of his assertions, his criticisms or his comments is as wide as, and no wider than that of any other subject". The Preamble of the Indian Constitution ensures to all its citizens the liberty of expression. Freedom of the press has been included as part of freedom of speech and expression under the Article 19 of the UDHR. The heart of the Article 19 says: "Everyone has the right to freedom of opinion and expression, this right includes freedom to hold opinions without interference and to seek, receive and impart information and ideas through any media and regardless of frontiers."

In *Romesh Thapar v. State of Madras*, Patanjali Shastri, Chief Justice observed: "Freedom of speech and of the press lay at the foundation of all democratic organisations, for without free political discussion no public education, so essential for the proper functioning of the process of popular government, is possible."

The Supreme Court observed in *Union of India v. Assn. for Democratic Reforms*: "Onesided information, disinformation, misinformation and non-information, all equally create an uninformed citizenry which makes democracy a farce. Freedom of speech and expression includes right to impart and receive information which includes freedom to hold opinions".

In *Indian Express v. Union of India*, it has been held that the press plays a very significant role in the democratic machinery. The courts have duty to uphold the freedom of press and invalidate all laws and administrative actions that abridge that freedom. Freedom of press has three essential elements. They are:

1. freedom of access to all sources of information,
2. freedom of publication, and
3. freedom of circulation.

In India, the press has not been able to practise its freedom to express the popular views. In *Sakal Papers Ltd. v. Union of India*, the Daily Newspapers (Price and Page) Order, 1960, which fixed the number of pages and size which a newspaper could publish at a price was held to be violative of freedom of press and not a reasonable restriction under the Article 19(2). Similarly, in *Bennett Coleman and Co. v. Union of India*, the validity of the Newsprint Control Order, which fixed the maximum number of pages, was struck down by the Supreme Court of India holding it to be violative of provision of Article 19(1)(a) and not to be reasonable restriction under Article 19(2). The Court struck down the rebuttal of the Government that it would help small newspapers to grow.

In *Romesh Thapar v. State of Madras* (1950), entry and circulation of the English journal "Cross Road", printed and published in Bombay, was banned by the Government of Madras. The same was held to be violative of the freedom of speech and expression, as "without liberty of circulation, publication would be of little value". In *Prabha Dutt v. Union of India* (1982), the Supreme Court directed the Superintendent of Tihar Jail to allow representatives of a few newspapers to interview Ranga and Billa, the death sentence convicts, as they wanted to be interviewed.

There are instances when the freedom of press has been suppressed by the legislature. The authority of the government, in such circumstances, has been under the scanner of judiciary. In the case of *Brij Bhushan v. State of Delhi* (AIR 1950 SC 129), the validity of censorship previous to the publication of an English Weekly of Delhi, the Organiser was questioned. The court struck down the Section 7 of the East Punjab Safety Act, 1949, which directed the editor and publisher of a newspaper "to submit for scrutiny, in duplicate, before the publication, till the further orders , all communal matters all the matters and news and views about Pakistan, including photographs, and cartoons", on the ground that it was a restriction on the liberty of the press. Similarly, prohibiting newspaper from publishing its own views or views of correspondents about a topic has been held to be a serious encroachment on the freedom of speech and expression.

Restrictions

Under Indian law, the freedom of speech and of the press do not confer an absolute right to express one's thoughts freely. Clause (2) of Article 19 of the Indian constitution enables the legislature to impose certain restrictions on free speech under following heads:

- I. security of the State,
- II. friendly relations with foreign States,
- III. public order,
- IV. decency and morality,
- V. contempt of court,
- VI. defamation,
- VII. incitement to an offence, and
- VIII. sovereignty and integrity of India.

Reasonable restrictions on these grounds can be imposed only by a duly enacted law and not by executive action.

Security of the State

Reasonable restrictions can be imposed on the freedom of speech and expression, in the interest of the security of the State. All the utterances intended to endanger the security of the State by crimes of violence intended to overthrow the government, waging of war and rebellion against the government, external aggression or war, etc., may be restrained in the interest of the security of the State. It does not refer to the ordinary breaches of public order which do not involve any danger to the State.

Friendly Relations with Foreign States

This ground was added by the Constitution (First Amendment) Act of 1951. The State can impose reasonable restrictions on the freedom of speech and expression, if it tends to jeopardise the friendly relations of India with other States.

Public Order

This ground was added by the Constitution (First Amendment) Act, 1951 in order to meet the situation arising from the Supreme Court's decision in Romesh Thapar's case (AIR 1950 SC 124). The expression 'public order' connotes the sense of public peace, safety and tranquillity.

In *Kishori Mohan v. State of West Bengal*, the Supreme Court explained the differences between three concepts: law and order, public order, security of State. Anything that disturbs public peace or public tranquillity disturbs public order. But mere criticism of the government does not necessarily disturb public order. A law punishing the utterances deliberately tending to hurt the religious feelings of any class has been held to be valid as it is a reasonable restriction aimed to maintaining the public order. It is also necessary that there must be a reasonable nexus between the restriction imposed and the achievement of public order. In *Superintendent, Central Prison v. Ram Manohar Lohiya* (AIR 1960 SC 633), the Court held the Section 3 of U.P. Special Powers Act, 1932, which punished a person if he incited a single person not to pay or defer the payment of Government dues, as there was no reasonable nexus between the speech and public order. Similarly, the court upheld the validity of the provision empowering a Magistrate to issue directions to protect the public order or tranquillity.

Decency and Morality

The word 'obscenity' is identical with the word 'indecency' of the Indian Constitution. In an English case of *R. v. Hicklin*, the test was laid down according to which it is seen 'whether the tendency of the matter charged as obscene tend to deprave and corrupt the minds which are open to such immoral influences'. This test was upheld by the Supreme Court in Ranjit D. Udeshi v. State of Maharashtra (AIR 1965 SC 881). In this case the Court upheld the conviction of a book seller who was prosecuted under Section 292, I.P.C., for selling and keeping the book *Lady Chatterley's Lover*. The standard of morality varies from time to time and from place to place.

Contempt of Court

The constitutional right to freedom of speech would not allow a person to contempt the courts. The expression Contempt of Court has been defined Section 2 of the Contempt of Courts Act, 1971. The term contempt of court refers to civil contempt or criminal contempt under the Act. But judges do not have any general immunity from criticism of their judicial conduct, provided that it is made in good faith and is genuine criticism, and not any attempt to impair the administration of justice. In *In re Arundhati Roy* ((2002) 3 SCC 343), the Supreme Court of India followed the view taken in the American Supreme Court (Frankfurter, J.) in *Pennekamp v. Florida* (328 US 331 : 90 L Ed 1295 (1946)) in which the United States Supreme Court observed: "If men, including judges and journalists, were angels, there would be no problem of contempt of court. Angelic judges would be undisturbed by extraneous influences and angelic journalists would not seek to influence them. The power to punish for contempt, as a means of safeguarding judges in deciding on behalf of the community as impartially as is given to the lot of men to decide, is not a privilege accorded to judges. The power to punish for contempt of court is a safeguard not for judges as persons but for the function which they exercise". In *E.M.S. Namboodripad v. T.N. Nambiar* ((1970) 2 SCC 325; AIR 1970 SC 2015), the Supreme Court confirmed the decision of the High Court, holding Mr. Namboodripad guilty of contempt of court. In *M.R. Parashar v. Farooq Abdullah* ((1984) 2 SCC 343; AIR 1984 SC 615.), contempt proceedings were initiated against the Chief Minister of Jammu and Kashmir. But the Court dismissed the petition for want of proof.

Defamation

The clause (2) of Article 19 prevents any person from making any statement that injures the reputation of another. With the same view, defamation has been criminalised in India by inserting it into Section 499 of the I.P.C. Where defamation is concerned, in case of a criminal defamation suit as laid down in Sections 499 and Section 500 of the Indian Penal Code, the issue - in question - being the truth isn't considered a defence. Even if a person has spoken the truth, he can be prosecuted for defamation. Under the first exception to Section 499, truth will only be a defence if the statement was made 'for the public good.' And that, is a question of fact to be assessed by the judiciary. The erstwhile *Economic & Political Weekly* (EPW) Editor Paranjoy Guha Thakurta's resignation following a legal notice by the lawyers for Adani Power Limited (APL) to the owners – the trustees of Sameeksha Trust, which owns and runs the Journal, Editor and authors of an article later withdrawn for "failing to meet editorial standards," brought the reach of IPC's Section 499 back into limelight.

Incitement to an Offense

This ground was also added by the Constitution (First Amendment) Act, 1951. The Constitution also prohibits a person from making any statement that incites people to commit offense.

Sovereignty and Integrity of India

This ground was also added subsequently by the Constitution (Sixteenth Amendment) Act, 1963. This is aimed to prohibit anyone from making statements that challenge the integrity and sovereignty of India.

Freedom of the Press

The Indian Constitution, while not mentioning the word "press", provides for *"the right to freedom of speech and expression"* (Article 19(1) a). However this right is subject to restrictions under sub clause, whereby this freedom can be restricted for reasons of "sovereignty and integrity of India, the security of the State, friendly relations with foreign States, public order, preserving decency, preserving morality, in relation to contempt, court, defamation, or incitement to an offense". Laws such as the Official Secrets Act and Prevention of Terrorist Activities Act (PoTA) have been used to limit press freedom. Under PoTA, person could be detained for up to six months for being in contact with a terrorist or terrorist group. PoTA was repealed in 2006, but the Official Secrets Act 1923 continues.

For the first half-century of independence, media control by the state was the major constraint on press freedom. Indira Gandhi famously stated in 1975 that All India Radio is "a Government organ, it is going to remain a Government organ..." With the liberalization starting in the 1990s, private control of media has burgeoned, leading to increasing independence and greater scrutiny of government.

It ranks poorly at 138th rank out of 180 listed countries in the Press Freedom Index 2018 released by Reporters Without Borders (RWB). Analytically India's press freedom, as could be deduced by the Press Freedom Index, has constantly reduced since 2002, when it culminated in terms of apparent freedom, achieving a rank of 80 among the reported countries. In 2018, India's freedom of press ranking declined two placed to 138. In explaining the decline, RWB cited growing intolerance from Hindu nationalist supporters of Indian Prime Minister Narendra Modi, and the murders of journalists such as Gauri Lankesh.

In August 2022, more than 100 international writers and artists expressed concern over the attacks on freedom of expression in India. These writers joined the writers' organisations - PEN America and PEN International - to sign a letter addressed to President of India Droupadi Murmu and urged her to support democratic principles.

Practical Constraints and Curtailments

Hate speech laws in India are regularly abused by political organisations and other influential people. Although these cases rarely result in a conviction, it is used as a form of intimidation which leads to wide spread self-censorship by the people. Apart from hate speech laws there are many other sections in the Indian Penal Code that curtails free speech. Books about history and religion are often targeted due to their very nature of promoting historical criticism.

The vague phrase "decency or morality" used in article 19(2) of the constitution has long enabled the state to engage in wide spread moral policing of mass media and the film and entertainment industry as religious groups often object to liberal ideas and deem all progressive values as indecent.

Freedom of speech and expression, which enable an individual to participate in public activities. The phrase, "freedom of press" has not been used in Article 19, though freedom activists, as well as most scholars and industrialised jurisdictions throughout the world recognise that freedom of expression includes freedom of press. Reasonable restrictions can be imposed in the interest of public order, security of State, decency or morality.

According to the estimates of Reporters Without Borders, India ranks 138th worldwide in press freedom index (The press freedom index for India is 43.24 for 2018). The Indian Constitution, while not mentioning the word "press", provides for *"the right to freedom of speech and expression"* (Article 19(1) a). However this right is subject to restrictions under subclause (2), whereby this freedom can be restricted for reasons of "sovereignty and integrity of India, the security of the State, friendly relations with foreign States, public order, preserving decency, preserving morality, in relation to contempt of court, defamation, or incitement to an offence". Laws such as the Official Secrets Act and Prevention of Terrorism Act(POTA) have been used to limit press freedom. Under POTA, person could be detained for up to six months before the police were required to bring charges on allegations for terrorism-related offences. POTA was repealed in 2004, but was replaced by amendments to UAPA. The Official Secrets Act 1923 remains in effect.

For the first half-century of independence, media control by the state was the major constraint on press freedom. Indira Gandhi famously stated in 1975 that All India Radio is "a Government organ, it is going to remain a Government organ..." On 26 June 1975, the day after the so-called emergency was declared in violation of the natural rights of Indian citizens, the Mumbai edition of *The Times of India* in its obituary column carried an entry that read "D.E.M O'Cracy beloved husband of T.Ruth, father of L.I.Bertie, brother of Faith, Hope and Justica expired on 26 June". With the liberalisation starting in the 1990s, private control of media has increased, leading to increasing independence and greater scrutiny of government.

Organisations like Tehelka and NDTV have been particularly influential, e.g. in bringing about the resignation of powerful Haryana minister Venod Sharma. In addition, laws like Prasar Bharati act passed in recent years contribute significantly to reducing the control of the press by the government. In recent times, the Indian government has been accused of trying to curtail this freedom through various means.

Sedition

According to the English Law, sedition embraces all the practices whether by word or writing which are calculated to disturb the tranquillity of the State and lead an ignorant person to subvert the Government. Basic criticism of the government is not seen as sedition unless the Government believes that it was calculated to undermine the respect for the government in such a way so as to make people cease to obey it. Section 124A of the Indian Penal Code defines the offence of sedition as follows: "Sedition. Whoever by words, either spoken or written, or by signs, or by visible representation, or otherwise, brings or attempts to bring into hatred or contempt, or excites or attempts to excite disaffection towards, the Government established by law in India, shall be punished with imprisonment for life, to which fine may be added, or with imprisonment which may extend to three years, to which fine may be added, or with fine". But Explanation 3 says "Comments expressing disapprobation of the administrative or other action of the Government without exciting or attempting to excite hatred, contempt or disaffection, do not constitute an offence under this section". In Kedar Nath v. State of Bihar (AIR 1962 SC 955), the court upheld the constitutional validity of the Section 124A of I.P.C and also upheld the view taken in Niharendu's case.

- National security Act. and Unlawful Activities Prevention act.

National Security Act (NSA) introduced in 1980. Unlawful Activities Prevention Act where the conviction rate is 2% enacted in 1967.

The sedition laws have empowered the executive branch of the government to use the ambiguously defined provision as an instrument to regulate public opinion and indiscriminately wield power.

Media's Role in Upholding Constitutional Values

In democratic societies, a vibrant and responsible media serves as a cornerstone in upholding constitutional values. It plays a crucial role in safeguarding fundamental rights, ensuring transparency, and fostering an informed citizenry.

The Guardian of Democracy:

- **The Fourth Estate:** The media is often referred to as the "Fourth Estate" due to its crucial role as an independent check on the three branches of government. It acts as a vigilant watchdog, holding those in power accountable for their actions and decisions.
- **Promoting Accountability and Transparency:** Through investigative journalism and in-depth reporting, the media sheds light on government actions, policies, and potential abuses of power. This scrutiny promotes transparency and ensures that public officials are answerable to the citizens they serve.

Safeguarding Freedom of Expression:

- **Constitutional Protections:** Many constitutions worldwide enshrine freedom of expression as a fundamental right. This protection empowers the media to report, analyze, and comment on matters of public interest without fear of censorship or reprisal.
- **Platform for Diverse Voices:** Media outlets provide a platform for a diverse

range of voices, allowing for the expression of different perspectives, opinions, and ideas. This diversity of voices is essential for a healthy and inclusive democratic discourse.

Advocating for Civil Liberties:

- **Defending Individual Rights:** Media often serves as a champion for individual rights, advocating for the protection of civil liberties and human rights. It highlights cases of injustice, discrimination, and violations of constitutional guarantees.
- **Raising Awareness and Mobilizing Public Opinion:** Through investigative reporting and in-depth analysis, the media educates the public about constitutional issues and mobilizes opinion on matters of legal and social significance. This can lead to advocacy for legal reform and policy change.

Promoting Civic Education and Engagement:

- **Informing the Citizenry:** An informed citizenry is essential for the functioning of a democracy. The media provides citizens with the information they need to make informed decisions, whether in elections or in advocacy for policy changes.
- **Educating on Constitutional Matters:** Media outlets play a crucial role in explaining complex legal and constitutional issues to the general public. This helps citizens understand the implications of legal decisions and policy choices on their rights and freedoms.

Fostering Social Progress:

- **Advocating for Change:** Media can serve as a catalyst for social progress by highlighting pressing issues and advocating for reforms that align with constitutional values. This includes areas such as civil rights, gender equality, and social justice.
- **Championing Inclusivity and Diversity:** The media plays a role in promoting inclusivity by giving voice to marginalized communities and shedding light on their experiences. This fosters a more inclusive understanding of constitutional rights and protections.

3

Freedom of Speech and Expression

Concept and Scope of Freedom of Speech and Expression

Freedom of speech and expression is a fundamental human right that is enshrined in international law and national constitutions around the world. It is the right to express one's thoughts and opinions without fear of government censorship or punishment. This right is essential for a democratic society, as it allows individuals to participate in public debate and to hold their government accountable.

Concept

The concept of freedom of speech and expression is based on the idea that individuals have the right to express themselves freely without fear of government interference. This right is essential for a number of reasons, including:

- Individual autonomy: Freedom of speech and expression allows individuals to develop their own thoughts and opinions and to express them freely. This is essential for individual autonomy and self-determination.
- Public discourse: Freedom of speech and expression allows for a free and open exchange of ideas. This is essential for public discourse and the development of a well-informed citizenry.
- Democratic participation: Freedom of speech and expression allows individuals to participate in the political process and to hold their government accountable. This is essential for a democratic society.

Scope

The scope of freedom of speech and expression is generally considered to include the following:

- Speech: This includes spoken words, as well as written words, such as books, articles, and online posts.
- Expression: This includes nonverbal forms of expression, such as art, music, and protest.
- Media: This includes the right to own and operate media outlets, such as newspapers, television stations, and websites.
- Internet: This includes the right to access and use the internet without government censorship.

Limitations

The right to freedom of speech and expression is not absolute. There are some limitations that are considered to be necessary to protect public order, morality, and national security. These limitations may include restrictions on:

- Hate speech: Speech that incites violence or hatred against a particular group of people.
- Obscenity: Speech that is considered to be offensive or indecent.
- Sedition: Speech that incites or advocates for the overthrow of the government.
- Espionage: Speech that reveals classified information.

The limitations on freedom of speech and expression are generally narrowly construed and are subject to judicial review. This means that the government must be able to justify any restriction on freedom of speech and expression in a court of law.

Restrictions on Freedom of Speech and Expression

Freedom of speech and expression is a fundamental human right that is enshrined in international law and national constitutions around the world. However, this right is not absolute and may be subject to certain restrictions. These restrictions are typically put in place to protect public order, morality, and national security.

Common Restrictions on Freedom of Speech and Expression

- Hate Speech: Speech that incites violence or hatred against a particular group of people based on their race, ethnicity, religion, sexual orientation, or other protected characteristics is often restricted.
- Obscenity: Speech that is considered to be offensive or indecent may also be restricted. However, the definition of obscenity can vary widely from one jurisdiction to another.
- Sedition: Speech that incites or advocates for the overthrow of the government may be considered seditious and subject to restrictions.

- Espionage: Speech that reveals classified information may be considered espionage and subject to restrictions.
- Defamation: Speech that is false and damages another person's reputation may be considered defamation and subject to civil lawsuits.
- Copyright and Trademark Infringement: Speech that violates copyright or trademark laws may be restricted.
- Commercial Speech: Speech that is solely for the purpose of advertising or promoting a product or service may be subject to certain regulations.
- Time, Place, and Manner Restrictions: Governments may also impose restrictions on the time, place, and manner of speech. For example, a government may prohibit loud protests in residential areas at night.

Justification for Restrictions

Governments typically justify restrictions on freedom of speech and expression by arguing that they are necessary to protect the following:

- Public Order: Restrictions on hate speech and sedition are often justified by the need to maintain public order and prevent violence.
- Morality: Restrictions on obscenity may be justified by the need to protect public morality.
- National Security: Restrictions on espionage may be justified by the need to protect national security.
- Individual Rights: Restrictions on defamation may be justified by the need to protect individual reputations.
- Intellectual Property Rights: Restrictions on copyright and trademark infringement may be justified by the need to protect intellectual property rights.
- Consumer Protection: Regulations on commercial speech may be justified by the need to protect consumers from false or misleading advertising.

Balancing Rights and Responsibilities in Media

Balancing Rights

Balancing rights is a complex and delicate process that involves weighing the competing interests and values involved in a particular situation. It is an essential part of a democratic society, as it allows us to protect the fundamental rights of individuals while also ensuring that society functions effectively. There are a number of factors to consider when balancing rights, including:

- The importance of the right: The more important the right, the more weight it should be given in the balancing process. For example, the right to life is often considered to be more important than the right to property.

- The extent of the infringement: The more significant the infringement of a right, the more justification there needs to be for it. For example, a minor restriction on freedom of speech may be justified, but a more severe restriction would require a stronger justification.
- The availability of alternative means: If there are alternative means of achieving a goal that do not infringe on a right, then those means should be used instead. For example, if a government wants to reduce crime, it should focus on measures that do not infringe on individual liberties, such as improving education and social services.
- The proportionality of the infringement: The infringement of a right should be proportionate to the goal that is being sought to be achieved. For example, a government should not impose a blanket ban on all protests in order to prevent a few violent incidents.

Balancing rights is not always easy, and there is no easy formula to follow. It is a process that requires careful consideration of the specific facts and circumstances of each case. However, it is an essential part of a democratic society, as it allows us to protect the fundamental rights of individuals while also ensuring that society functions effectively.

- In criminal law: The right to a fair trial is balanced with the need to protect society from crime. This means that the government may be able to restrict certain rights in order to ensure a fair trial, such as the right to privacy.
- In civil law: The right to free speech is balanced with the right to privacy. This means that individuals may be able to sue for defamation if their reputation is damaged by false or misleading speech.
- In constitutional law: The right to freedom of religion is balanced with the government's right to maintain order and protect public safety. This means that the government may be able to restrict certain religious practices if they are deemed to be a threat to public safety.

Balancing rights is an ongoing process that requires constant vigilance and debate. It is a reminder that our rights are not absolute, and that they must sometimes be balanced against other important interests and values.

Responsibilities in Media

Media holds a unique and powerful position in society, serving as a conduit for information, a platform for public discourse, and a watchdog over those in power. With this influence comes a set of profound responsibilities. This stage delves into the multifaceted responsibilities that the media carries, including the pursuit of truth, maintaining integrity, promoting diversity, and upholding democratic principles.

Understanding and adhering to these responsibilities are essential for a thriving and accountable media ecosystem.

Pursuit of Truth and Accuracy:

- **The Bedrock of Journalism:** The primary responsibility of media is to seek and report the truth. This demands rigorous fact-checking, verification of sources, and a commitment to accuracy in reporting.
- **Consequences of Misinformation:** In an era of information overload, spreading false or misleading information can have far-reaching consequences. It erodes public trust, distorts public discourse, and can even lead to real-world harm.

Fostering Transparency and Accountability:

- **Accountability to the Public:** Media organizations have a responsibility to be transparent about their sources, methodologies, and any potential conflicts of interest. This transparency builds trust with the audience.
- **Holding Power to Account:** A crucial role of the media is to act as a check on power, scrutinizing the actions and decisions of governments, institutions, and individuals in positions of authority.

Respecting Diversity and Inclusivity:

- **Representing Diverse Perspectives:** Media has a responsibility to accurately represent the diversity of voices and experiences within society. This includes different cultural, social, political, and demographic perspectives.
- **Avoiding Stereotypes and Bias:** Media should be vigilant in avoiding stereotypes and biases that can perpetuate discrimination and inequality. Fair and balanced reporting requires a commitment to impartiality.

Ethical Considerations in Reporting:

- **Balancing Privacy and the Public Interest:** Media professionals must carefully weigh the public's right to know against an individual's right to privacy. Ethical reporting should avoid unnecessary intrusion into private lives.
- **Sensitivity in Reporting:** Sensitivity is crucial when reporting on sensitive topics such as tragedies, emergencies, or issues that impact vulnerable populations. Ethical reporting takes into account the potential emotional impact on the audience.

Accountability for Errors and Corrections:

- **Transparent Handling of Errors:** When mistakes occur, media organizations have a responsibility to promptly acknowledge and correct them. This transparency is essential for maintaining credibility.
- **Learning and Improvement:** Accountability extends to learning from mistakes

and implementing measures to prevent similar errors in the future. Continuous improvement is a hallmark of responsible journalism.

Upholding Democratic Principles:

- **Facilitating Informed Citizenship:** Media has a responsibility to provide citizens with the information they need to make informed decisions in a democratic society. This includes reporting on elections, policy issues, and civic engagement.
- **Protecting Press Freedom:** Media plays a crucial role in advocating for and protecting press freedom. This includes resisting censorship, legal threats, and other forms of interference in journalistic work.

4

Defamation, Sedition and Contempt of Court

Defamation Laws: IPC Sections 499-502

Defamation

Defamation, at a first approximation, is any form of *communication* that can injure a third party's reputation. This can include all modes of human-understandable communications: gestures, images, signs, words. It is not necessarily restricted to making assertions that are falsifiable, and can extend to concepts that are more abstract than reputation – like dignity and honour. For a communication to be considered defamatory, it must be conveyed to someone other than the defamed. Depending on the permanence or transience of the communication medium, defamation may be distinguished between libel (written, printed, posted online, published in mass media) and slander (spoken off the record). It is treated as a civil wrong (tort, delict), as a criminal offence, or both. The exact definition of defamation and related acts, as well as the ways they are dealt with, can vary greatly between countries and jurisdictions; for example, whether they constitute crimes or not, to what extent insults and opinions are included in addition to allegations of facts, to what extent proving the alleged facts is a valid defence.

Defamation and related laws can encompass a variety of acts (from general defamation and insult – as applicable to every citizen – to specialized provisions covering specific entities and social structures):

- Defamation against a legal person in general
- Insult against a legal person in general
- Acts against public officials

- Acts against state institutions (government, ministries, government agencies, armed forces)
- Acts against state symbols
- Acts against the state itself
- Acts against heads of state
- Acts against religions (blasphemy)
- Acts against the judiciary or legislature (contempt of court)

History

Defamation law has a long history stretching back to classical antiquity. While defamation has been recognized as an actionable wrong in various forms across historical legal systems and in various moral and religious philosophies, defamation law in contemporary legal systems can primarily be traced back to Roman and early English law.

Roman law was aimed at giving sufficient scope for the discussion of a man's character, while it protected him from needless insult and pain. The remedy for verbal defamation was long confined to a civil action for a monetary penalty, which was estimated according to the significance of the case, and which, although punitive in its character, doubtless included practically the element of compensation. But a new remedy was introduced with the extension of the criminal law, under which many kinds of defamation were punished with great severity. At the same time increased importance attached to the publication of defamatory books and writings, the *libri* or *libelli famosi*, from which is derived the modern use of the word *libel*; and under the later emperors the latter term came to be specially applied to anonymous accusations or *pasquils*, the dissemination of which was regarded as particularly dangerous, and visited with very severe punishment, whether the matters contained in them were true or false.

The Praetorian Edict, codified circa AD 130, declared that an action could be brought up for shouting at someone contrary to good morals: "*qui, adversus bonos mores convicium cui fecisse cuiusve opera factum esse dicitur, quo adversus bonos mores convicium fieret, in eum iudicium dabo.*" In this case, the offence was constituted by the unnecessary act of shouting. According to Ulpian, not all shouting was actionable. Drawing on the argument of Labeo, he asserted that the offence consisted in shouting contrary to the morals of the city ("*adversus bonos mores huius civitatis*") something apt to bring in disrepute or contempt ("*quae... ad infamiam vel invidiam alicuius spectaret*") the person exposed thereto. Any act apt to bring another person into disrepute gave rise to an *actio injurarum*. In such a case the truth of the statements was no justification for the public and insulting manner in which they had been made, but, even in public matters, the accused had the opportunity to justify his actions by openly stating what he considered necessary for public safety to be denounced by the libel and proving his assertions to be true. The second head included defamatory statements made in private, and in this case the offense lay in the content of the imputation, not in the manner of its publication. The truth was therefore a sufficient defense, for no man had a right to demand legal protection for a false reputation.

In Anglo-Saxon England, whose legal tradition is the predecessor of contemporary common law jurisdictions, slander was punished by cutting out the tongue. Historically, while defamation of a commoner in England was known as libel or slander, the defamation of a member of the English aristocracy was called *scandalum magnatum,* literally "the scandal of magnates".

Human Rights

Following the Second World War and with the rise of contemporary international human rights law, the right to a legal remedy for defamation was included in Article 17 of the United Nations International Covenant on Civil and Political Rights (ICCPR), which states that:

1. No one shall be subjected to arbitrary or unlawful interference with his privacy, family, home or correspondence, nor to unlawful attacks on his honour and reputation.
2. Everyone has the right to the protection of the law against such interference or attacks.

This implies a right to legal protection against defamation; however, this right co-exists with the right to freedom of opinion and expression under Article 19 of the ICCPR as well as Article 19 of the Universal Declaration of Human Rights. Article 19 of the ICCPR expressly provides that the right to freedom of opinion and expression may be limited so far as it is necessary "for respect of the rights or reputations of others". Consequently, international human rights law provides that while individual's should have the right to a legal remedy for defamation, this right must be balanced with the equally protected right to freedom of opinion and expression. In general, ensuring that domestic defamation law adequately balances individuals' right to protect their reputation with freedom of expression and of the press entails:

- Providing for truth (i.e., demonstrating that the content of the defamatory statement is true) to be a valid defence,
- Recognising reasonable publication on matters of public concern as a valid defence, and
- Ensuring that defamation may only be addressed by the legal system as a tort.

In most of Europe, article 10 of the European Convention on Human Rights permits restrictions on freedom of speech when necessary to protect the reputation or rights of others. Additionally, restrictions of freedom of expression and other rights guaranteed by international human rights laws (including the European Convention on Human Rights (ECHR)) and by the constitutions of a variety of countries are subject to some variation of the three-part test recognised by the United Nations Human Rights Committee which requires that limitations be: 1) "provided by law that is clear and accessible to everyone", 2) "proven to be necessary and legitimate to protect the rights or reputations of others", and 3) "proportionate and the least restrictive to achieve the purported aim". This test is analogous to the Oakes Test applied domestically by the Supreme Court of Canada in assessing whether limitations on constitutional rights are "demonstrably justifiable in a free and democratic society" under Section 1 of the Canadian Charter of Rights and Freedoms, the "necessary in a democratic society" test applied by the European Court of Human Rights in assessing limitations on rights under the ECHR, Section 36 of the post-Apartheid Constitution of South Africa, and Section 24 of the 2010 Constitution of Kenya.

General Comment No. 34

In 2011, the United Nations Human Rights Committee published their General comment No. 34 (CCPR/C/GC/34) – regarding Article 19 of the ICCPR.

Paragraph 47 states:

- Defamation laws must be crafted with care to ensure that they comply with paragraph 3 [of Article 19 of the ICCPR], and that they do not serve, in practice, to stifle freedom of expression. All such laws, in particular penal defamation laws, should include such defences as the defence of truth and they should not be applied with regard to those forms of expression that are not, of their nature, subject to verification. At least with regard to comments about public figures, consideration should be given to avoiding penalizing or otherwise rendering unlawful untrue statements that have been published in error but without malice. In any event, a public interest in the subject matter of the criticism should be recognized as a defence. Care should be taken by States parties to avoid excessively punitive measures and penalties. Where relevant, States parties should place reasonable limits on the requirement for a defendant to reimburse the expenses of the successful party. States parties should consider the decriminalization of defamation and, in any case, the application of the criminal law should only be countenanced in the most serious of cases and imprisonment is never an appropriate penalty. It is impermissible for a State party to indict a person for criminal defamation but then not to proceed to trial expeditiously – such a practice has a chilling effect that may unduly restrict the exercise of freedom of expression of the person concerned and others.

Defamation as a Tort

While each legal tradition approaches defamation differently, it is typically regarded as a tort for which the offended party can take civil action. The range of remedies available to successful plaintiffs in defamation cases varies between jurisdictions and range from damages to court orders requiring the defendant to retract the offending statement or to publish a correction or an apology.

Common Law

Background

Modern defamation in common law jurisdictions are historically derived from English defamation law. English law allows actions for libel to be brought in the High Court for any published statements alleged to defame a named or identifiable individual or individuals (under English law companies are legal persons, and allowed to bring suit for defamation) in a manner that causes them loss in their trade or profession, or causes a reasonable person to think worse of them.

Overview

In contemporary common law jurisdictions, to constitute defamation, a claim must generally be false and must have been made to someone other than the person defamed. Some common law jurisdictions distinguish between spoken defamation, called *slander*, and defamation in other media such as printed words or images, called *libel*. The fundamental distinction between libel and slander lies solely in the *form* in which the defamatory matter is published. If the offending material is published in some fleeting form, such as spoken words or sounds, sign language, gestures or the like, then it is slander. In contrast, libel encompasses defamation by written or printed words, pictures, or in any form other than spoken words or gestures. The law of libel originated in the 17th century in England. With the growth of publication came the growth of libel and development of the tort of libel. The highest award in an American defamation case, at US$222.7 million was rendered in 1997 against Dow Jones in favour of MMAR Group Inc; however, the verdict was dismissed in 1999 amid allegations that MMAR failed to disclose audiotapes made by its employees.

In common law jurisdictions, civil lawsuits alleging defamation have frequently been used by both private businesses and governments to suppress and censor criticism. A notable example of such lawsuits being used to suppress political criticism of a government is the use of defamation claims by politicians in Singapore's ruling People's Action Party to harass and suppress opposition leaders such as J. B. Jeyaretnam Over the first few decades of the twenty first century, the phenomenon of strategic lawsuits against public participation has gained prominence in many common law jurisdictions outside Singapore as activists, journalists, and critics of corporations, political leaders, and public figures are increasingly targeted with vexatious defamation litigation. As a result, tort reform measures have been enacted in various jurisdictions; the California Code of Civil Procedure and Ontario's Protection of Public Participation Act do so by enabling defendants to make a special motion to strike or dismiss during which discovery is suspended and which, if successful, would terminate the lawsuit and allow the party to recover its legal costs from the plaintiff.

Defences

There are a variety of defences to defamation claims in common law jurisdictions. The two most fundamental defences arise from the doctrine in common law jurisdictions that only a false statement of fact (as opposed to opinion) can be defamatory. This doctrine gives rise to two separate but related defences: opinion and truth. Statements of opinion cannot be regarded as defamatory as they are inherently non-falsifiable. Where a statement has been shown to be one of fact rather than opinion, the most common defence in common law jurisdictions is that of truth. Proving the truth of an allegedly defamatory statement is always a valid defence. Where a statement is partially true, certain jurisdictions in the Commonwealth have provided by statute that the defence "shall not fail by reason only that the truth of every charge is not proved if the words not proved to be true do not materially injure the claimant's reputation having regard to the truth of the remaining charges". Similarly, the American doctrine of substantial truth provides that a statement is not defamatory if it has "slight inaccuracies of expression" but is otherwise true. Since a statement can only be defamatory if it harms another person's reputation, another defence tied to the ability of a statement to be defamatory is to demonstrate that, regardless of whether the statement is true or is a statement of fact, it does not actually harm someone's reputation.

It is also necessary in these cases to show that there is a well-founded public interest in the specific information being widely known, and this may be the case even for public figures. Public interest is generally not "what the public is interested in", but rather "what is in the interest of the public".

Other defences recognised in one or more common law jurisdictions include:

- Privilege: A circumstance that justifies or excuses an act that would otherwise constitute a tort on the ground that it stemmed from a recognised interest of social importance, provides a complete bar and answer to a defamation suit, though conditions may have to be met before this protection is granted. While some privileges have long been recognised, courts may create a new privilege for particular circumstances – privilege as an affirmative defence is a potentially ever-evolving doctrine. Such newly created or circumstantially recognised privileges are referred to as residual justification privileges. There are two types of privilege in common law jurisdictions:
    - Absolute privilege has the effect that a statement cannot be sued on as defamatory, even if it were made maliciously; a typical example is evidence given in court (although this may give rise to different claims, such as an action for malicious prosecution or perjury) or statements made in a session of the legislature by a member thereof (known as 'Parliamentary privilege' in Commonwealth countries).
    - Qualified privilege: A more limited, or 'qualified', form of privilege may be available to journalists as a defence in circumstances where it is considered important that the facts be known in the public interest; an example would be public meetings, local government documents, and information relating to public bodies such as the police and fire departments. Another example would be that a professor – acting in good

faith and honesty – may write an unsatisfactory letter of reference with unsatisfactory information.

- Mistake of fact: Statements made in a good faith and reasonable belief that they were true are generally treated the same as true statements; however, the court may inquire into the reasonableness of the belief. The degree of care expected will vary with the nature of the defendant: an ordinary person might safely rely on a single newspaper report, while the newspaper would be expected to carefully check multiple sources.
- Mere vulgar abuse: An insult that is not necessarily defamatory if it is not intended to be taken literally or believed, or likely to cause real damage to a reputation. Vituperative statements made in anger, such as calling someone "an arse" during a drunken argument, would likely be considered mere vulgar abuse and not defamatory.
- Fair comment: Statements made with an honest belief in their soundness on a matter of public interest (such as regarding official acts) are defendable against a defamation claim, even if such arguments are logically unsound; if a reasonable person could honestly entertain such an opinion, the statement is protected.
- Consent: In rare cases, a defendant can argue that the plaintiff consented to the dissemination of the statement.
- Innocent dissemination: A defendant is not liable if they had no actual knowledge of the defamatory statement or no reason to believe the statement was defamatory. Thus, a delivery service cannot be held liable for delivering a sealed defamatory letter. The defence can be defeated if the lack of knowledge was due to negligence.
- Incapability of further defamation: Historically, it was a defence at common law that the claimant's position in the community is so poor that defamation could not do further damage to the plaintiff. Such a claimant could be said to be "libel-proof", since in most jurisdictions, actual damage is an essential element for a libel claim. Essentially, the defence was that the person had such a bad reputation before the libel, that no further damage could possibly have been caused by the making of the statement.
- Statute of limitations: Most jurisdictions require that a lawsuit be brought within a limited period of time. If the alleged libel occurs in a mass media publication such as a newspaper or the Internet, the statute of limitations begins to run at the time of publication, not when the plaintiff first learns of the communication.
- No third-party communication: If an employer were to bring an employee into a sound-proof, isolated room, and accuse him of embezzling company money, the employee would have no defamation recourse, since no one other than the would-be plaintiff and would-be defendant heard the false statement.

- No actual injury: If there *is* third-party communication, but the third-party hearing the defamatory statement does not believe the statement, or does not care, then there is no injury, and therefore, no recourse.

Defamation per se

Many common law jurisdictions recognise that some categories of statements are considered to be defamatory *per se*, such that people making a defamation claim for these statements do not need to prove that the statement was defamatory. In an action for defamation *per se*, the law recognises that certain false statements are so damaging that they create a presumption of injury to the plaintiff's reputation, allowing a defamation case to proceed to verdict with no actual proof of damages. Although laws vary by state, and not all jurisdictions recognise defamation *per se*, there are four general categories of false statement that typically support a *per se* action:

1. accusing someone of a crime;
2. alleging that someone has a foul or loathsome disease;
3. adversely reflecting on a person's fitness to conduct their business or trade; and
4. imputing serious sexual misconduct.

If the plaintiff proves that such a statement was made and was false, to recover damages the plaintiff need only prove that someone had made the statement to any third party. No proof of special damages is required. However, to recover full compensation a plaintiff should be prepared to prove actual damages. As with any defamation case, truth remains an absolute defence to defamation *per se*. This means that even if the statement would be considered defamatory *per se* if false, if the defendant establishes that it is in fact true, an action for defamation *per se* cannot survive. The conception of what type of allegation may support an action for defamation per se can evolve with public policy. For example, in May 2012 an appeals court in New York, citing changes in public policy with regard to homosexuality, ruled that describing someone as gay is not defamation.

Variations within Common Law Jurisdictions

While defamation torts are broadly similar across common law jurisdictions; differences have arisen as a result of diverging case law, statutes and other legislative action, and constitutional concerns specific to individual jurisdictions.

Some jurisdictions have a separate tort or delict of injury, intentional infliction of emotional distress, involving the making of a statement, even if truthful, intended to harm the claimant out of malice; some have a separate tort or delict of "invasion of privacy" in which the making of a true statement may give rise to liability: but neither of these comes under the general heading of "defamation". The tort of harassment created by Singapore's Protection from Harassment Act 2014 is an example of a tort of this type being created by statute. There is also, in almost all jurisdictions, a tort or delict of "misrepresentation", involving the making of a statement that is untrue even though not defamatory. Thus a surveyor who states a house is free from risk of flooding has not defamed anyone, but may still be liable to someone who purchases the house relying on this statement. Other increasingly common claims similar to defamation in U.S. law are claims that a famous trademark has been diluted through tarnishment. In America, for example, the unique tort of false light protects plaintiffs against statements which are not technically false but are misleading. Libel and slander both require publication.

Although laws vary by state; in America, a defamation action typically requires that a plaintiff claiming defamation prove that the defendant:

1. made a false and defamatory statement concerning the plaintiff;
2. shared the statement with a third party (that is, somebody other than the person defamed by the statement);
3. if the defamatory matter is of public concern, acted in a manner which amounted at least to negligence on the part of the defendant; and
4. caused damages to the plaintiff.

Additionally, American courts apply special rules in the case of statements made in the press concerning public figures, which can be used as a defence. While plaintiff alleging defamation in an American court must usually prove that the statement caused harm, and was made without adequate research into the truthfulness of the statement; where the plaintiff is a celebrity or public official, they must additionally prove that the statement was made with actual malice (i.e. the intent to do harm or with reckless disregard for the truth). A series of court rulings led by *New York Times Co. v. Sullivan*, 376 U.S. 254 (1964) established that for a public official (or other legitimate public figure) to win a libel case in an American court, the statement must have been published knowing it to be false or with reckless disregard to its truth (i.e. actual malice).

The Associated Press estimates that 95% of libel cases involving news stories do not arise from high-profile news stories, but "run of the mill" local stories like news coverage of local criminal investigations or trials, or business profiles. Media liability insurance is available to newspapers to cover potential damage awards from libel lawsuits. An early example of libel is the case of John Peter Zenger in 1735. Zenger was hired to publish the *New York Weekly Journal*.

When he printed another man's article criticising William Cosby, the royal governor of Colonial New York, Zenger was accused of seditious libel. The verdict was returned as *not guilty* on the charge of seditious libel, because it was proven that all the statements Zenger had published about Cosby had been true, so there was not an issue of defamation. Another example of libel is the case of *New York Times Co. v. Sullivan* (1964). The Supreme Court of the United States overruled a state court in Alabama that had found *The New York Times* guilty of libel for printing an advertisement that criticised Alabama officials for mistreating student civil rights activists. Even though some of what *The Times* printed was false, the court ruled in its favour, saying that libel of a public official requires proof of actual malice, which was defined as a "knowing or reckless disregard for the truth".

Many jurisdictions within the Commonwealth (e.g. Singapore, Ontario, and the United Kingdom) have enacted legislation to:

- Codify the defences of fair comment and qualified privilege
- Provide that, while most instances of slander continue to require special damage to be proved (i.e. prove that pecuniary loss was caused by the defamatory statement), instances such as slander of title shall not
- Clarify that broadcast statements (including those that are only broadcast in spoken form) constitute libel rather than slander.

Libel law in England and Wales was overhauled even further by the Defamation Act 2013.

Defamation in Indian tort law largely resembles that of England and Wales. Indian courts have endorsed the defences of absolute and qualified privilege, fair comment, and justification. While statutory law in the United Kingdom provides that, if the defendant is only successful in proving the truth of some of the several charges against him, the defence of justification might still be available if the charges not proved do not materially injure the reputation, there is no corresponding provision in India, though it is likely that Indian courts would treat this principle as persuasive precedent. Recently, incidents of defamation in relation to public figures have attracted public attention.

The origins of U.S. defamation law pre-date the American Revolution. Though the First Amendment of the American Constitution was designed to protect freedom of the press, it was primarily envisioned to prevent censorship by the state rather than defamation suits; thus, for most of American history, the Supreme Court did not interpret the First Amendment as applying to libel cases involving media defendants. This left libel laws, based upon the traditional common law of defamation inherited from the English legal system, mixed across the states. The 1964 case *New York Times Co. v. Sullivan* dramatically altered the nature of libel law in the country by elevating the fault element for public officials to actual malice – that is, public figures could win a libel suit only if they could demonstrate the publisher's "knowledge that the information was false" or that the information was published "with reckless disregard of whether it was false or not". Later the Supreme Court held that statements that are so ridiculous to be clearly not true are protected from libel claims, as are statements of opinion relating to matters of public concern that do not contain a provably false factual connotation. Subsequent state and federal cases have addressed defamation law and the Internet.

American defamation law is much less plaintiff-friendly than its counterparts in European and the Commonwealth countries. A comprehensive discussion of what is and is not libel or slander under American law is difficult, as the definition differs between different states and is further affected by federal law. Some states codify what constitutes slander and libel together, merging the concepts into a single defamation law.

New Zealand received English law with the signing of the Treaty of Waitangi in February 1840. The current Act is the Defamation Act 1992 which came into force on 1 February 1993 and repealed the Defamation Act 1954. New Zealand law allows for the following remedies in an action for defamation: compensatory damages; an injunction to stop further publication; a correction or a retraction; and in certain cases, punitive damages. Section 28 of the Act allows for punitive damages only when a there is a flagrant disregard of the rights of the person defamed. As the law assumes that an individual suffers loss if a statement is defamatory, there is no need to prove that specific damage or loss has occurred. However, Section 6 of the Act allows for a defamation action brought by a corporate body to proceed only when the body corporate alleges and proves that the publication of the defamation has caused or is likely to cause pecuniary loss to that body corporate.

As is the case for most Commonwealth jurisdictions, Canada follows English law on defamation issues (except in Quebec where the private law is derived from French civil law). In common law provinces and territories, defamation covers any communication that tends to lower the esteem of the subject in the minds of ordinary members of the public. Probably true statements are not excluded, nor are political opinions. Intent is always presumed, and it is not necessary to prove that the defendant intended to defame. In *Hill v. Church of Scientology of Toronto* (1995), the Supreme Court of Canada rejected the *actual malice* test adopted in the US case *New York Times Co. v. Sullivan*. Once a claim has been made, the defendant may avail themselves of a defence of justification (the truth), fair comment, responsible communication, or privilege. Publishers of defamatory comments may also use the defence of innocent dissemination where they had no knowledge of the nature of the statement, it was not brought to their attention, and they were not negligent.

Roman Dutch and Scots Law

Defamation in jurisdictions applying Roman Dutch law (i.e. most of Southern Africa, Indonesia, Suriname, and the Dutch Caribbean) gives rise to a claim by way of "actio iniuriarum". For liability under the *actio iniuriarum*, the general elements of delict must be present, but specific rules have been developed for each element. Causation, for example, is seldom in issue, and is assumed to be present. The elements of liability under the *actio iniuriarum* are as follows:

- harm, in the form of a violation of a personality interest (one's *corpus*, *dignitas* and *fama*);
- wrongful conduct; and
- intention.

Under the *actio iniuriarum*, harm consists in the infringement of a personality right, either "corpus", "dignitas", or "fama". *Dignitas* is a generic term meaning 'worthiness, dignity, self-respect', and comprises related concerns like mental tranquillity and privacy. Because it is such a wide concept, its infringement must be serious. Not every insult is humiliating; one must prove *contumelia*. This includes insult (*iniuria* in the narrow sense), adultery, loss of consortium, alienation of affection, breach of promise (but only in a humiliating or degrading manner), et cetera. "Fama" is a generic term referring to reputation and actio iniuriarum pertaining to it encompasses defamation more broadly Beyond simply covering actions that fall within the broader concept of defamation, "actio iniuriarum" relating to infringements of a person's *corpus* provides civil remedies for assaults, acts of a sexual or indecent nature, and 'wrongful arrest and detention'.

In Scots law, which is closely related to Roman Dutch law, the remedy for defamation is similarly the actio iniuriarium and the most common defence is "veritas" (i.e. proving the truth of otherwise defamatory statement). Defamation falls within the realm of non-patrimonial (i.e. dignitary) interests. The Scots law pertaining to the protection of non-patrimonial interests is said to be 'a thing of shreds and patches'. This notwithstanding, there is 'little historical basis in Scots law for the kind of structural difficulties that have restricted English law' in the development of mechanisms to protect so-called 'rights of personality'. The *actio iniuriarum* heritage of Scots law gives the courts scope to recognise, and afford reparation in, cases in which no patrimonial (or 'quasi-patrimonial') 'loss' has occurred, but a recognised dignitary interest has nonetheless been invaded through the wrongful conduct of the defender. For such reparation to be offered, however, the non-patrimonial interest must be deliberately affronted: negligent interference with a non-patrimonial interest will not be sufficient to generate liability. An *actio iniuriarum* requires that the conduct of the defender be 'contumelious' - that is, it must show such hubristic disregard of the pursuer's recognised personality interest that an intention to affront (*animus iniuriandi*) might be imputed.

Defamation as a Crime

In addition to tort law, many jurisdictions treat defamation as a criminal offence and provide for penalties as such. Article 19, a British free expression advocacy group, has published global maps charting the existence of criminal defamation law across the globe, as well as showing countries that have special protections for political leaders or functionaries of the state.

There can be regional statutes that may differ from the national norm. For example, in the United States, criminal defamation is generally limited to the living. However, there are 7 states (Idaho, Kansas, Louisiana, Nevada, North Dakota, Oklahoma, Utah) that have criminal statutes regarding defamation of the dead.

The Organization for Security and Co-operation in Europe (OSCE) has also published a detailed database on criminal and civil defamation provisions in 55 countries, including all European countries, all member countries of the Commonwealth of Independent States, America, and Canada. Questions of group libel have been appearing in common law for hundreds of years. One of the earliest known cases of a defendant being tried for defamation of a group was the case of *R v Orme and Nutt* (1700). In this case, the jury found that the defendant was guilty of libeling several subjects, though they did not specifically identify who these subjects were. A report of the case told that the jury believed that "where a writing ... inveighs against mankind in general, or against a particular order of men, as for instance, men of the gown, this is no libel, but it must descend to particulars and individuals to make it libel." This jury believed that only individuals who believed they were specifically defamed had a claim to a libel case. Since the jury was unable to identify the exact people who were being defamed, there was no cause to identify the statements were a libel.

Another early English group libel which has been frequently cited is *King v. Osborne* (1732). In this case, the defendant was on trial "for printing a libel reflecting upon the Portuguese Jews". The printing in question claimed that Jews who had arrived in London from Portugal burned a Jewish woman to death when she had a child with a Christian man, and that this act was common. Following Osborne's anti-Semitic publication, several Jews were attacked. Initially, the judge seemed to believe the court could do nothing since no individual was singled out by Osborne's writings. However, the court concluded that "since the publication implied the act was one Jews frequently did, the whole community of Jews was defamed." Though various reports of this case give differing accounts of the crime, this report clearly shows a ruling based on group libel. Since laws restricting libel were accepted at this time because of its tendency to lead to a breach of peace, group libel laws were justified because they showed potential for an equal or perhaps greater risk of violence. For this reason, group libel cases are criminal even though most libel cases are civil torts.

In a variety of Common Law jurisdictions, criminal laws prohibiting protests at funerals, sedition, false statements in connection with elections, and the use of profanity in public, are also often used in contexts similar to criminal libel actions. The boundaries of a court's power to hold individuals in "contempt of court" for what amounts to alleged defamatory statements about judges or the court process by attorneys or other people involved in court cases is also not well established in many common law countries.

Criticism

While defamation torts are less controversial as they ostensibly involve plaintiffs seeking to protect their right to dignity and their reputation, criminal defamation is more controversial as it involves the state expressly seeking to restrict freedom of expression. Human rights organisations, and other organisations such as the Council of Europe and Organization for Security and Co-operation in Europe, have campaigned against strict defamation laws that criminalise defamation. The freedom of expression advocacy group Article 19 opposes criminal defamation, arguing that civil defamation laws providing defences for statements on matters of public interest are better compliant with international human rights law. The European Court of Human Rights has placed restrictions on criminal libel laws because of the freedom of expression provisions of the European Convention on Human Rights. One notable case was *Lingens v. Austria* (1986).

In India

In India, a defamation case can be filed under either criminal law or civil law or cyber crime law, together or in sequence.

According to the Constitution of India, the fundamental right to free speech (Article 19) is subject to "reasonable restrictions":

19. Protection of certain rights regarding freedom of speech, etc.

- (1) All citizens shall have the right—

  (a) to freedom of speech and expression;

- (2) Nothing in sub-clause (a) of clause (1) shall affect the operation of any existing law, or prevent the State from making any law, in so far as such law imposes reasonable restrictions on the exercise of the right conferred by the said sub-clause in the interests of [the sovereignty and integrity of India], the security of the State, friendly relations with foreign States, public order, decency or morality, or in relation to contempt of court, defamation or incitement to an offence.

Accordingly, for the purpose of criminal defamation, "reasonable restrictions" are defined in Section 499 of the Indian Penal Code, 1860. This section defines defamation and provides ten valid exceptions when a statement is not considered to be defamation. It says that defamation takes place, when someone "by words either spoken or intended to be read, or by signs or by visible representations, makes or publishes any imputation concerning any person intending to harm, or knowing or having reason to believe that such imputation will harm, the reputation of such person". The punishment is simple imprisonment for up to two years, or a fine, or both (Section 500).

Some other offences related to false allegations: false statements regarding elections (Section 171G), false information (Section 182), false claims in court (Section 209), false criminal charges (Section 211).

Some other offences related to insults: against public servants in judicial proceedings (Section 228), against religion or religious beliefs (Section 295A), against religious feelings (Section 298), against breach of peace (Section 504), against modesty of women (Section 509).

According to the Indian Code of Criminal Procedure, 1973 defamation is prosecuted only upon a complaint (within six months from the act) (Section 199), and is a bailable, non-cognisable and compoundable offence.

Section 499 in The Indian Penal Code

Defamation

Whoever, by words either spoken or intended to be read, or by signs or by visible representations, makes or publishes any imputation concerning any person intending to harm, or knowing or having reason to believe that such imputation will harm, the reputation of such person, is said, except in the cases hereinafter expected, to defame that person.

Explanation 1

It may amount to defamation to impute anything to a deceased person, if the imputation would harm the reputation of that person if living, and is intended to be hurtful to the feelings of his family or other near relatives.

Explanation 2

It may amount to defamation to make an imputation concerning a company or an association or collection of persons as such.

Explanation 3

An imputation in the form of an alternative or expressed ironically, may amount to defamation.

Explanation 4

No imputation is said to harm a person's reputa-tion, unless that imputation directly or indirectly, in the estimation of others, lowers the moral or intellectual character of that person, or lowers the character of that person in respect of his caste or of his calling, or lowers the credit of that person, or causes it to be believed that the body of that person is in a loathsome state, or in a state generally considered as disgrace-ful. Illustrations

- (a) A says—"Z is an honest man; he never stole B's watch"; in-tending to cause it to be believed that Z did steal B's watch. This is defamation, unless it fall within one of the exceptions.
- (b) A is asked who stole B's watch. A points to Z, intending to cause it to be believed that Z stole B's watch. This is defama-tion unless it fall within one of the exceptions.
- (c) A draws a picture of Z running away with B's watch, intending it to be believed that Z stole B's watch. This is defamation, unless it fall within one of the exceptions. First Exception.—Imputation of truth which public good requires to be made or published.—It is not defamation to impute anything which is true concerning any person, if it be for the public good that the imputation should be made or published. Whether or not it is for the public good is a question of fact. Second Exception.—Public conduct of public servants.—It is not defamation to express in a good faith any opinion whatever re-specting the conduct of a public servant in the discharge of his public functions, or respecting his character, so far as his character appears in that conduct, and no further. Third Exception.—Conduct of any person touching any public question.—It is

not defamation to express in good faith any opinion whatever respecting the conduct of any person touching any public question, and respecting his character, so far as his character appears in that conduct, and no further. Illustration It is not defamation in A to express in good faith any opinion whatever respecting Z's conduct in petitioning Government on a public question, in signing a requisition for a meeting on a public question, in presiding or attending a such meeting, in forming or joining any society which invites the public support, in voting or canvassing for a particular candidate for any situa-tion in the efficient discharges of the duties of which the public is interested. Fourth Exception.—Publication of reports of proceedings of Courts.—It is not defamation to publish substantially true report of the proceedings of a Court of Justice, or of the result of any such proceedings. Explanation.—A Justice of the Peace or other officer holding an inquiry in open Court preliminary to a trial in a Court of Jus-tice, is a Court within the meaning of the above section. Fifth Exception.—Merits of case decided in Court or conduct of witnesses and others concerned.—It is not defamation to express in good faith any opinion whatever respecting the merits of any case, civil or criminal, which has been decided by a Court of Justice, or respecting the conduct of any person as a party, witness or agent, in any such case, or respecting the character of such person, as far as his character appears in that conduct, and no further. Illustrations

- (a) A says—"I think Z's evidence on that trial is so contradic-tory that he must be stupid or dishonest". A is within this exception if he says this is in good faith, in as much as the opin-ion which he expresses respects Z's character as it appears in Z's conduct as a witness, and no further.
- (b) But if A says—"I do not believe what Z asserted at that trial because I know him to be a man without veracity"; A is not within this exception, in as much as the opinion which he express of Z's character, is an opinion not founded on Z's conduct as a witness. Sixth Exception.—Merits of public performance.—It is not defa-mation to express in good faith any opinion respecting the merits of any performance which its author has submitted to the judgment of the public, or respecting the character of the author so far as his character appears in such performance, and no further. Explanation.—A performance may be substituted to the judgment of the public expressly or by acts on the part of the author which imply such submission to the judgment of the public. Illustrations
- (a) A person who publishes a book, submits that book to the judgment of the public.
- (b) A person who makes a speech in public, submits that speech to the judgment of the public.
- (c) An actor or singer who appears on a public stage, submits his acting or signing in the judgment of the public.

- (d) A says of a book published by Z—"Z's book is foolish; Z must be a weak man. Z's book is indecent; Z must be a man of impure mind". A is within the exception, if he says this in good faith, in as much as the opinion which he expresses of Z respects Z's character only so far as it appears in Z's book, and no further.

- (e) But if A says—"I am not surprised that Z's book is foolish and indecent, for he is a weak man and a libertine". A is not within this exception, in as much as the opinion which he expresses of Z's character is an opinion not founded on Z's book. Seventh Exception.—Censure passed in good faith by person having lawful authority over another.—It is not defamation in a person having over another any authority, either conferred by law or arising out of a lawful contract made with that other, to pass in good faith any censure on the conduct of that other in matters to which such lawful authority relates. Illustration A Judge censuring in good faith the conduct of a witness, or of an officer of the Court; a head of a department censuring in good faith those who are under his orders; a parent censuring in good faith a child in the presence of other children; a school-master, whose authority is derived from a parent, censuring in good faith a pupil in the presence of other pupils; a master censuring a servant in good faith for remissness in service; a banker censur-ing in good faith the cashier of his bank for the conduct of such cashier as such cashier—are within this exception. Eighth Exception.—Accusation preferred in good faith to autho-rised person.—It is not defamation to prefer in good faith an accusation against any person to any of those who have lawful authority over that person with respect to the subject-matter of accusation. Illustration If A in good faith accuse Z before a Magistrate; if A in good faith complains of the conduct of Z, a servant, to Z's master; if A in good faith complains of the conduct of Z, and child, to Z's father—A is within this exception. Ninth Exception.—Imputation made in good faith by person for protection of his or other's interests.—It is not defamation to make an imputation on the character of another provided that the imputation be made in good faith for the protection of the inter-ests of the person making it, or of any other person, or for the public good. Illustrations

- (a) A, a shopkeeper, says to B, who manages his business—"Sell nothing to Z unless he pays you ready money, for I have no opin-ion of his honesty". A is within the exception, if he has made this imputation on Z in good faith for the protection of his own interests.

- (b) A, a Magistrate, in making a report of his own superior offi-cer, casts an imputation on the character of Z. Here, if the imputation is made in good faith, and for the public good, A is within the exception. Tenth Exception.—Caution intended for good of person to whom conveyed or for public good.—It is not defamation to convey a caution, in good faith, to one person against another, provided that such caution be intended for the good of the person to whom it is conveyed, or of some person in whom that person is inter-ested, or for the public good. COMMENTS Imputation without publication In section 499 the words "makes or publishes any imputation" should be interpreted as words supple-menting to each other. A maker of imputation without publication is not liable to be punished under that section; Bilal Ahmed Kaloo v. State of Andhra Pradesh, (1997) 7 Supreme Today 127.

Section 500 in The Indian Penal Code

Punishment for Defamation

Whoever defames another shall be punished with simple imprisonment for a term which may extend to two years, or with fine, or with both

Section 501 in the Indian Penal Code

Printing or Engraving Matter Known to be Defamatory

Whoev-er prints or engraves any matter, knowing or having good reason to believe that such matter is defamatory of any person, shall be punished with simple imprisonment for a term which may extend to two years, or with fine, or with both.

Section 502 in the Indian Penal Code

Sale of Printed or Engraved Substance Containing Defamatory Matter

Whoever sells or offers for sale any printed or engraved substance containing defamatory matter, knowing that it contains such matter, shall be punished with simple imprisonment for a term which may extend to two years, or with fine, or with both.

Sedition Laws: IPC Section 124(A)

Sedition is overt conduct, such as speech or organization, that tends toward rebellion against the established order. Sedition often includes subversion of a constitution and incitement of discontent toward, or insurrection against, established authority. Sedition may include any commotion, though not aimed at direct and open violence against the laws. Seditious words in writing are seditious libel. A seditionist is one who engages in or promotes the interest of sedition. Because sedition is overt, it is typically not considered a subversive act, and the overt acts that may be prosecutable under sedition laws vary by jurisdiction.

Roman Origin

Seditio was the offence, in the later Roman Republic, of collective disobedience to a magistrate, including both military mutiny and civilian mob action. Leading or instigating *seditio* was punishable by death. Civil *seditio* became frequent during the political crisis of the first century BCE, as populist politicians sought to check the privileged classes by appealing to public assemblies. The Julio-Claudian emperors addressed this situation by abolishing elections and other duties of the assemblies. Under Tiberius the crime of *seditio* was subsumed in the law of *majestas*, which prohibited any utterance against the dignity of the emperor.

Section 124A of the Indian Penal Code

Section 124A of the Indian Penal Code lays down the punishment for sedition. The Indian Penal Code was enacted in 1860, under the British Raj. Section 124A forms part of Chapter VI of the Code which deals with offences against the state. Chapter VI comprises sections from 121 to 130, wherein section 121A and 124A were introduced in 1870. The then British government of India feared that the Khilafat movement on the Indian subcontinent would wage a war against them. Particularly after the successful suppression of Wahabi/Waliullah Movement, the need was felt for such a law. Throughout the Raj, the section was used to suppress political dissent in favour of independence, including Lokmanya Tilak and Mahatma Gandhi, both of whom were found guilty and imprisoned.

The section kept drawing criticism in the independent India as well for being a hindrance to free speech. Sedition was made a cognisable offence for the first time in history in India, during the tenure of PM Indira Gandhi in 1973, that is, arrest without a police warrant was now permissible. In 1962 the Supreme Court of India interpreted the section to apply only if there is, say, "incitement to violence" or "overthrowing a democratically elected government through violent means".

As of 11 May 2022 : This law has been put on temporary hold by Supreme Court of India citing re-examination.

Text

Section 124A. Sedition

Whoever, by words, either spoken or written, or by signs, or by visible representation, or otherwise, brings or attempts to bring into hatred or contempt, or excites or attempts to excite disaffection towards, the Government established by law in India, shall be punished with imprisonment for life, to which fine may be added, or with imprisonment which may extend to three years, to which fine may be added, or with fine.

- *Explanation 1.*—The expression "disaffection" includes disloyalty and all feelings of enmity.
- *Explanation 2.*—Comments expressing disapprobation of the measures of the Government with a view to obtain their alteration by lawful means, without exciting or attempting to excite hatred, contempt or disaffection, do not constitute an offence under this section.

- *Explanation 3.*—Comments expressing disapprobation of the administrative or other action of the Government without exciting or attempting to excite hatred, contempt or disaffection, do not constitute an offence under this section.

Development and Current Status

The section related to sedition initially had its place in the code, as Section 113, when Thomas Babington Macaulay drafted the Penal Code in 1837. However, for reasons unknown, it was omitted from the actual Code. It was finally added in 1870 on the suggestion of James Fitzjames Stephen, at the time handling legal issues in the colonial Government of Indian. Due to increasing Wahabi activities, and fearing that Muslim preachers would incite religious war in the Indian subcontinent, the Raj introduced this section under the title "Exciting disaffection". Stephen's version of 1870 was amended to a large extent through IPC Amendment Act of 1898. The current section stands very much similar to this 1898's section; however minor alterations were made at various points in India's colonial and post-colonial history—in 1937, 1948, 1950, and by Part B States (Law) Act, 1951.

A case in 1958, *Ram Nandan v State,* heard by the Allahabad High Court declared the sedition law void. The Punjab high court had also struck down the law. A Supreme Court judgement in 1962 brought back sedition into the Constitution, interpreting the section to say that it only applies if there is "incitement to violence".

Sedition was made cognizable for the first time during the tenure of Indira Gandhi via the 1973 Code of Criminal Procedure (CrPC) which replaced the 1898 CrPC.

On May 11, 2022, the Supreme Court of India suspended the colonial era law. The court said that the law has been misused by governments to quash dissent and that it was not in tune with the times. Due to this, hundreds of people who were jailed under the law have become eligible for bail. The ruling does not overturn the sedition law, the law has only been put on temporary hold and no further cases can be registered under this law until the ongoing review by the government is completed.

Notable Cases

Pre-independence

The first known registered case under the section was in Calcutta High Court in 1891; *Queen Empress v Jogendra Chunder Bose.* Bose's article, published in his own Bengali magazine *Bangobasi,* criticized the Age of Consent Act, 1891. The Act was described as "forced Europeanisation" and a gag on Hindus, who were described as legally incapable and prevented from rebelling against the Act. The authorities put forth a claim that Bose had incited rebellion; in his instructions to the jury, the Chief Justice William Comer Petheram explained the meaning of "disaffection" as "a feeling contrary to affection, in other words, dislike or hatred" and linked it with disobedience towards the government. Bose was nevertheless released on bail, and the case was dropped.

The sedition trial of 1897 against Lokmanya Tilak is historically famous. Tilak, a lawyer by training, was also politically active in support of independence. He established and published two dailies—*Kesari* in Marathi and *Mahratta* in English; both being published from Pune. In 1894, Professor R. P. Karkaria presented his paper on the Maratha king Shivaji to the Royal Asiatic Society in Bombay. This turned into an annual celebration commemorating the anniversary of Shivaji's coronation. Three years later, Tilak published reports of this celebration, as "Shivaji's Utterances"; this essay doubled as an attack on the colonial government. Justice Arthur Strachey, who presided over Tilak's case, widened the understanding of Section 124A. Under Strachey's definition, the attempt to excite "feelings of enmity" against government was also a form of sedition. Tilak was found guilty by the jury and sentenced to 18 months of rigorous imprisonment. Tilak again faced charges against sedition for two *Kesari* articles, titled "The Country's Misfortune" (12 May 1908) and "These Remedies Are Not Lasting" (9 June 1908). Once again Tilak was found guilty under the newly drafted section 124A, and sentenced to six years of imprisonment in Burma. Despite the verdict, this trial, according to historian Mithi Mukherjee, "marked a fundamental discursive rupture in the history of empire and paved the way for mass anticolonial movements under the leadership of Gandhi. In 1922, Mahatma Gandhi's three articles for *Young India* resulted into his and Shankarlal Banker's imprisonment under the sedition section. While appearing in court, Gandhi referred to Section 124A as the "prince among the political sections of the Indian Penal Code designed to suppress the liberty of the citizen".

Post-independence

In 1951, the Punjab High Court ruled Section 124A to be unconstitutional. A similar ruling was passed in 1959 by the Allahabad High Court, which also concluded that it struck at the very root of free speech. The Government of India appealed to the Supreme Court of India, which in 1962 ruled that speeches against the government or political parties was not illegal, while upholding it as applicable to separatism by persuasion or force; this pronouncement had the effect of diluting the law.

During the 21st century, various notable authors, creative professionals, activists and politicians have been charged with sedition under Section 124A. Cases include the then Vishva Hindu Parishad (VHP) general secretary Praveen Togadia (2003), Simranjit Singh Mann (2005), Binayak Sen (2007), author Arundhati Roy (2010), cartoonist Aseem Trivedi (2012), student activist Rinshad Reera (2019), climate activist Disha Ravi (2020).

Low Conviction Rate

Between 2014 and 2019, 326 sedition cases were filed in India, charge sheets were filed in 141 cases which resulted in only 6 convictions.

On 15 July 2021, the Chief Justice of India N.V. Ramana drew attention to the fact that the rate of conviction under sedition is very low and that this law has been misused by the executive powers. Some critics of the law further elaborate on this point by claiming that the purpose of this law is not to convict the charged, but to harass and to silence critics of the government by the means of a long drawn out process.

Criticism

In post-independence India, Section 124A came under criticism at numerous intervals, being singled out for its curbing of free speech. When the First Amendment of the Constitution of India was passed in 1951, Prime Minister Jawaharlal Nehru proposed to "get rid of it [Section 124A]" as written, and favoured handling sedition-related by other means. Several opinion-makers have called for the abolishing of sedition laws in the context of the 2016 protests at the Jawaharlal Nehru University. In 2018, the Law Commission of India published a consultation paper that asked for a possible amendment or repeal of the law. During the 2019 Indian general election, the opposition Indian National Congress (INC) included a specific proposal to abolish Section 124A in their manifesto. However, while the INC-led United Progressive Alliance had been in power (2004–2014), the section had remained intact and was used to file charges on various citizens; following 2012-2013 protests against Kudankulam Nuclear Power Plant in Tamil Nadu, an "astonishing number" of citizens faced trial under Section 124A: 23,000 were in temporary custody, of whom 9,000 were arrested only for sedition.

Critics of the law claim that sedition is an outdated law from the colonial era and it curtails the freedom of speech and that it has no place in a modern democracy. Critics further point out that the law was introduced by the colonial government in India to curtail dissent and that Britain has since abolished this law in 2009. The then Parliamentary Under Secretary of State at the Ministry of Justice of UK, Claire Ward said:

- "The existence of these obsolete offences in this country had been used by other countries as justification for the retention of similar laws which have been actively used to suppress political dissent and restrict press freedom. Abolishing these offences will allow the UK to take a lead in challenging similar laws in other countries, where they are used to suppress free speech."

The Editor's Guild of India has called this a *"draconian law"*, and has demanded the repeal of this law and has also expressed that *"this law has no space in any modern liberal democracy"*. The Indian Women Press Corps (IWPC) also has said:

- "We have noticed, with dismay, a growing trend in India in recent times where both central and state governments have routinely slapped sedition charges on journalists for articles, tweets, Facebook posts that criticise government policies...In January 2021, IWPC founder member *Mrinal Pande* and some other journalists were booked for sedition for tweets relating to farmers' protest."

The Press Club of India has condemned the use of this law by state governments against senior journalists for the coverage of the farmers protests. Furthermore, some critics of the law say that the purpose of this law is not to convict, but for the government to harass its critics through the drawn out process.

Alternatives

The following laws in India address the same aspects covered by the sedition law—

- Unlawful Activities Act
- Public Safety Acts (such as the JK PSA)
- National Security Act

Amending and Repealing Section 124A

Numerous critics, students, former government employees including Indian Police Service and Indian Administrative Service officers, legal thinkers and judges, scholars, human rights and civil liberty advocates, journalists, and so on have commented against the sedition law, calling for it to be scrapped or undergo amendments.

A law student proposes "the following modification to the law is suggested. Section 124A should be retained subject to three conditions: first, that, the offender must be in a position of authority...; second, that, the offending words must be understood in context...; and, third, they should have a tendency to actually cause violence or disorder...."

In 2021, Kishorechandra Wangkhemcha and Kanhaiya Lal Shukla, petitioned the Supreme Court against the law. The court admitted the case.

As of 11 May 2022,the law has been put on hold by Supreme Court citing re-examination.

Contempt of Court Act 1971

In India, the offence of contempt of court is committed when a person either disobeys a court order (civil contempt), or when a person says or does anything that scandalizes, prejudices, or interferes with judicial proceedings and the administration of justice (criminal contempt). Contempt of court can be punished with imprisonment or a fine, or both.

History and Legislation

The offence of contempt of courts was established in common law, and can also be traced to colonial legislation, with the earliest recorded penalties contained in the Regulating Act of 1773, which stated that the newly formed Mayor's Court of Calcutta would have the same powers as a court of the English King's Bench to punish persons for contempt. Courts established in India under colonial rule followed the common law principle that all 'courts of record' had the inherent power to punish for contempt. High Courts established in Bombay, Calcutta, and Madras as courts of record subsequently exercised the power of contempt to penalise persons for interfering with the administration of justice.

The Contempt of Courts Act 1926 was enacted to resolve a conflict of opinions between High Courts in India on whether they had the power to penalise offences of contempt committed against other, subordinate courts that fell under their jurisdiction. The 1926

Act specifically affirmed this power, and allowed the High Courts to penalise contempt against subordinate courts as well as against their own judgments and proceedings. In 1952, the Contempt of Courts Act was replaced by a new legislation of the same name, which expanded the power to punish for contempt from High Courts to other courts as well.

The Constitution of India, enacted in 1950, specifically established the Supreme Court of India as well as High Courts in the states of India as courts of record with the power to punish for acts of contempt. Contempt of court is also a ground on which the right to freedom of speech in India can be restricted.

In 1961, a committee headed by H.N. Sanyal, an Additional Solicitor General for the Government of India, was appointed to examine the application of contempt laws in India. The Sanyal Committee recommended that contempt proceedings should be initiated not by the courts themselves, but on the recommendation of a law officer of the government. These recommendations were incorporated in the Contempt of Courts Act 1971, enacted by the Parliament of India, which is the current legislation governing contempt of courts in India. The Contempt of Courts Act 1971 defines civil and criminal contempt, and lays down the powers and procedures by which courts can penalise contempt, as well as the penalties that can be given for the offence of contempt. The Act was amended in 2006, to limit the power of courts to punish for contempt, only when such contempt "interfered with the due course of justice," and to allow truth as a defense to contempt.

Commission of Contempt of Court

The Contempt of Courts Act 1971 categorises the offence of contempt into civil and criminal contempt. The Act specifies that High Courts and the Supreme Court of India have the power to try and punish the offence of contempt, and High Courts have the power to punish acts of contempt against courts subordinate to them; however, the Supreme Court of India has clarified that any court of record has the inherent power to punish for contempt. In addition to these courts, certain administrative tribunals also have been given the power to punish for contempt, in their governing statutes.

Civil Contempt

Civil contempt, defined in Section 2(b) of the Contempt of Courts Act, is "wilful disobedience to any judgment, decree, direction, order, writ or other process of a court or wilful breach of an undertaking given to a court".

Criminal Contempt

Criminal contempt, defined in Section 2(c), is committed when anything is published, or done, which "scandalises, or tends to scandalise, or lowers or tends to lower the authority of, any court", or "prejudices, or interferes or tends to interfere with, the due course of any judicial proceeding," or "interferes or tends to interfere with, or obstructs or tends to obstruct, the administration of justice in any other manner." The offence of criminal contempt has been held to cover false statements made to or about the judiciary, coercion and attempts to pervert judicial proceedings by attacking witnesses, parties, or judges, recording court proceedings without permission from the court, obstructing officers of the court from performing their functions, as well as verbal abuse and accusations of incompetence or bias against judges.

Procedure

The procedure for trying cases of contempt of court is provided in the Contempt of Courts Act 1971. Proceedings can be initiated by courts *suo motu*, i.e. by themselves, and require a notice in writing to be sent to person alleged to have committed contempt to appear before the court, when the contemptuous act or words occur in the presence of the court.

Courts are required to conduct these hearings as soon as possible, and preferably on the same day when it concerns acts of contempt committed in their presence. Persons accused of contempt have the right to be heard in their defence and courts can hear evidence regarding the case as well. Detention in custody is permissible during a trial for contempt.

When contemptuous acts or words are alleged to have occurred outside a courtroom, proceedings for contempt in the High Courts or Supreme Courts can only be carried out if with the permission of the relevant law officer. In the case of High Courts, the consent of the State's Advocate General is required, and in the case of the Supreme Court, the consent of either the Attorney General of India or the Solicitor General of India is required. Proceedings for contempt in the Supreme Court are also subject an additional set of regulations, known as the 'Rules to Regulate Proceedings for Contempt of Supreme Court'.

Defenses

The Contempt of Courts Act allows three defenses to charges of contempt. It allows an exemption for those who innocently publish or commit acts that would otherwise amount to contempt, if they reasonably believed that there were no ongoing judicial proceedings regarding these acts, or if they reasonably believe that the content of their words or actions did not contain anything contemptuous. The Act also specifically exempts fair and accurate reporting on judicial proceedings, and fair criticism of the judiciary. In 2006, the Contempt of Courts Act 1971 was amended to allow truth as a defense to contempt, provided that the person claiming this defence was acting in public interest.

Punishment and Sentencing

Both civil and criminal contempt share the same punishment under the Contempt of Courts Act 1971. The Act allows for a maximum term of imprisonment for six months, and this can be supplemented with a fine of up to [1] 2000. The Contempt of Courts Act 1971 also specifically allows courts to forgo the punishment if an apology is made to the court, and may use their discretion to determine whether the apology has been sufficient.

Criticism

In 1969, a challenge to the constitutional validity of the Contempt of Courts Act 1971 was dismissed by the Supreme Court of India, which found the law to be substantively valid. In 2020, lawyer and activist Prashant Bhushan, along with journalist and politician Arun Shourie, and publisher N. Ram, filed a petition challenging the constitutional validity of the Contempt of Courts Act again

Courts' powers to punish for criminal contempt have been repeatedly criticized by former judges and lawyers as having a chilling effect on freedom of speech, being too broad and vague in its definition and lending itself to misuse to shield the judiciary from criticism. Senior advocate Sanjay Hegde has argued that the offence of "scandalizing the court" is "incapable of precise definition," and that it derives from English law, where it has since been abolished.

In 2011, retired Supreme Court judge and former Press Council of India Chairman, Markandeya Katju, called for amendments to the Contempt of Courts Act 1971 in order to allow the media to report better on law and judiciary-related matters.

In March 2018, the Law Commission of India was tasked by the Government of India with re-examining Section 2 of the Contempt of Courts Act 1971, which defines the offence of contempt. The Commission was asked to examine a proposal that suggested that contempt of court should be limited to cases of civil contempt, i.e. disobedience of court orders, and should not include the offence of 'scandalising the court', i.e. criminal contempt. The Commission recommended the retention of the offence of 'criminal contempt' in India, noting that courts in India continue to use it widely, unlike other countries in which offences such as 'scandalising the court' have fallen into disuse. The Commission also noted that the power of courts to penalise contempt was inherent, and would continue to exist even if the Act was amended or deleted altogether.

Act, 1971

Section 1. Short Title and Extent

(1) This Act may be called the Contempt of Courts Act, 1971.

(2) It extends to the whole of India: Provided that it shall not apply to the State of Jammu and Kashmir except to the extent to which the provisions of this Act relate to contempt of the Supreme Court.

Section 2. Definitions.—In this Act, Unless the Context otherwise Requires

(a) "contempt of court" means civil contempt or criminal contempt;

(b) "civil contempt" means wilful disobedience to any judgment, decree, direction, order, writ or other process of a court or wilful breach of an undertaking given to a court;

(c) "criminal contempt" means the publication (whether by words, spoken or written, or by signs, or by visible representation, or otherwise) of any matter or the doing of any other act whatsoever which—

(i) scandalises or tends to scandalise, or lowers or tends to lower the authority of, any court; or

(ii) prejudices, or interferes or tends to interfere with, the due course of any judicial proceeding; or

(iii) interferes or tends to interfere with, or obstructs or tends to obstruct, the administration of justice in any other manner;

(d) "High Court" means the High Court for a State or a Union territory, and includes the court of the Judicial Commissioner in any Union territory.

Section 3. Innocent Publication and Distribution of Matter not Contempt

(1) A person shall not be guilty of contempt of court on the ground that he has published (whether by words, spoken or written, or by signs, or by visible representations, or otherwise) any matter which interferes or tends to interfere with, or obstructs or tends to obstruct, the course of justice in connection with any civil or criminal proceeding pending at that time of publication, if at that time he had no reasonable grounds for believing that the proceeding was pending. —(1) A person shall not be guilty of contempt of court on the ground that he has published (whether by words, spoken or written, or by signs, or by visible representations, or otherwise) any matter which interferes or tends to interfere with, or obstructs or tends to obstruct, the course of justice in connection with any civil or criminal proceeding pending at that time of publication, if at that time he had no reasonable grounds for believing that the proceeding was pending."

(2) Notwithstanding anything to the contrary contained in this Act or any other law for the time being in force, the publication of any such matter as is mentioned in sub-section (1) in connection with any civil or criminal proceeding which is not pending at the time of publication shall not be deemed to constitute contempt of court.

(3) A person shall not be guilty of contempt of court on the ground that he has distributed a publication containing any such matter as is mentioned in sub-section (1), if at the time of distribution he had no reasonable grounds for believing that it contained or was likely to contain any such matter as aforesaid: Provided that this sub-section shall not apply in respect of the distribution of—

(i) any publication which is a book or paper printed or published otherwise than in conformity with the rules contained in section 3 of the Press and Registration of Books Act, 1867 (25 of 1867);

(ii) any publication which is a newspaper published otherwise than in conformity with the rules contained in section 5 of the said Act. Explanation.—For the purposes of this section, a judicial proceeding—

(a) is said to be pending—

(A) in the case of a civil proceeding, when it is instituted by the filing of a plaint or otherwise,

(B) in the case of a criminal proceeding under the Code of Criminal Procedure, 1898 (5 of 1898) , or any other law—

(i) where it relates to the commission of an offence, when the charge-sheet or challan is filed, or when the court issues summons or warrant, as the case may be, against the accused, and

(ii) in any other case, when the court takes cognizance of the matter to which the proceeding relates, and in the case of a civil or criminal proceeding, shall be deemed to continue to be pending until it is heard and finally decided, that is to say, in a case where an appeal or revision is competent, until the appeal or revision is heard and finally decided or, where no appeal or revision is preferred, until the period of limitation prescribed for such appeal or revision has expired;

(b) which has been heard and finally decided shall not be deemed to be pending merely by reason of the fact that proceedings for the execution of the decree, order or sentence passed therein are pending.

Section 4. Fair and Accurate Report of Judicial Proceeding not Contempt

Subject to the provisions contained in section 7, a person shall not be guilty of contempt of court for publishing a fair and accurate report of a judicial proceeding or any stage thereof. —Subject to the provisions contained in section 7, a person shall not be guilty of contempt of court for publishing a fair and accurate report of a judicial proceeding or any stage thereof."

Section 5. Fair Criticism of Judicial Act not Contempt

A person shall not be guilty of contempt of court for publishing any fair comment on the merits of any case which has been heard and finally decided. —A person shall not be guilty of contempt of court for publishing any fair comment on the merits of any case which has been heard and finally decided."

Section 6. Complaint against Presiding Officers of Subordinate Courts when not Contempt

A person shall not be guilty of contempt of court in respect of any statement made by him in good faith concerning the presiding officer of any subordinate court to—

(a) any other subordinate court, or

(b) the High Court, to which it is subordinate. Explanation.—In this section, "subordinate court" means any court subordinate to a High Court.

Section 7. Publication of Information Relating to Proceedings in Chambers or in Camera not Contempt Except in Certain Cases

(1) Notwithstanding anything contained in this Act, a person shall not be guilty of contempt of court for publishing a fair and accurate report of a judicial proceeding before any court sitting in chambers or in camera except in the following cases, that is to say,—

(a) where the publication is contrary to the provisions of any enactment for the time being in force;

(b) where the court, on grounds of public policy or in exercise of any power vested in it, expressly prohibits the publication of all information relating to the proceeding or of information of the description which is published;

(c) where the court sits in chambers or in camera for reasons connected with public order or the security of the State, the publication of information relating to those proceedings;

(d) where the information relates to a secret process, discovery or invention which is an issue in the proceedings.

(2) Without prejudice to the provisions contained in sub-section (1), a person shall not be guilty of contempt of court for publishing the text or a fair and accurate summary of the whole, or any part, of an order made by a court sitting in chambers or in camera, unless the court has expressly prohibited the publication thereof on grounds of public policy, or for reasons connected with public order or the security of the State, or on the ground that it contains information relating to a secret process, discovery or invention, or in exercise of any power vested in it.

Section 8. Other Defences not Affected

Nothing contained in this Act shall be construed as implying that any other defence which would have been a valid defence in any proceedings for contempt of court has ceased to be available merely by reason of the provisions of this Act. —Nothing contained in this Act shall be construed as implying that any other defence which would have been a valid defence in any proceedings for contempt of court has ceased to be available merely by reason of the provisions of this Act."

Section 9. Act not to Imply Enlargement of Scope of Contempt

Nothing contained in this Act shall be construed as implying that any disobedience, breach, publication or other act is punishable as contempt of court which would not be so punishable a part from this Act. —Nothing contained in this Act shall be construed as implying that any disobedience, breach, publication or other act is punishable as contempt of court which would not be so punishable a part from this Act."

Section 10. Power of High Court to Punish Contempts of Subordinate Courts

Every High Court shall have and exercise the same jurisdiction, powers and authority, in accordance with the same procedure and practice, in respect of contempts of courts subordinate to it as it has and exercises in respect of contempts of itself: —Every High Court shall have and exercise the same jurisdiction, powers and authority, in accordance with the same procedure and practice, in respect of contempts of courts subordinate to it as it has and exercises in respect of contempts of itself\:" Provided that no High Court shall take cognizance of a contempt alleged to have been committed in respect of a court subordinate to it where such contempt is an offence punishable under the Indian Penal Code (45 of 1860).

Section 11. Power of High Court to Try Offences Committed or Offenders Found Outside Jurisdiction

A High Court shall have jurisdiction to inquire into or try a contempt of itself or of any court subordinate to it, whether the contempt is alleged to have been committed within or outside the local limits of its jurisdiction, and whether the person alleged to be guilty of contempt is within or outside such limits. —A High Court shall have jurisdiction to inquire into or try a contempt of itself or of any court subordinate to it, whether the contempt is alleged to have been committed within or outside the local limits of its jurisdiction, and whether the person alleged to be guilty of contempt is within or outside such limits."

Section 12. Punishment for Contempt of Court

(1) Save as otherwise expressly provided in this Act or in any other law, a contempt of court may be punished with simple imprisonment for a term which may extend to six months, or with fine which may extend to two thousand rupees, or with both: —(1) Save as otherwise expressly provided in this Act or in any other law, a contempt of court may be punished with simple imprisonment for a term which may extend to six months, or with fine which may extend to two thousand rupees, or with both\:" Provided that the accused may be discharged or the punishment awarded may be remitted on apology being made to the satisfaction of the court. Explanation.—An apology shall not be rejected merely on the ground that it is qualified or conditional if the accused makes it bona fide.

(2) Notwithstanding anything contained in any other law for the time being in force, no court shall impose a sentence in excess of that specified in sub-section (1) for any contempt either in respect of itself or of a court subordinate to it.

(3) Notwithstanding anything contained in this section, where a person is found

guilty of a civil contempt, the court, if it considers that a fine will not meet the ends of justice and that a sentence of imprisonment is necessary shall, instead of sentencing him to simple imprisonment, direct that he be detained in a civil prison for such period not exceeding six months as it may think fit.

(4) Where the person found guilty of contempt of court in respect of any undertaking given to a court is a company, every person who, at the time the contempt was committed, was in charge of, and was responsible to, the company for the conduct of business of the company, as well as the company, shall be deemed to be guilty of the contempt and the punishment may be enforced, with the leave of the court, by the detention in civil prison of each such person: Provided that nothing contained in this sub-section shall render any such person liable to such punishment if he proves that the contempt was committed without his knowledge or that he exercised all due diligence to prevent its commission.

(5) Notwithstanding anything contained in sub-section (4), where the contempt of court referred to therein has been committed by a company and it is proved that the contempt has been committed with the consent or connivance of, or is attributable to any neglect on the part of, any director, manager, secretary or other officer of the company, such director, manager, secretary or other officer shall also be deemed to be guilty of the contempt and the punishment may be enforced, with the leave of the court, by the detention in civil prison of such director, manager, secretary or other officer. Explanation.—For the purposes of sub-sections (4) and (5),—

(a) "company" means any body corporate and includes a firm or other association of individuals; and

(b) "director", in relation to a firm, means a partner in the firm.

Section 13. Contempts not Punishable in Certain Cases

Notwithstanding anything contained in any law for the time being in force,—

(a) no court shall impose a sentence under this Act for a contempt of court unless it is satisfied that the contempt is of such a nature that it substantially interferes, or tends substantially to interfere with the due course of justice;

(b) the court may permit, in any proceeding for contempt of court, justification by truth as a valid defence if it is satisfied that it is in public interest and the request for invoking the said defence is bona fide.]

Section 14. Procedure where Contempt is in the Face of the Supreme Court or a High Court

(1) When it is alleged, or appears to the Supreme Court or the High Court upon its own view, that a person has been guilty of contempt committed in its presence

or hearing, the Court may cause such person to be detained in custody, and, at any time before the rising of the Court, on the same day, or as early as possible thereafter, shall— —(1) When it is alleged, or appears to the Supreme Court or the High Court upon its own view, that a person has been guilty of contempt committed in its presence or hearing, the Court may cause such person to be detained in custody, and, at any time before the rising of the Court, on the same day, or as early as possible thereafter, shall—"

(a) cause him to be informed in writing of the contempt with which he is charged;

(b) afford him an opportunity to make his defence to the charge;

(c) after taking such evidence as may be necessary or as may be offered by such person and after hearing him, proceed, either forthwith or after adjournment, to determine the matter of the charge; and

(d) make such order for the punishment or discharge of such person as may be just.

(2) Notwithstanding anything contained in sub-section (1), where a person charged with contempt under that sub-section applies, whether orally or in writing, to have the charge against him tried by some Judge other than the Judge or Judges in whose presence or hearing the offence is alleged to have been committed, and the Court is of opinion that it is practicable to do so and that in the interests of proper administration of justice the application should be allowed, it shall cause the matter to be placed, together with a statement of the facts of the case, before the Chief Justice for such directions as he may think fit to issue as respects the trial thereof.

(3) Notwithstanding anything contained in any other law, in any trial of a person charged with contempt under sub-section (1) which is held, in pursuance of a direction given under sub-section (2), by a Judge other than the Judge or Judges in whose presence or hearing the offence is alleged to have been committed, it shall not be necessary for the Judge or Judges in whose presence or hearing the offence is alleged to have been committed to appear as a witness and the statement placed before the Chief Justice under sub-section (2) shall be treated as evidence in the case.

(4) Pending the determination of the charge, the Court may direct that a person charged with contempt under this section shall be detained in such custody as it may specify: Provided that he shall be released on bail, if a bond for such sum of money as the Court thinks sufficient is executed with or without sureties conditioned that the person charged shall attend at the time and place mentioned in the bond and shall continue to so attend until otherwise directed by the Court: Provided further that the Court may, if it thinks fit, instead of taking bail from such person, discharge him on his executing a bond without sureties for his attendance as aforesaid.

Section 15. Cognizance of Criminal Contempt in other Cases

(1) In the case of a criminal contempt, other than a contempt referred to in section 14, the Supreme Court or the High Court may take action on its own motion or on a motion made by—

(a) the Advocate-General, or

(b) any other person, with the consent in writing to the Advocate-General, [or]

(c) in relation to the High Court for the Union territory of Delhi, such Law Officer as the Central Government may, by notification in the Official Gazette, specify in this behalf, or any other person, with the consent in writing of such Law Officer.]

(2) In the case of any criminal contempt of a subordinate court, the High Court may take action on a reference made to it by the subordinate court or on a motion made by the Advocate-General or, in relation to a Union territory, by such Law Officer as the Central Government may, by notification in the Official Gazette, specify in this behalf.

(3) Every motion or reference made under this section shall specify the contempt of which the person charged is alleged to be guilty. Explanation.—In this section, the expression "Advocate-General" means—

(a) in relation to the Supreme Court, the Attorney-General or the Solicitor-General;

(b) in relation to the High Court, the Advocate-General of the State or any of the States for which the High Court has been established;

(c) in relation to the Court of a Judicial Commissioner, such Law Officer as the Central Government may, by notification in the Official Gazette, specify in this behalf.

Section 16. Contempt by Judge, Magistrate or other Person Acting Judicially

(1) Subject to the provisions of any law for the time being in force, a Judge, Magistrate or other person acting judicially shall also be liable for contempt of his own court or of any other court in the same manner as any other individual is liable and the provisions of this Act shall, so far as may be, apply accordingly. —(1) Subject to the provisions of any law for the time being in force, a Judge, Magistrate or other person acting judicially shall also be liable for contempt of his own court or of any other court in the same manner as any other individual is liable and the provisions of this Act shall, so far as may be, apply accordingly."

(2) Nothing in this section shall apply to any observations or remarks made by a Judge, Magistrate or other person acting judicially, regarding a subordinate court in an appeal or revision pending before such Judge, Magistrate or other person against the order or judgment of the subordinate court.

Section 17. Procedure after Cognizance

(1) Notice of every proceeding under section 15 shall be served personally on the person charged, unless the court for reasons to be recorded directs otherwise. —(1) Notice of every proceeding under section 15 shall be served personally on the person charged, unless the court for reasons to be recorded directs otherwise."

(2) The notice shall be accompanied—

(a) in the case of proceedings commenced on a motion, by a copy of the motion as also copies of the affidavits, if any, on which such motion is founded; and

(b) in case of proceedings commenced on a reference by a subordinate court, by a copy of the reference.

(3) The Court may, if it is satisfied that a person charged under section 15 is likely to abscond or keep out of the way to avoid service of the notice, order the attachment of his property of such value or amount as it may deem reasonable.

(4) Every attachment under sub-section (3) shall be effected in the manner provided in the Code of Civil Procedure, 1908 (5 of 1908) , for the attachment of property in execution of a decree for payment of money, and if, after such attachment, the person charged appears and shows to the satisfaction of the court that he did not abscond or keep out of the way to avoid service of the notice, the Court shall order the release of his property from attachment upon such terms as to costs or otherwise as it may think fit.

(5) Any person charged with contempt under section 15 may file an affidavit in support of his defence, and the court may determine the matter of the charge either on the affidavits filed or after taking such further evidence as may be necessary, and pass such order as the justice of the case requires.

Section 18. Hearing of Cases of Criminal Contempt to be by Benches

(1) Every case of criminal contempt under section 15 shall be heard and determined by a Bench of not less than two Judges.

(2) Sub-section (1) shall not apply to the Court of a Judicial Commissioner.

Section 19. Appeals

(1) An appeal shall lie as of right from any order or decision of High Court in the exercise of its jurisdiction to punish for contempt— —(1) An appeal shall lie as of right from any order or decision of High Court in the exercise of its jurisdiction to punish for contempt—"

(a) where the order or decision is that of a single Judge, to a Bench of not less than two Judges of the Court;

(b) where the order or decision is that of a Bench, to the Supreme Court: Provided that where the order or decision is that of the Court of the Judicial Commissioner in any Union territory, such appeal shall lie to the Supreme Court.

(2) Pending any appeal, the appellate Court may order that—

(a) the execution of the punishment or order appealed against be suspended;

(b) if the appellant is in confinement, he be released on bail; and

(c) the appeal be heard notwithstanding that the appellant has not purged his contempt.

(3) Where any person aggrieved by any order against which an appeal may be filed satisfies the High Court that he intends to prefer an appeal, the High Court may also exercise all or any of the powers conferred by sub-section (2).

(4) An appeal under sub-section (1) shall be filed—

(a) in the case of an appeal to a Bench of the High Court, within thirty days;

(b) in the case of an appeal to the Supreme Court, within sixty days, from the date of the order appealed against.

Section 20. Limitation for Actions for Contempt

No court shall initiate any proceedings of contempt, either on its own motion or otherwise, after the expiry of a period of one year from the date on which the contempt is alleged to have been committed. —No court shall initiate any proceedings of contempt, either on its own motion or otherwise, after the expiry of a period of one year from the date on which the contempt is alleged to have been committed."

Section 21. Act not to Apply to Nyaya Panchayats or other Village Courts

Nothing contained in this Act shall apply in relation to contempt of Nyaya Panchayats or other village courts, by whatever name known, for the administration of justice, established under any law. —Nothing contained in this Act shall apply in relation to contempt of Nyaya Panchayats or other village courts, by whatever name known, for the administration of justice, established under any law."

Section 22. Act to be in Addition to, and not in Derogation of, other Laws relating to Contempt

The provisions of this Act shall be in addition to, and not in derogation of the provisions of any other law relating to contempt of courts. —The provisions of this Act shall be in addition to, and not in derogation of the provisions of any other law relating to contempt of courts."

Section 23. Power of Supreme Court and High Courts to Make Rules

The Supreme Court or, as the case may be, any High Court, may make rules, not inconsistent with the provisions of this Act, providing for any matter relating to its procedure.

Section 24. Repeal

The Contempt of Courts Act, 1952 (32 of 1952), is hereby repealed.

Case Studies on Defamation, Sedition, and Contempt of Court

Case Studies on Defamation

Case Study 1: Tata Sons Ltd. v. Greenpeace International

Overview: In 2013, Tata Sons, the holding company of the Tata Group, filed a defamation suit against Greenpeace International, an environmental advocacy organization. The suit was filed in response to a Greenpeace report that alleged Tata's involvement in illegal mining operations in the Kalinganagar area of Odisha.

Key Details:

- Tata Sons argued that the report contained false and damaging statements that harmed their reputation and business interests.
- The court issued an injunction against Greenpeace, restraining them from publishing or disseminating the report further.
- The case highlighted the tension between freedom of expression and the protection of reputation, emphasizing the need for responsible reporting on sensitive issues.

Case Study 2: Ram Jethmalani v. Subramanian Swamy

Overview: Renowned lawyers Ram Jethmalani and Subramanian Swamy were involved in a defamation suit in 2016. Swamy accused Jethmalani of receiving illegal payments from a public sector undertaking, leading to Jethmalani filing a defamation suit.

Key Details:

- The case exemplified a high-profile legal battle, with both parties being prominent figures in Indian politics and law.
- The court deliberated on the statements made by Swamy and determined whether they were based on fact or constituted defamatory remarks.
- The case underscored the importance of evidence and factual accuracy in defamation claims.

Case Study 3: MJ Akbar v. Priya Ramani

Overview: In 2018, former Union Minister and journalist MJ Akbar filed a defamation suit against journalist Priya Ramani, who had accused him of sexual harassment during the #MeToo movement. Ramani had made the allegations in a tweet and an article.

Key Details:

- The case raised important questions about the #MeToo movement, freedom of speech, and the right to reputation.
- The court considered whether Ramani's allegations were true and made in public interest, or if they constituted defamatory statements.
- The verdict ultimately highlighted the significance of addressing allegations of sexual harassment in a fair and just manner.

Case Study 4: Asha Parekh v. Outlook

Overview: Veteran Bollywood actress Asha Parekh filed a defamation suit against Outlook magazine in 2017 over an article that alleged her involvement in the underworld during her acting career. Key Details:

- The case centered on the publication's responsibility to fact-check and verify information before making serious allegations against public figures.
- The court examined whether the article was based on credible evidence or if it amounted to reckless reporting.
- The case served as a reminder of the ethical obligations of media organizations when reporting on sensitive matters.

Case Study 5: Arun Jaitley v. Arvind Kejriwal

Overview: In 2015, Finance Minister Arun Jaitley filed a defamation suit against Delhi Chief Minister Arvind Kejriwal and five other members of the Aam Aadmi Party (AAP) for making defamatory statements in connection with financial irregularities during Jaitley's tenure as president of the Delhi and District Cricket Association (DDCA). Key Details:

- The case highlighted the political context in which defamation suits can arise, especially between rival political parties.
- The court examined the veracity of the allegations and whether they were made with a malicious intent to tarnish Jaitley's reputation.
- The verdict emphasized the need for responsible political discourse and the consequences of making false and damaging statements about public figures.

Case Studies on Sedition

Case Study 6: Bal Gangadhar Tilak's Sedition Trial (1897)

Overview: Bal Gangadhar Tilak, a prominent nationalist leader, was charged with sedition in 1897 for his articles published in his Marathi newspaper, Kesari. The British colonial government accused him of inciting disaffection against the British rule.

Key Details

- Tilak's defense argued that he was advocating for self-rule and not violence against the British government.
- He was convicted and sentenced to 18 months of rigorous imprisonment.

Impact

Tilak's trial galvanized the Indian nationalist movement and led to increased calls for self-rule and independence from British colonial rule.

Case Study 7: Kanhaiya Kumar's Sedition Case (2016)

Overview: Kanhaiya Kumar, then president of the Jawaharlal Nehru University (JNU) Students' Union, was charged with sedition in 2016 for allegedly raising anti-India slogans during a protest on the university campus.

Key Details

- The case sparked a nationwide debate on freedom of expression and the use of sedition charges against dissenting voices.
- Kumar maintained that he did not raise any anti-India slogans and was advocating for social justice issues.

Outcome

Kumar was granted bail, and the case against him eventually led to discussions on the appropriate application of sedition laws in modern India.

Case Study 8: Sedition Case Against Hardik Patel (2015)

Overview: Hardik Patel, a leader of the Patidar community in Gujarat, was charged with sedition in 2015 for allegedly advocating violence and demanding reservation for the Patidar community in government jobs and educational institutions.

Key Details

- Patel's agitation for reservation rights gained significant traction and led to widespread protests in Gujarat.
- The sedition charge was based on his alleged calls for violent agitation.

Outcome

The sedition charges against Hardik Patel were eventually dropped, but the case highlighted the contentious nature of sedition laws in addressing public protests and demands for social justice.

Case Study 9: Sedition Case Against Adivasi Activists in Chhattisgarh (2010)

Overview: Several Adivasi activists in Chhattisgarh were charged with sedition in 2010 for allegedly supporting and aiding Maoist insurgents. They were accused of being sympathizers or supporters of armed rebellion against the state.

- The activists were advocating for the rights of Adivasi communities and critiquing government policies in Maoist-affected regions.
- The case raised questions about the broad interpretation and application of sedition laws in cases involving tribal communities.

Outcome

The sedition charges were eventually dropped against some of the activists, highlighting the need for a nuanced approach when applying sedition laws in cases involving marginalized communities.

Case Study 10: Sedition Case Against Amnesty International India (2016)

Overview: Amnesty International India faced allegations of sedition in 2016 for organizing an event titled "Broken Families" in Bangalore, which focused on human rights violations in Jammu and Kashmir. It was alleged that anti-India slogans were raised during the event.

Key Details

- Amnesty International maintained that it had organized the event in accordance with Indian law and that it was meant to promote discussion on human rights issues.
- The case raised concerns about the space for free expression and human rights advocacy in India.

Outcome

The sedition case against Amnesty International India brought attention to the broader debate on the appropriate use of sedition laws in cases involving advocacy for human rights and freedom of expression.

Case Studies on Contempt of Court

Case Study 11: Duda S. P. Jain v. State of Maharashtra (1998)

Overview

In this landmark case, Duda S. P. Jain, an advocate, was found guilty of contempt of court for making scandalous and derogatory statements against the judiciary in a letter written to the Chief Justice of India. Jain's statements were deemed to undermine the authority and dignity of the court.

Key Details

- The Supreme Court held that freedom of speech and expression does not grant an absolute license to criticize the judiciary in a manner that scandalizes or tends to lower its authority.

Outcome

Duda S. P. Jain was found guilty of contempt of court, emphasizing the need for respectful and responsible criticism of the judiciary.

Case Study 12: In Re: Arundhati Roy (2002)

Overview

Author Arundhati Roy faced contempt of court proceedings for her article in Outlook magazine, which criticized the judiciary's handling of a case concerning the construction of the Narmada Dam. Roy expressed her views on the matter, which were deemed to be scurrilous and scandalous.

Key Details

- The Supreme Court held that while constructive criticism of the judiciary is permissible, making scurrilous remarks with an intention to scandalize the court is contemptuous.

Outcome

Arundhati Roy was found guilty of contempt of court, highlighting the importance of maintaining decorum and respect for the judiciary in public discourse.

Case Study 13: A. M. Mathai v. S. K. Kochunny (1992)

This case involved a dispute between two lawyers, A. M. Mathai and S. K. Kochunny. Mathai filed a contempt petition against Kochunny for making disparaging remarks against him during a court proceeding.

Key Details

- The Kerala High Court held that while lawyers have a right to criticize the conduct of opposing counsel, such criticism must be within the bounds of decency and should not be derogatory.

Outcome

S. K. Kochunny was held guilty of contempt of court, emphasizing the importance of maintaining professional decorum in legal proceedings.

Case Study 14: Delhi Judicial Service Association v. State of Gujarat (1991)

Overview

In this case, a resolution passed by the Delhi Judicial Service Association criticizing certain actions of the Gujarat High Court was challenged on grounds of contempt.

Key Details

- The Supreme Court held that a resolution passed by a body of judicial officers criticizing the actions of another high court can amount to contempt of court if it tends to undermine the authority of the judiciary.

Outcome

The resolution was held to be contemptuous, underlining the need for judicial officers to exercise caution in their public statements about other courts.

Case Study 15: Pritam Ashok Sadaphule v. State of Maharashtra (2003)

Overview

Pritam Ashok Sadaphule, an advocate, was held in contempt of court for filing false affidavits and making false statements before the court. The court found that Sadaphule had deliberately misled the court in a criminal case.

Key Details

- The Bombay High Court emphasized that filing false affidavits and providing false information to the court undermines the administration of justice and constitutes contempt.

Outcome

Pritam Ashok Sadaphule was held guilty of contempt of court, emphasizing the importance of honesty and integrity in interactions with the judiciary.

5

Media Laws and Regulations

Press and Registration of Books Act 1867

The Press and Registration of Books Act, 1867 is a legislative enactment that was enacted during the British colonial period in India. Its primary objective was to regulate the printing and publication of books and newspapers. The Act sought to impose certain obligations on publishers, including the requirement to provide information about the ownership and management of printing presses and publications.

Key Provisions of the Press and Registration of Books Act, 1867:

- Registration of Printing Presses and Publications: The Act mandates that all printing presses and newspapers must be registered with the government. This registration is intended to provide a degree of oversight and accountability over the publishing industry.
- Statement of Ownership and Circulation: Publishers are required to file a statement providing details about the ownership, including names and addresses of owners, as well as information about the circulation of the publication. This aims to ensure transparency and prevent anonymity in the publication of materials.
- Renewal of Registration: Registration under the Act is not indefinite. Publishers are required to renew their registration periodically, ensuring that the government maintains up-to-date information about the publishing industry.
- Prohibition of Anonymous Publications: The Act prohibits the printing and publication of newspapers and books without providing the required information about ownership and circulation. This provision is aimed at preventing anonymous or clandestine publications.

- Penalties for Non-Compliance: The Act prescribes penalties for non-compliance with its provisions. This may include fines or, in some cases, the seizure of printing presses or publications.
- Inspection of Registered Printing Presses: The Act grants authorities the power to inspect registered printing presses to ensure compliance with the law. This serves as a means of oversight and enforcement.
- Exceptions and Exemptions: The Act provides certain exceptions, such as for publications by or under the authority of the government. These exceptions recognize the special status of official publications.
- Offenses and Prosecution: The Act outlines offenses related to non-compliance, including providing false information or failing to comply with registration requirements. It also establishes procedures for prosecution in case of violations.
- Amendments and Modifications: Over the years, the Act has been subject to amendments and modifications to adapt to changing circumstances and technologies in the publishing industry.

Act

Section 1. Interpretation-clause

(1) In this Act, unless there shall be something repugnant in the subject or context,— "Book" includes every volume, part or division of a volume, and pamphlet, in any language, and every sheet of music, map, chart or plan separately printed"editor" means the person who controls the selection of the matter that is published in a newspaper;] "Magistrate" means any person exercising the full powers of a 6Magistrate, and includes a Magistrate of police ["newspaper" means any printed periodical work containing public news or comments on public news;] ["paper" means any document, including a newspaper, other than a book; "prescribed" means prescribed by rules made by the Central Government under section 20A; "Press Registrar" means the Registrar of newspapers for India appointed by the Central Government under section 19A and includes any other person appointed by the Central Government to perform all or any of the functions of the Press Registrar; "printing" includes cyclostyling and printing by lithography; "Register" means the Register of newspapers maintained under section 19B.]

(2) Any reference in this Act to any law which is not in force in the State of Jammu and Kashmir shall, in relation to that State, be construed as a reference to the corresponding law in force in that State.]

Section 2. Repeal of Act 11 of 1835

[Rep. by the Repealing Act, 1870 (14 of 1870), sec. 1 and Sch., Pt. II.]

Section 3. Particulars to be Printed on Books and Papers

Every book or paper printed within [India] shall have printed legibly on it the name of the printer and the place of printing, and (if the book or paper be published) [the name] of the publisher, and the place of publication.

Section 4. Keeper of Printing Press to Make Declaration

(1) No person shall within [India], keep in his possession any press for the printing of books or papers, who shall not have made and subscribed the following declaration before 2[the District, Presidency or Sub-divisional Magistrate] within whose local jurisdiction such press may be: "I, A.B., declare that I have a press for printing at—". And this last blank shall be filled up with a true and precise description of the place where such press may be situate.

(2) As often as the place where a press is kept is changed, a new declaration shall be necessary: Provided that where the change is for a period not exceeding sixty days and the place where the press is kept after the change is within the local jurisdiction of the Magistrate referred to in sub-section (1), no new declaration shall be necessary if—

(a) a statement relating to the change is furnished to the said Magistrate within twenty-four hours thereof; and

(b) the keeper of the press continues to be the same.]

Section 5. Rules as to Publication of Newspapers

No [newspaper] shall be published in [India], except in conformity with the rules hereinafter laid down:

(1) Without prejudice to the provisions of section 3, every copy of every such newspaper shall contain the names of the owner and editor thereof printed clearly on such copy and also the date of its publication.

(2) The printer and the publisher of every such [newspaper] shall appear [in person or by agent authorised in this behalf in accordance with rules made under section 20, before a District, Presidency or Sub-divisional Magistrate within whose local jurisdiction such newspaper shall be printed or published and shall make and subscribe, in duplicate, the following declaration: "I A.B., declare that I am the printer (or publisher, or printer and publisher) of the [newspaper] entitled— [and to be printed or published, or to be printed and published], as the case may be at—". And the last blank in this form of declaration shall be filled up with a true and precise account of the premises where the printing or publication is conducted.

(2A) Every declaration under rule (2) shall specify the title of the newspaper, the language in which it is to be published and the periodicity of its publication and shall contain such other particulars as may be prescribed.]

(2B) Where the printer or publisher of a newspaper making a declaration under rule (2) is not the owner thereof, the declaration shall specify the name of the owner and shall also be accompanied by an authority in writing from the owner authorising such person to make and subscribe such declaration.

(2C) A declaration in respect of a newspaper made under rule (2) and authenticated under section 6 shall be necessary before the newspaper can be published.

(2D) Where the title of any newspaper or its language or the periodicity of its publication is changed, the declaration shall cease to have effect and a new declaration shall be necessary before the publication of the newspaper can be continued.

(2E) As often as the ownership of a newspaper is changed, a new declaration shall be necessary.

(3) As often as the place of printing or publication is changed, a new declaration shall be necessary: [Provided that where the change is for a period not exceeding thirty days and the place of printing or publication after the change is within the local jurisdiction of the Magistrate referred to in rule (2), no new declaration shall be necessary if—

(a) a statement relating to the change is furnished to the said Magistrate within twenty-four hours thereof; and

(b) the printer or publisher or the printer and publisher of the newspaper continues to be the same.

(4) As often as the printer or the publisher who shall have made such declaration as is aforesaid shall leave India for a period exceeding ninety days or where such printer or publisher is by infirmity or otherwise rendered incapable of carrying out his duties for a period exceeding ninety days in circumstances not involving the vacation of his appointment, a new declaration shall be necessary.]

(5) Every declaration made in respect of a newspaper shall be void, where the newspaper does not commence publication—

(a) within six weeks [of the authentication of the declaration under section 6], in the case of a newspaper to be published once a week or oftener; and

(b) within three months [of the authentication of the declaration under section 6], in the case of any other newspaper, and in every such case, a new declaration shall be necessary before the newspaper can be published.

(6) Where, in any period of three months, any daily, tri-weekly, bi-weekly, weekly or fortnightly newspaper publishes issues the number of which is less than half of what should have been published in accordance with the declaration made in respect thereof, the declaration shall cease to have effect and a new declaration shall be necessary before the publication of the newspaper can be continued.

(7) Where any other newspaper has ceased publication for a period, exceeding twelve months, every declaration made in respect thereof shall cease to have effect, and a new declaration shall be necessary before the newspaper can be re-published.

(8) Every existing declaration in respect of a newspaper shall be cancelled by the Magistrate before whom a new declaration is made and subscribed in respect of the same:] [Provided that no person [who does not ordinarily reside in India, or] who has not attained majority in accordance with the provisions of the Indian Majority Act, 1875 (9 of 1875), or of the law to which he is subject in respect of the attainment of majority, shall be permitted to make the declaration prescribed by this section, nor shall any such person edit a newspaper.]

5A. Keepers of printing presses and printers and publishers of newspapers in Jammu and Kashmir to make and subscribe fresh declarations within specified period.—

(1) No person who has made and subscribed a declaration in respect of any press under section 4 of the Jammu and Kashmir State Press and Publications Act, S. 1989 (Jammu and Kashmir Act, No. I of S. 1989) shall keep the press in his possession for the printing of books or papers [after the 31st day of December, 1968, unless before the expiry of that date] he makes and subscribes a fresh declaration in respect of that press under section 4 of this Act.

(2) Every person who has subscribed to any declaration in respect of a newspaper under section 5 of the Jammu and Kashmir State Press and Publications Act, S. 1989 (Jammu and Kashmir Act, No. 1 of S. 1989) shall cease to be the editor, printer or publisher of the newspaper mentioned in such declaration 2[after the 31st day of December, 1968 unless before the expiry of that date] he makes and subscribes a fresh declaration in respect of that newspaper under rule (2) of the rules laid down in section 5 of this Act.]

Section 6. Authentication of Declaration

Each of the two originals of every declaration so made and subscribed as is aforesaid, shall be authenticated by the signature and official seal of the Magistrate before whom the said declaration shall have been made: [Provided that where any declaration is made and subscribed under section 5 in respect of a newspaper, the declaration shall not, save in the case of newspapers owned by the same person, be so authenticated unless the Magistrate [is, on inquiry from the Press Registrar, satisfied] that the newspaper proposed to be published does not bear a title which is the same as, or similar to, that of any other newspaper published either in the same language or in the same State.]

(Deposit) —One of the said originals shall be deposited among the records of the office of the Magistrate, and the other shall be deposited among the records of the High Court of Judicature, or [other principal Civil Court of original jurisdiction for the place where] the said declaration shall have been made. Inspection and supply of copies.—The

Officer-in -charge of each original shall allow any person to inspect that original on payment of a fee of one rupee, and shall give to any person applying a copy of the said declaration, attested by the seal of the Court which has the custody of the original, on payment of a fee of two rupees. [A copy of the declaration attested by the official seal of the Magistrate, or a copy of the order refusing to authenticate the declaration, shall be forwarded as soon as possible to the person making and subscribing the declaration and also to the Press Registrar.]

Section 7. Office Copy of Declaration to be Prima Facie Evidence

In any legal proceeding whatever, as well civil as criminal, the production of a copy of such declaration as is aforesaid, attested by the seal of some Court empowered by this Act to have the custody of such declarations, 1[or, in the case of the editor, a copy of the newspaper containing his name printed on it as that of the editor] shall be held (unless the contrary be proved) to be suficient evidence, as against the person whose name shall be subscribed to such declaration, 1[or printed on such newspaper, as the case may be] that the said person was printer or publisher, or printer and publisher (according as the words of the said declaration may be) of every portion of every 2[newspaper] whereof the title shall correspond with the title of the 2[newspaper] mentioned in the declaration, 5[or the editor of every portion of that issue of the newspaper of which a copy is produced].

Section 8. New Declaration by Persons who have Signed a Declaration and Subsequently Ceased to be Printers or Publishers

If any person has subscribed to any declaration in respect of a newspaper under section 5 and the declaration has been authenticated by a Magistrate under section 6 and subsequently that person ceases to be the printer or publisher of the newspaper mentioned in such declaration, he shall appear before any District, Presidency or Sub-divisional Magistrate, and make and subscribe in duplicate the following declaration:— "I, A.B., declare that I have ceased to be the printer or publisher or printer and publisher of the newspaper entitled—". Authentication and filing.—Each original of the latter declaration shall be authenticated by the signature and seal of the Magistrate before whom the said latter declaration shall have been made, and one original of the said latter declaration shall be filed along with each original of the former declaration. Inspection and supply of copies.—The Officer-in-charge of each original of the latter declaration shall allow any person applying to inspect that original on payment of a fee of one rupee, and shall give to any person applying a copy of the said latter declaration, attested by the seal of the Court having custody of the original, on payment of a fee of two rupees. Putting copy in evidence.—In all trials in which a copy, attested as is aforesaid, of the former declaration shall have been put in evidence, it shall be lawful to put in evidence a copy, attested as is aforesaid, of the latter declaration, and the former declaration shall not be taken to be evidence that the declarant was, at any period subsequent to the date of the latter declaration, printer or publisher of the [newspaper] therein mentioned. [A copy of the latter declaration attested by the official seal of the Magistrate shall be forwarded to the Press Registrar.]

8A. Person whose name has been incorrectly published as editor may make a declaration before a Magistrate.—If any person, whose name has appeared as editor on a copy of a newspaper, claims that he was not the editor of the issue on which his name has so appeared, he may, within two weeks of his becoming aware that his name has been so published, appear before a District, Presidency or Sub-Divisional Magistrate and make a declaration that his name was incorrectly published in that issue as that of the editor thereof, and if the Magistrate after making such inquiry or causing such inquiry to be made as he may consider necessary is satisfied that such declaration is true, he shall certify accordingly, and on that certificate being given the provisions of section 7 shall not apply to that person in respect of that issue of the newspaper. The Magistrate may extend the period allowed by this section in any case where he is satisfied that such person was prevented by sufficient cause from appearing and making the declaration within that period.]

8B. Cancellation of declaration.—If, on an application made to him by the Press Registrar or any other person or otherwise, the Magistrate empowered to authenticate a declaration under this Act, is of opinion that any declaration made in respect of a newspaper should be cancelled, he may, after giving the person concerned an opportunity of showing cause against the action proposed to be taken, hold an inquiry into the matter and if, after considering the cause, if any, shown by such person and after giving him an opportunity of being heard, he is satisfied that—

(i) the newspaper, in respect of which the declaration has been made is being published in contravention of the provisions of this Act or rules made thereunder; or

(ii) the newspaper mentioned in the declaration bears a title which is the same as, or similar to, that of any other newspaper published either in the same language or in the same State; or

(iii) the printer or publisher has ceased to be the printer or publisher of the newspaper mentioned in such declaration; or

(iv) the declaration was made on false representation or on the concealment of any material fact or in respect of a periodical work which is not a newspaper; the Magistrate may, by order, cancel the declaration and shall forward as soon as possible a copy of the order to the person making or subscribing the declaration and also to the Press Registrar.

8C. Appeal.—

(1) Any person aggrieved by an order of a Magistrate refusing to authenticate a declaration under section 6 or cancelling a declaration under section 8B may, within sixty days from the date on which such order is communicated to him, prefer an appeal to the Appellate Board to be called the Press and Registration Appellate Board [consisting of a Chairman and another member to be nominated by the Press Council of India, established under section 4 of the Press Council Act, 1978 (37 of 1978), from among its members]: Provided that the Appellate

Board may entertain an appeal after the expiry of the said period, if it is satisfied that the appellant was prevented by sufficient cause from preferring the appeal in time.

(2) On receipt of an appeal under this section, the Appellate Board may, after calling for the records from the Magistrate and after making such further inquiries as it thinks fit, confirm, modify or set aside the order appealed against.

(3) Subject to the provisions contained in sub-section (2), the Appellate Board may, by order, regulate its practice and procedure.

(4) The decision of the Appellate Board shall be final.]

Section 9. Copies of Books Printed after Commencement of Act to be Delivered Gratis to Government

Printed copies of the whole of every book which shall be printed in [India] after this Act shall come into force, together with all maps, prints or other engravings belonging thereto, finished and coloured in the same manner as the best copies of the same, shall, notwithstanding any agreement (if the book be published) between the printer and publisher thereof, be delivered by the printer at such place and to such officer as the State Government shall, by notification in the Official Gazette, from time to time direct, and free of expense to the Government, as follows, that is to say:—

(a) in any case, within one calendar month after the day on which any such book shall first be delivered out of the press, one such copy, and,

(b) if within one calendar year from such day the State Government shall require the printer to deliver other such copies not exceeding two in number, then within one calendar month after the day on which any such requisition shall be made by the State Government on the printer, another such copy, or two other such copies, as the State Government may direct, the copies so delivered being bound, sewed or stitched together and upon the best paper on which any copies of the book shall be printed . The publisher or other person employing the printer shall, at a reasonable time before the expiration of the said month, supply him with all maps, prints and engravings finished and coloured as aforesaid, which may be necessary to enable him to comply with the requirements aforesaid. Nothing in the former part of this section shall apply to—

(i) any second or subsequent edition of a book in which edition no additions or alterations either in the letter-press or in the maps, prints or other engravings belonging to the book have been made, and a copy of the first or some preceding edition of which book has been delivered under this Act, or

(ii) any [newspaper] published in conformity with the rules laid down in section 5 of this Act.

Section 10. Receipt for Copies Delivered under Section 9

The officer to whom a copy of a book is delivered under the last foregoing section shall give to the printer a receipt in writing therefor. foregoing section shall give to the printer a receipt in writing therefor."

Section 11. Disposal of Copies Delivered under Section 9

The copy delivered pursuant to clause

(a) of the first paragraph of section 9 of this Act shall be disposed of as the State Government shall from time to time determine. Any copy or copies delivered pursuant to clause (b) of the said paragraph shall be [transmitted to the Central Government].

11A. Copies of newspapers printed in India to be delivered gratis to Government.—The printer of every newspaper in [India] shall deliver at such place and to such officer as the State Government may, by notification in the Official Gazette, direct, and free of expense to the Government, two copies of each issue of such newspaper as soon as it is published.]

11B. Copies of newspapers to be delivered to Press Registrar.—Subject to any rules that may be made under this Act, the publisher of every newspaper in India shall deliver free of expense to the Press Registrar one copy of each issue of such newspaper as soon as it is published.]

Section 12. Penalty for Printing Contrary to Rule in Section 3

Whoever shall print or publish any book or paper otherwise than in conformity with the rule contained in section 3 of this Act, shall, on conviction before a Magistrate, be punished by fine not exceeding 1[two thousand] rupees, or by simple imprisonment for a term not exceeding 2[six months], or by both.

Section 13. Penalty for Keeping Press without Making Declaration Required by Section 4

Whoever shall keep in his possession any such press as aforesaid. [In contravention of any of the provisions contained in section 4 of this Act], shall, on conviction before a Magistrate, be punished by fine not exceeding [two thousand] rupees, or by simple imprisonment for a term not exceeding [six months] or by both.

Section 14. Punishment for Making False Statement

Any person who shall, in making [any declaration or other statement] under the authority of this Act, make a statement which is false, and which he either knows or believes to be false, or does not believe to be true, shall, on conviction before a Magistrate, be punished by fine not exceeding [two thousand] rupees, and imprisonment for a term not exceeding [six months].

Section 15. Penalty for Printing or Publishing Newspaper without Conforming to Rules

(1) Whoever shall 2[edit], print or publish any 3[newspaper], without conforming to the rules hereinbefore laid down, or whoever shall 2[edit], print or publish, or shall cause to be 2[edited], printed or published, any 4[newspaper], knowing that the said rules have not been observed with respect to 5[that newspaper], shall, on conviction before a Magistrate, be punished with fine not exceeding 6[two thousand] rupees, or imprisonment for a term not exceeding 7[six months] or both. 8[(2) Where an offence is committed in relation to a newspaper under sub-section (1), the Magistrate may, in addition to the punishment imposed under the said sub-section, also cancel the declaration in respect of the newspaper.]

15A. Penalty for failure to make a declaration under section 8.—If any person who has ceased to be a printer or publisher of any newspaper fails or neglects to make a declaration in compliance with section 8, he shall, on conviction before a Magistrate, be punishable by fine not exceeding two hundred rupees.]

The Press and Registration of Books Act, 1867

Section 16. Penalty for not Delivering Books or not Supplying Printer with Maps

If any printer of any such book as is referred to in section 9 of this Act shall neglect to deliver copies of the same pursuant to that section, he shall for every such default forfeit to the Government such sum not exceeding fifty rupees as a Magistrate having jurisdiction in the place where the book was printed may, on the application of the officer to whom the copies should have been delivered or of any person authorised by that officer in this behalf, determine to be in the circumstances a reasonable penalty for the default, and, in addition to such sum, such further sum as the Magistrate may determine to be the value of the copies which the printer ought to have delivered.

If any publisher or other person employing any such printer shall neglect to supply him, in the matter prescribed in the second paragraph of section 9 of this Act with the maps, prints or engravings which may be necessary to enable him to comply with the provisions of that section, such publisher or other person shall for every such default forfeit to the Government such sum not exceeding fifty rupees as such a Magistrate as aforesaid may, on such an application as aforesaid, determine to be in the circumstances a reasonable penalty for the default, and, in addition to such sum, such further sum as the Magistrate may determine to be the value of the maps, prints or engravings which such publisher or other person ought to have supplied.]

16A. Penalty for failure to supply copies of newspapers gratis to Government.—If any printer of any newspaper published in 2[India] neglects to deliver copies of the same in compliance with section 11A, he shall, on the complaint of the officer to whom copies should have been delivered or of any person authorised by that officer in this behalf, be punishable, on conviction by a Magistrate having jurisdiction in the place where the newspaper was printed, with fine which may extend to fifty rupees for every default.]

16B. Penalty for failure to supply copies of newspapers to Press Registrar.—If any publisher of any newspaper published in India neglects to deliver copies of the same in compliance with section 11B, he shall, on the complaint of the Press Registrar, be punishable, on conviction by a Magistrate having jurisdiction in the place where the newspaper was printed, by fine which may extend to fifty rupees for every default.]

Section 17

Recovery of forfeitures and disposal thereof and of fines.—Any sum forfeited to the Government under 2[section 16] may be recovered, under the warrant of the Magistrate determining the sum, or of his successor in office, in the manner authorised by the Code of Criminal Procedure (10 of 1882)3 for the time being in force, and within the period prescribed by the Indian Penal Code (45 of 1860), for the levy of a fine. 4

Section 18. Registration of Memoranda of Books

There shall be kept at such office, and by such officer as the State Government shall appoint in this behalf, a book to be called a Catalogue of Books printed in 1[India], wherein shall be registered a memorandum of every book which shall have been delivered 2[pursuant to clause

(a) of the first paragraph of section 9] of this Act. Such memorandum shall (so far as may be practicable) contain the following particulars (that is to say):—

(1) the title of the book and the contents of the title-page, with a translation into English of such title and contents, when the same are not in the English language;

(2) the language in which the book is written;

(3) the name of the author, translator, or editor of the book or any part thereof;

(4) the subject;

(5) the place of printing and the place of publication;

(6) the name of firm of the printer and the name of firm of the publisher;

(7) the date of issue from the press or of the publication;

(8) the number of sheets, leaves or pages;

(9) the size;

(10) the first, second or other number of the edition;

(11) the number of copies of which the edition consists;

(12) whether the book is printed, 3[cyclostyled or lithographed];

(13) the price at which the book is sold to the public; and

(14) the name and residence of the proprietor of the copyright or of any portion of such copyright. Such memorandum shall be made and registered in the case of each book as soon as practicable after the delivery of the 4[copy thereof pursuant to clause (a) of the first paragraph of section 9] 5

Section 19. Publication of Memoranda Registered

The memoranda registered during each quarter in the said Catalogue shall be published in the Official Gazette, as soon as may be after the end of such quarter, and a copy of the memoranda so published shall be sent 1 to the Central Government 2.

19A. Appointment of Press Registrar and other officers.—The Central Government may appoint a Registrar of newspapers for India and such other officers under the general superintendence and control of the Press Registrar as may be necessary for the purpose of performing the functions assigned to them by or under this Act, and may, by general or special order, provide for the distribution or allocation of functions to be performed by them under this Act.

19B. Register of newspapers.—

(1) The Press Registrar shall maintain in the prescribed manner a Register of newspapers.

(2) The Register shall, as far as may be practicable, contain the following particulars about every newspaper published in India, namely:—

(a) the title of the newspaper;

(b) the language in which the newspaper is published;

(c) periodicity of the publication of the newspaper;

(d) the name of the editor, printer and publisher of the newspaper;

(e) the place of printing and publication;

(f) the average number of pages per week;

(g) the number of days of publication in the year;

(h) the average number of copies printed, the average number of copies sold to the public and the average number of copies distributed free to the public, the average being calculated with reference to such period as may be prescribed;

(i) retail selling price per copy;

(j) the names and addresses of the owners of the newspaper and such other particulars relating to ownership as may be prescribed;

(k) any other particulars which may be prescribed.

(3) On receiving information from time to time about the aforesaid particulars, the Press Registrar shall cause relevant entries to be made in the Register and may make such necessary alterations or corrections therein as may be required for keeping the Register up-to-date.

19C. Certificates of registration.—On receiving from the Magistrate under section 6 a copy of the declaration in respect of a newspaper 1[and on the publication of such newspaper, the Press Registrar shall], as soon as practicable thereafter, issue a certificate of registration in respect of that newspaper to the publisher thereof.

19D. Annual statement, etc., to be furnished by newspapers.—It shall be the duty of the publisher of every newspaper—

(a) to furnish to the Press Registrar an annual statement in respect of the newspaper at such time and containing such of the particulars referred to in sub-section (2) of section 19B as may be prescribed;

(b) to publish in the newspaper at such times and such of the particulars relating to the newspaper referred to in sub-section (2) of section 19B as may be specified in this behalf by the Press Registrar.

19E. Returns and reports to be furnished by newspapers.—The publisher of every newspaper shall furnish to the Press Registrar such returns, statistics and other information with respect to any of the particulars referred to in sub- section (2) of section 19B as the Press Registrar may from time to time require.

19F. Right of access to records and documents.—The Press Registrar or any gazetted officer authorised by him in writing in this behalf shall, for the purpose of the collection of any information relating to a newspaper under this Act, have access to any relevant record or document relating to the newspaper in the possession of the publisher thereof, and may enter at any reasonable time any premises where he believes such record or document to be and may inspect or take copies of the relevant records or documents or ask any question necessary for obtaining any information required to be furnished under this Act.

19G. Annual report.—The Press Registrar shall prepare, in such form and at such time each year as may be prescribed, an annual report containing a summary of the information obtained by him during the previous year in respect of the newspapers in India and giving an account of the working of such newspapers, and copies thereof shall be forwarded to the Central Government.

19H. Furnishing of copies of extracts from Register.—On the application of any person for the supply of the copy of any extract from the Register and on payment of such fee as may be prescribed, the Press Registrar shall furnish such copy to the applicant in such form and manner as may be prescribed.

19-I. Delegation of powers.—Subject to the provisions of this Act and regulations made thereunder, the Press Registrar may delegate all or any of his powers under this Act to any officer subordinate to him.

19J. Press Registrar and other officers to be public servants.—The Press Registrar and all officers appointed under this Act shall be deemed to be public servants within the meaning of section 21 of the Indian Penal Code (45 of 1860).

19K. Penalty for contravention of section 19D or section 19E, etc.—If the publisher of any newspaper—

(a) refuses or neglects to comply with the provisions of section 19D or section 19E; or 1

(c) publishers in the newspaper in pursuance of clause (b) of section 19D any particulars relating to the newspaper which he has reason to believe to be false, he shall be punishable with fine which may extend to five hundred rupees.

19L. Penalty for improper disclosure of information.—If any person engaged in connection with the collection of information under this Act wilfully discloses any information or the contents of any return given or furnished under this Act otherwise than in the execution of his duties under this Act or for the purposes of the prosecution of an offence under this Act or under the Indian Penal Code (45 of 1860), he shall be punishable with imprisonment for a term which may extend to six months, or with fine which may extend to one thousand rupees, or with both.

Section 20. Power of State Government to make Rules

(1) The State Government may, by notification in the Official Gazette, make such rules (not inconsistent with the rules made by the Central Government under section 20A) as may be necessary or desirable for carrying out the objects of this Act.

(2) Every rule made by the State Government under this section shall be laid, as soon as may be after it is made, before the State Legislature.]

20A. Power of Central Government to make rules.—

(1) The Central Government may, by notification in the Official Gazette, make rules—

(a) prescribing the particulars which a declaration made and subscribed under section 5 may contain; 2[and the form and manner in which the names of the printer, publisher, owner and editor of a newspaper and the place of its printing and publication may be printed on every copy of such newspaper]; 3[(b) prescribing the manner in which copies of any declaration attested by the official seal of a Magistrate or copies of any order refusing to authenticate any declaration may be forwarded to the person making and subscribing the declaration and to the Press Registrar;]

(c) prescribing the manner in which copies of any newspaper may be sent to the Press Registrar under section 11B;

(d) prescribing the manner in which a Register may be maintained under section 19B and the particulars which it may contain;

(e) prescribing the particulars in which an annual statement to be furnished by the publisher of a newspaper to the Press Registrar may contain;

(f) prescribing the form and manner in which an annual statement under clause (a) of section 19D, or any returns, statistics or other information under section 19E, may be furnished to the Press Registrar;

(g) prescribing the fees for furnishing copies of extracts from the Register and the manner in which such copies may be furnished;

(h) prescribing the manner in which a certificate of registration may be issued in respect of a newspaper;

(i) prescribing the form in which, and the time within which, annual reports may be prepared by the Press Registrar and forwarded to the Central Government. 4[(2) Every rule made under this section shall be laid as soon as may be after it is made, before each House of Parliament, while it is in session, for a total period of thirty days which may be comprised in one session or 5[in two or more successive sessions and if, before the expiry of the session immediately following the session or the successive sessions aforesaid] both houses agree in making any modification in the rule or both Houses agree that the rule should not be made, the rule shall thereafter have effect only in such modified form or be of no effect, as the case may be; so, however, that any such modification or annulment shall be without prejudice to the validity of anything previously done under that rule.]

20B. Rules made under this Act may provide that contravention thereof shall be punishable.— Any rule made under any provision of this Act may provide that any contravention thereof shall be punishable with fine which may extend to one hundred rupees.]

Section 21. Power to Exclude any Class of Books from Operation of Act

[The State Government may, by notification in the Official Gazette], exclude any class of books 2[or papers] from the operation of the whole or any part or parts of this Act: 3[Provided that no such notification in respect of any class of newspapers shall be issued without consulting the Central Government.]

Section 22. Extent

This Act Extends to the Whole of India 2.]

Section 23. Commencement of Act

Working Journalists and other Newspaper Employees (Conditions of Service) and Miscellaneous Provisions Act 1955

The Working Journalists and other Newspaper Employees (Conditions of Service) and Miscellaneous Provisions Act, 1955 is a legislative framework enacted by the Government of India to establish certain conditions of service for journalists and other newspaper employees. The Act aims to protect the rights and interests of journalists and newspaper employees, ensuring fair employment practices within the newspaper industry.

Key Provisions of the Act:

- Definition of Working Journalist: The Act defines a "working journalist" as any person whose principal occupation is that of a journalist and is employed either wholly or mainly in, or in relation to, any newspaper establishment.
- Fixation of Rates of Wages and Working Hours: The Act provides for the fixation and revision of rates of wages and working hours for working journalists and other newspaper employees. Wages must be paid within a specified period after the end of the wage period.
- Conditions of Service and Employment: The Act lays down provisions regarding the conditions of service, including hours of work, leave, holidays, termination of service, and other related matters. These conditions are aimed at ensuring fair treatment and job security for journalists and newspaper employees.
- Appointment of Wage Boards: The Act empowers the appropriate government to constitute Wage Boards for the purpose of fixing and revising rates of wages, determining working hours, and other related matters. These Wage Boards comprise representatives of employers, employees, and independent members.
- Maintenance of Records: Newspaper establishments are required to maintain records and registers containing particulars of employees, hours of work, wages paid, and other relevant information. This ensures transparency and compliance with labor laws.
- Prohibition of Certain Disputes: The Act prohibits certain disputes related to wages, hours of work, and other conditions of service from being adjudicated upon by any court or authority, except as provided under the Act.
- Press Council of India: The Act establishes the Press Council of India, which serves as an autonomous body for the purpose of preserving the freedom of the press and maintaining and improving the standards of newspapers and news agencies.
- Penalties for Violations: The Act provides for penalties in case of non-compliance with its provisions. This may include fines or other forms of legal action against newspaper establishments or employers.
- Protection of Service Conditions: The Act contains provisions that protect the

service conditions of working journalists and newspaper employees in the event of a change in ownership or control of a newspaper establishment.

- Application of the Act: The Act applies to newspaper establishments employing a minimum specified number of persons, as notified by the appropriate government.

Laws of Obscenity: IPC Sections 292-294

The Indian Penal Code (IPC) Sections 292 to 294 pertain to laws regarding obscenity. These sections define and regulate what is considered obscene and outline the legal consequences for actions related to obscenity.

- Section 292 - Sale, etc., of Obscene Books, etc.: This section makes it a criminal offense to sell, distribute, publicly exhibit, or circulate any material (including books, pamphlets, or drawings) that is considered obscene, or any material that contains lascivious or sexually explicit content. The section aims to prohibit the dissemination of materials that are likely to corrupt public morals.
- Section 293 - Sale, etc., of Obscene Objects to Young Persons: This section extends the prohibition of obscene materials to include selling, distributing, or publicly exhibiting such materials to a person under the age of twenty years. It aims to protect young persons from exposure to explicit or harmful content.
- Section 294 - Obscene Acts and Songs: This section addresses public acts or performances that are considered obscene. It prohibits the uttering of any obscene words, making any obscene gestures, or singing, reciting, or uttering any obscene songs or ballads in or near a public place. The section aims to maintain public decency and prevent the public display of explicit content.

Key Considerations:

- Definition of Obscenity: The determination of what constitutes obscenity is often subjective and may vary based on cultural, social, and legal interpretations. The courts in India have established certain criteria to assess obscenity, considering factors like prurient appeal, artistic or literary merit, and community standards.
- Protection of Freedom of Expression: While these sections aim to regulate obscenity, they must be balanced with the right to freedom of expression enshrined in the Indian Constitution. Courts may weigh the right to free speech against the need to protect public decency and morals.
- Exceptions: The law does provide certain exceptions for works of art, literature, science, or other objects that have historical, archaeological, or scientific significance. These exceptions are meant to protect legitimate forms of expression from being unjustly penalized.

- Penalties: Violation of these sections may result in criminal penalties, including fines and imprisonment, depending on the severity of the offense.

Indecent Representation of Women (Prohibition) Act 1986

The Indecent Representation of Women (Prohibition) Act, 1986 is an Indian legislation enacted to prohibit the indecent representation of women through advertisements, publications, writings, paintings, figures, or in any other manner. The Act was put in place to combat the objectification and demeaning portrayal of women in media and other forms of visual representation. Key Provisions of the Act:

- Prohibition of Indecent Representation: The Act makes it illegal to produce, publish, distribute, or exhibit any form of material that contains indecent representation of women, either directly or indirectly. This includes visual, auditory, or written material that tends to dehumanize or demean women.
- Definitions: The Act provides clear definitions for terms such as "indecent representation of women," "advertisement," and "distribution," to offer precise guidelines for interpretation and enforcement.
- Exceptions for Artistic and Educational Purposes: The Act acknowledges that there may be instances where the representation of women may be necessary for artistic, cultural, educational, or religious purposes. It provides exceptions for such instances, provided that the representation is not obscene or indecent.
- Regulation of Advertisements: The Act empowers the Central Government to regulate advertisements to prevent indecent representation of women. This includes the power to issue guidelines and instructions to ensure compliance with the law.
- Penalties for Offenses: The Act prescribes penalties for violations, including fines and imprisonment, depending on the severity of the offense. Repeat offenders may face more severe penalties.
- Seizure and Confiscation of Materials: The Act provides for the seizure and confiscation of materials that violate its provisions. This ensures that such material does not continue to be disseminated.
- Designation of Authorities: The Act designates specific authorities, both at the Central and State levels, responsible for the enforcement and implementation of its provisions. These authorities have the power to investigate complaints and take legal action against offenders.
- Advisory Boards: The Act establishes advisory boards at both the Central and State levels to advise the government on matters related to the Act's implementation. These boards may consist of experts in the fields of law, women's rights, and media.

- Procedure for Investigation and Trial: The Act outlines the procedures to be followed in the investigation and trial of offenses under its purview. This includes provisions for search and seizure, as well as the legal process to be followed in cases of violations.

Scheduled Castes and Tribes (Prevention of Atrocities) Act, 1989

The Scheduled Castes and the Scheduled Tribes (Prevention of Atrocities) Act, 1989 (its correct name) was enacted by the Parliament of India to prevent atrocities and hate crimes against the scheduled castes and scheduled tribes. The Act is popularly known as the SC/ST Act, PoA, or simply the 'Atrocities Act'.

It was enacted when the existing legal provisions (such as the Protection of Civil Rights Act, 1955 and the Indian Penal Code) were found to be inadequate to check these crimes (defined as 'atrocities' in Section 3 of the Act). Recognising the continuing gross indignities and offences against Scheduled Castes and Tribes, the Parliament passed the Scheduled Castes and the Scheduled Tribes (Prevention of Atrocities) Act, 1989.

The Act was passed in Parliament of India on 11 September 1989 and notified on 30 January 1990. It was comprehensively amended in 2015 (including renumbering sub-sections of Section 3), and notified on 26 January 2016. It was subsequently amended in 2018 and 2019.

The rules were notified on 31 March 1995. They were comprehensively amended and notified on 14 April 2016. There were a few amendments to the rules and annexures in 2018.

Necessity

Atrocities Rooted in Caste System

A study conducted by the National Commission for SCs and STs in 1990 on *Atrocities on Scheduled Castes and Scheduled Tribes: Causes and Remedies* pointed out various causal factors for atrocities: land disputes; land alienation; bonded labour; indebtedness; non-payment of minimum wages; caste prejudice and practice of untouchability; political factions on caste lines; refusal to perform traditional works such as digging burial pits, arranging cremations, removing carcasses of dead animals and beating drums; etc. The deep root for such atrocities is traceable to the caste system, which "encompasses a complete ordering of social groups on the basis of the so-called ritual purity. A person is considered a member of the caste into which s/he is born and remains within that caste until death…."

Considered ritually impure, Dalits have been physically and socially excluded from caste Hindu society, denied basic resources and services, and discriminated against in all areas of life. Consequently, they face various forms of exploitation, insults, and violence, as well as degrading practices of untouchability. The Scheduled Tribes are equally exploited on grounds of not falling within the caste system but having a distinct culture and worldview of their own. "Women belonging to these castes and tribes bore double burden. They were exploited by caste and gender, and were vulnerable and powerless against sexual exploitation".

The post-Independence era was marked by frequent instances of atrocities springing up across the country: for example, the assassination of the young, educated Dalit leader Emmanuel Sekaran in Tamil Nadu for defying the untouchability-based interdicts on Scheduled Castes (SCs, also called Dalits), which resulted in the Ramanathapuram riots of 1957; the Kilavenmani massacre of 42 Dalits in 1968 in Tamil Nadu; the gruesome killing of Dalit Kotesu in Kanchikacherla in 1969 in Andhra Pradesh; the killings of 10 Scheduled Tribes (STs, also called Adivasis, literally 'first dweller') by police in connection with a land dispute in Indravalli in Andhra Pradesh in 1978. All such events shook the then national leadership. Hence, under pressure from Dalit MPs, the Government of India started monitoring atrocities against Dalits from 1974, and in the case of Adivasis from 1981 onwards, with special focus on murder, rape, arson and grievous hurt.

Atrocities continued to increase in ferocity and frequency – for example, in Bihar the massacres of Dalits at Belchi in 1979 and at Pipra in 1980; in Uttar Pradesh the massacre following a Dalit bridegroom riding on horseback at Kafalta in 1980; in Madhya Pradesh the killing of Bacchdas in Mandsaur district in 1982; in Bihar the killing in police firing on 15 tribals at Banjhi in Sahebganj district in 1985. In all such cases, the Indian state at both the national and state levels avoided addressing basic contradictions, vulnerabilities and causative factors; the treatment was mainly symptomatic and palliative instead of the required radical solutions.

Continuing Widespread Prevalence

As late as October 2021, the Supreme Court of India was constrained to observe that *Atrocities against members of the SCs and STs are not a thing of the past. They continue to be a reality in our society even today. Hence the statutory provisions which have been enacted by Parliament as a measure of protecting the constitutional rights of persons belonging to the Scheduled Castes and Scheduled Tribes must be complied with and enforced conscientiously* (Justices Dhananjaya Y Chandrachud and BV Nagarathna).

They went on to note that several members of the scheduled communities "*face insurmountable hurdles in accessing justice from the stage of filing the complaint to the conclusion of the trial" and that they "specifically suffer on account of procedural lapses in the criminal justice system*".

They noted that due to the fear of retribution from members of dominant caste groups, ignorance, or police apathy, many victims do not register complaints in the first place and when they do so, the police officials are reluctant to register complaints or do not record allegations accurately.

"*Eventually, if the case does get registered, the victims and witnesses are vulnerable to intimidation, violence, and social and economic boycott. Further, many perpetrators of caste-based atrocities get away scot free due to shoddy investigations and the negligence of prosecuting advocates," rued the bench. "This results in low conviction rates under the SC/ST Act, giving rise to the erroneous perception that cases registered under the Act are false and that it is being misused. On the contrary, the reality is that many acquittals are a result of improper investigation and prosecution of crime, leading to insufficient evidence".*

Legislative History

The Constitutional Roots

The Act is rooted in Articles 15 and 17 of the Indian Constitution. Article 15 prohibits discrimination on the basis of caste. Article 17 of the Constitution of India states that 'Untouchability is abolished and its practice in any form is forbidden. The enforcement of any disability arising out of "Untouchability" shall be an offence punishable in accordance with law'.

The Untouchability (Offences) Act, 1955

Five years after the Constitution of India was adopted, the necessary legislation - the Untouchability (Offences) Act (UOA) 1955 - was enacted. It was amended and renamed in 1976 as the Protection of Civil Rights Act (PCRA).

Though UOA did not precisely define the offence, it was a major step forward, and had several enabling provisions. UOA recognised 'wilful negligence' [UOA S10] and was proactive in that it stated clearly that the presumption of court would be that the crime arose from 'untouchability' and it was the defendant who should prove that it wasn't [UOA S12]. The Act was farsighted in that it recognised the culpability of companies and those in charge, including their directors [UOA S14].

However, due to legal loopholes, the levels of punishments being less (compared to those of the Indian Penal Code, 1860 (IPC)), and the law and order machinery being neither professionally trained nor socially inclined to implement such social legislation, a more comprehensive deterrent Act was required to protect the scheduled communities from inter-community violence committed by the dominant communities.

The Protection of Civil Rights Act, 1955

It was later recognised that the Untouchability (Offences) Act 1955 was not sufficient to eradicate untouchability and to punish the perpetrators. So the parliament brought about many changes to UOA after 21 years on 19 November 1976 (the then prime minister's birthday), and renamed it the Protection of Civil Rights Act (PCRA), 1955. In the 1976 amendment, discrimination on the basis of untouchability was also brought under this Act [PCRA S4]. 'Untouchability' as a result of religious and social disabilities was made punishable. The amendments made it clear that all offences under this Act are cognisable [PCRA S15(1)]. It made mandatory the provision of legal aid, appointment of supervising officers, setting up of special courts and committees, and periodic survey of the working of the provisions of this Act to suggest measures for the better implementation [PCRA S15A2]. It even had provision for state and central government annual implementation reports being placed before parliament [PCRA S15A4]. Much of this is carried forward to POA and its amendments, though the liability of companies has been removed.

However, PCRA suffered from severe infirmities, chief among them being that it did not even recognise many of the caste based crimes, was too lenient, and did not have an empowered mechanism to monitor the implementation of the Act (especially given that the police and judiciary were drawn from the same social milieu).

Consequently, caste based crimes continued and even increased both in intensity and scale. Under continued pressure from Dalit MPs and political leaders, the magnitude and gravity of the problem was finally recognised by Prime Minister Rajiv Gandhi. In his Independence day address on 15 August 1987, he announced that an Act would be passed, if necessary, to check atrocities. This nudged the parliament to legislate the Scheduled Castes and the Scheduled Tribes (Prevention of Atrocities) Act, 1989.

The POA and Amendments

Instead of tinkering with the PCRA, the parliament of India passed a new legislation to explicitly *prevent* offences against the scheduled communities by members of non-scheduled communities, that would set up speedy justice, monitoring, accountability, relief, and rehabilitation mechanisms. The Scheduled Castes and the Scheduled Tribes (Prevention of Atrocities) Act (POA), 1989 was thus passed on 11 September 1989. The Act was notified in the Gazette of India, Extraordinary, Part II, sec. 3(ii), dated 29 January 1990 (notification No. S.O. 106(E)) and came into force on 30 January 1990. The rules were notified on 31 March 1995.

The 1989 Act and 1995 rules underwent substantial amendments in 2013, 2014, 2015, 2018, and 2019. The 8 November 2013 amendment to the Rules inserted Rule 17A that added vigilance and monitoring committees at the sub-divisional level, and provided for nominees of the union government in the vigilance and monitoring committees.

The rules were amended on 23 June 2014 to enhance relief and rehabilitation.

The Amendment Ordinance 2014 was signed by the president on 4 March 2014 - the last day before the model code of conduct for parliamentary elections came into force - and came into force immediately. Unsurprisingly, dominant communities campaigned for the total repeal of the Act during the parliamentary elections. Since it was an ordinance, and was not ratified by (the next) parliament within six months, it lapsed. It was then referred back to the cabinet.

It was later passed as the Amendment Act 2015 and the Amendment Rules 2016. The Amendment Act 2015 and Amendment Rules 2016 comprehensively overhauled the parent Act and Rules. The Act added Chapter IVA Section 15A (the rights of victims and witnesses), and defined dereliction of duty by officials and accountability mechanisms more precisely. It added several new offences in Section 3 and (bizarrely) renumbered the entire section since the recognised crime almost doubled. It filled several gaps in the previous version of the Act (such as adding a schedule for Section 3(2)(va) showing which offence under Section 3 should be invoked for which IPC crime) apart from making accountability of officials clearer. Section 14A to ensure time bound trials was also inserted. The amended Act 2015 came into effect on 26 January 2016.

The amended rules enhance and streamline relief and rehabilitation, with clear timelines and deliverables. The amended Rules came into effect on 14 April 2016.

The Supreme Court of India, in its verdict of 20 March 2018, banned immediate arrest of a person accused of insulting or injuring a member of a scheduled community to prevent arbitrary arrest. This led to a furore, which in turn led to a stunned parliament voting to overturn the judgement. In August 2018, the parliament passed an amendment to override the ruling (with effect from 20 August 2018) by inserting section 18A(1)(a) '*preliminary enquiry shall not be required for registration of an FIR against any person* and section 18A(1)(b), *the investigating officer shall not require approval for the arrest, if necessary, of any person against whom an accusation of having committed an offence under this Act has been made and no procedure, other than that provided under this Act or the Code, shall apply*. The amendments categorically rule out anticipatory bail for a person accused of atrocities against the scheduled communities, notwithstanding any court order. The Supreme Court of India upheld the constitutional validity of the amendment on 10 February 2020.

On 27 June 2018 the Rules were amended to clarify that the relief provided in the Rule 15(1) contingency plan and Rule 12(4) Annexe Schedule I was in addition to relief from other sources [Rule 12(5)], removed the restriction of 25 members in the State Vigilance and Monitoring Committee [Rule 16(1)], and tweaked the relief provisions in the Rule 12(4) Annexe Schedule I.

On 31 October 2019, Section 1(2) was amended to extend the Act to the whole of India.

Key Features of the Amendment Act 2015 (No 1 of 2016)

The Amendment Ordinance 2014 (No 1 of 2014) was signed by the president on 4 March 2014 and came into force immediately. Since it was an ordinance, and was not ratified by (the next) parliament within six months, it lapsed. It was then referred back to the cabinet.

The Amendment Act 2015 (No 1 of 2016) was passed to replace the ordinance of 2014. The bill was introduced in parliament on 7 July 2014 and referred to the standing committee on 17 July 2014. Subsequently, it was passed by the Lok Sabha on 4 August 2015 and then by the Rajya Sabha in December 2015. The amended Act received presidential assent on 31 December 2015, was notified as Act 1 of 2016 on 1 January 2016 in the Gazette of India Extraordinary, and came into force on 26 January 2016.

The key features of the Amendment Act of 2015 are

- Addition of new categories of offences to the existing 19 punishable offences. The following new offences were added. To cite a few: tonsuring of head, moustache, or similar acts which are derogatory to the dignity of Dalits and Adivasis; garlanding with chappals; denying access to irrigation facilities or forest rights ; dispose or carry human or animal carcasses, or to dig graves; using or permitting manual scavenging; dedicating Dalit women as devadasi; abusing in caste name; perpetrating witchcraft atrocities; imposing social or economic boycott; preventing Dalit and Adivasi candidates filing of nomination to contest elections; hurting the modesty of Dalit/Adivasi woman by removing her garments; forcing to leave house, village or residence; defiling objects sacred to SCs and STs; touching a woman or uses words, acts or gestures of a sexual nature against women.
- Addition of IPC offences attracting committed against Dalits or Adivasis as punishable offences under the POA Act. Presently, only those offences listed in IPC as attracting punishment of 10 years or more and committed on Dalits/ Adivasis are accepted as offences falling under the POA Act. A number of commonly committed offences (hurt, grievous hurt, intimidation, kidnapping etc.) were excluded from the Act. This loophole enabled the perpetrators of the atrocities to escape punishment. Therefore, a Schedule of list of IPC offences is provided in the amended Act.
- Establishment of Exclusive Special Courts and Special Public Prosecutors to exclusively try the offences falling under the Act to enable speedy and expeditious disposal of cases.
- Power of Exclusive Courts to take cognizance of offence and completion of trial in two months. Courts so established or specified have the power to directly take cognizance of offences under this Act and the trial shall, as far as possible, be completed within a period of two months from the date of filing the charge sheet.
- Addition of chapter IVA, Section 15A on the 'Rights of Victims and Witnesses' and the duties and responsibilities of the State. They include the right to be treated fairly and with respect, protection of victims, witnesses, informants, and their dependants against any kind of intimidation, coercion, inducement, violence, or threats of violence, timebound relief and rehabilitation, and the right to assistance from concerned individuals, organisations, and advocates.
- Defining clearly the term 'wilful negligence' of public servants at all levels, starting from the registration of complaint, and covering aspects of dereliction of duty under this Act.
- Addition of presumption to the offences – If the accused was acquainted with the victim or his family, the court will presume that the accused was aware of the caste or tribal identity of the victim unless proved otherwise.

Objectives

The basic objective and purpose of this more comprehensive legislation was enunciated when the Bill was introduced in the Lok Sabha:

- Despite various measures to improve the socio-economic conditions of the SCs and STs, they remain vulnerable... They have in several brutal incidents, been deprived of their life and property... Because of the awareness created... through spread of education, etc., when they assert their rights and resist practices of untouchability against them or demand statutory minimum wages or refuse to do any bonded and forced labour, the vested interests try to cow them down and terrorise them. When the SCs and STs try to preserve their self-respect or honour of their women, they become irritants for the dominant and the mighty...

Under the circumstances, the existing laws like the Protection of Civil Rights Act 1955 and the normal provisions of the Indian Penal Code have been found to be inadequate to check and deter crimes against them committed by non-SCs and non-STs... It is considered necessary that not only the term 'atrocity' should be defined, but also stringent measures should be introduced to provide for higher punishment for committing such atrocities. It is also proposed to enjoin on the States and Union Territories to take specific preventive and punitive measures to protect SCs and STs from being victimized and, where atrocities are committed, to provide adequate relief and assistance to rehabilitate them.

The preamble of the Act states that it is

- An Act to prevent the commission of offences of atrocities against the members of the Scheduled Castes and the Scheduled Tribes, to provide for Special Courts for the trial of such offences and for the relief and rehabilitation of the victims of such offences and for matters connected therewith or incidental thereto.

The objectives of the Act, therefore, very clearly emphasise the intention of the Indian state to deliver justice to the scheduled caste and scheduled tribe communities through affirmative action in order to enable them to live in society with dignity and self-esteem and without fear, violence or suppression from the dominant castes.

The Supreme Court of India too reiterated the significance and importance of the Act in 1995 and at periodic intervals.

On 25 October 2021, the Supreme Court bench consisting of Chief Justice N.V. Ramana, Justice J Surya Kant and Justice Hima Kohli held that

- The SC/ST Act has been specifically enacted to deter acts of indignity, humiliation and harassment against members of Scheduled Castes and Scheduled Tribes. The Act is also a recognition of the depressing reality that despite undertaking several measures, the Scheduled Castes/Scheduled Tribes continue to be subjected to various atrocities at the hands of uppercastes. The Courts have to be mindful of the fact that the Act has been enacted keeping in view the express constitutional safeguards enumerated in Articles 15, 17 and 21 of the Constitution, with a twinfold objective of protecting the members of these vulnerable communities as well as to provide relief and rehabilitation to the victims of castebased atrocities.

Salient Features

The provisions of the Act and Rules can be divided into three different categories, covering a variety of issues related to atrocities against the scheduled communities and their position in society.

- The first contains provisions of criminal law. It establishes criminal liability for a number of specifically defined atrocities, and extends the scope of certain categories of penalizations given in the Indian Penal Code (IPC).
- The second contains provisions for relief and rehabilitation for victims of atrocities.
- The third contains provisions that establish special authorities for the implementation and monitoring of the Act.

The salient features of the Act as amended to date are given below. (Please note that the section and rule references used here are as of the 2016 amendment. They - especially subsections of Section 3(1) - have changed significantly from the original Act of 1989).

- Creation of new types of offences not in the Indian Penal Code (IPC) or in the Protection of Civil Rights Act 1955 (PCRA).
- Commission of offences only by specified persons (atrocities can be committed only by members of the non-SC and non-ST communities on members of the SC or ST communities. Crimes among or between the scheduled communities (STs and SCs) do not come under the purview of this Act).
- Defines various types of atrocities against the scheduled communities (Section 3(1)(a) to 3(1)(zc) and 3(2)(i) to 3(2)(vii)).
- Prescribes stringent punishment for such atrocities (Section 3(1)(a) to 3(1)(zc) and 3(2)(i) to 3(2)(vii)).
- Enhanced punishment for some offences (Section 3(2)(i) to 3(2)(vii), 5).
- Enhanced minimum punishment for public servants (Section 3(2)(vii)).
- Punishment for neglect of duties by a public servant (Section 4).
- Attachment and forfeiture of property (Section 7).
- Externment of potential offenders (Section 10(1)).
- Creation of Special Courts (Section 14).
- Time-bound investigation: Chargesheeting within 60 days from registration of FIR (Rule 7(2)).

- Time-bound trials: Within 60 days of chargesheeting (Section 14(2)).
- Appointment of Special Public Prosecutors (Section 15).
- Rights of victims and witnesses (Section 15A).
- Empowers the government to impose collective fines (Section 16).
- Cancellation of arms licences in the areas identified where an atrocity may take place or has taken place (Rule 3(iii)) and seize all illegal fire arms (Rule 3(iv)).
- Grant arms licences to SCs and STs (Rule 3(v)).
- Denial of anticipatory bail (Section 18).
- Denial of probation to convict (Section 19).
- Provides relief and rehabilitation for victims of atrocities or their legal heirs (Sections 15A(6), 15A(11), 17(3), and 21(2)(iii), Rules 11 and 12(4)).
- Identification of atrocity prone areas (Section 17(1), 21(2)(vii), Rule 3(1)).
- Setting up deterrents to prevent atrocities on the scheduled communities by others (Rule 3(i) to 3(xi)).
- Setting up a mandatory, periodic monitoring system at different levels (Section 21(2)(v)):
  - Sub-divisional level (Rule 17A).
  - District level (Rule 3(xi), 4(2), 4(4), 17).
  - State level (Rule 8(xi), 14, 16, 18).
  - Union level (Section 21(2), 21(3), 21(4)). (All available annual reports placed on the table of each house of parliament by the union government under Section 21(4) are uploaded here.

Together, the Act and the Rules provide a framework for monitoring the state response to the atrocities against Scheduled Castes and Scheduled Tribes. According to the Act and Rules, there are to be monthly reports from the District Magistrates (Rule 4(4)), quarterly review meetings at the district level by the District Monitoring and Vigilance Committee (DVMC, Rule 17(3)) and reviews in January and July by a State Monitoring and Vigilance Committee (SVMC) chaired by the Chief Minister (Rule 16(2)). The performance of every Special Public Prosecutor (SPP) will also have to be reviewed by the Director of Public Prosecutions (DPP) every quarter (Rule 4(2)). Annual reports have to be sent to the union government by 31 March every year (Rule 18).

The Act and Rules are a potent mechanism and precision instruments that can be used in tandem with the Right To Information (RTI) Act 2005 to motivate the state to hold the mandatory meetings and enforce compliance. A Human Rights Defenders

Monitoring Calendar has been developed from the Act and rules to help human rights defenders and others to clarify the functions and duties of the monitoring authorities (the SVMC and DVMC).

Atrocity

An atrocity is a crime against the Scheduled Castes (SCs) or the Scheduled Tribes (STs) in India listed in Section 3 of the Scheduled Castes and the Scheduled Tribes (Prevention of Atrocities) Act, 1989 as amended to date. The term 'atrocity' was not defined until this Act was passed by the Parliament in 1989.

In specific terms:

- It is an offence punishable under sections 3(1) and 3(2) of the Act.
- It *denotes the quality of being shockingly cruel and inhumane, whereas the term* 'crime' *relates to an act punishable by law.*
- It implies *any offence under the Indian Penal Code (IPC) committed against SCs by non-SC persons, or against STs by non-ST persons. Caste consideration as a motive is not necessary to make such an offence in case of atrocity.*
- It signifies *crimes which have ingredients of infliction of suffering in one form or the other that should be included for reporting'. This is based on the assumption that 'where the victims of crime are members of Scheduled Castes and the offenders do not belong to Scheduled Castes caste considerations are really the root cause of the crime, even though caste considerations may not be the vivid and minimum motive for the crime.*

Section 3 of the Act lists offences shattering the self-respect and esteem of the scheduled communities, denial of economic, democratic and social rights, discrimination, exploitation and abuse of the legal process, etc. It contains:

- Offences in their own right (Section 3(1) contains 30 subsections with an equal number of offences. Section 3(2) contains four subsections with offences)
- Two derived offences (sections 3(2)(vi) and 3(2)(vii)). The derived offences only come into the picture when another offence under the Act has been committed.
- One subsection (Section 3(2)(v)) increases the punishment for certain offences under the Indian Penal Code (IPC).

These protections can be broadly divided into protection from

- Social disabilities (denial of access to certain places and to use customary passage and to get water from any spring, reservoir or any other source).
- Personal harm (forceful drinking or eating of inedible or obnoxious substance, against stripping, outrage of modesty, sexual exploitation, injury, or annoyance).

- Property denial or destruction (land, residential premises, existing property).
- Malicious prosecution.
- Political disabilities.
- Economic exploitation.

The common denominator of the offences is that criminal liability can only be established if the offence is committed by a person who is *not* a member of a Scheduled Caste or a Scheduled Tribe *against* a person who belongs to a Scheduled Caste or a Scheduled Tribe.

Investigation

The Act and Rules are very precise about who should do the investigation, the sequence, and the procedure at every stage.

- *Step 1*: When there is information (from any source) that an atrocity may be or may have been committed, an officer not below the rank of deputy superintendent of police (DSP) *or* sub-divisional magistrate (SDM) must visit the spot and conduct a preliminary inquiry (Rule 6(1)) and identify the perpetrators, the victims, and the extent of damage and prepare a report (Rule 6(2)).
- *Step 2*: On confirmation that an atrocity has taken place, *both* the superintendent of police (SP) *and* the district magistrate must visit the spot and conduct a preliminary inquiry to access the loss of life and property, and identify the victims and their dependents entitled to relief. (Rule 12(1)).
- *Step 3*: On confirmation, the SP will order the FIR to be filed (Rule 12(2)).
- *Step 4*: The SP will appoint an investigation officer (not below the rank of DSP) to continue the investigation (Rule 12(3)). According to Rule 7(1) investigation of an offence committed under the Act cannot be investigated by an officer below the rank of Deputy Superintendent of Police (DSP).
- *Step 5*: The investigation officer (DSP) should complete the investigation on *top priority* and file the charge sheet within 60 days of the FIR being filed (Rule 7(2)). If the investigation is not completed within 60 days, the DSP should file a written explanation (Rule 7(2A)). If the written explanation is not filed, the DSP is liable for prosecution under Section 4 for violation of Section 4(2)(e).

Various High Courts have set aside cases based on Rule 7(1). The rule is to ensure that the investigations are of high quality, and the assumption is that senior officials would not be as biased, nor as vulnerable to other pressures, as those in the lower rungs of the police force.

The Andhra Pradesh High Court, in *D. Ramlinga Reddy v. State of AP*, took the position that provisions of Rule 7 are mandatory and held that investigation under the SC/

ST (Prevention of Atrocities) Act has to be carried out by only an officer not below the rank of DSP. An investigation carried out and charge sheet filed by an incompetent officer is more than likely to be quashed. Similarly, the Madras High Court in *M. Kathiresam v. State of Tamil Nadu* held that investigation conducted by an officer other than a DSP is improper and bad in law and proceedings based on such an investigation are required to be quashed. The Courts without taking into consideration the inadequacies of the State, have been punishing SC/STs (the victims) for the same. Shri Pravin Rashtrapal, Member of Parliament rightly pointed out that there are insufficient officers at that level. His statement is supported by the Annual Report of 2005-2006 of Ministry of Home Affairs. Of the total posts sanctioned by the government under Indian Police Service (IPS) more than 15 percent of the posts are vacant. This basically means that there is one IPS officer for 77,000 SC/STs.

In the case of Karnataka, there were no officers of the required rank in three districts, as admitted by the government at the State Vigilance and Monitoring Committee (SVMC) in September 2010. Though officers of higher rank can conduct the investigation (the Act only says 'at least of rank'), in practice they seldom do.

Special Courts

For speedy trial, Section 14 of the Act provides for a Court of Session to be a Special Court to try offences under this Act in each district. Rule 13(i) mandates that the judge in a special court be sensitive with right aptitude and understanding of the problems of the scheduled communities.

However, that is seldom the case. Most states have declared a court as a 'special court'. The hitch is that they are designated courts (as opposed to exclusive special courts) and so have to hear many other cases too. Consequently, at any time about 80% of the cases are pending—defeating the very purpose of having special courts in the first place.

Special Court Justice Ramaswamy observed in the case of State of Karnataka v. Ingale that more than seventy-five percent of the cases brought under the SC/ST Act end in acquittal at all levels. The situation has not improved much since 1992 according to the figures given by the 2002 Annual Report dealing with SC/ST Act (of the Ministry of Social Justice and Empowerment) Of the total cases filed in 2002 only 21.72% were disposed of, and, of those, a mere 2.31% ended in conviction. The number of acquittals is 6 times more than the number of convictions and more than 70 percent of the cases are still pending. By 2019, pendency in courts had risen to 147,545 (92.97%) for scheduled castes and 26,025 (90.72%) for scheduled tribes.

Inaugurating a two-day annual conference of State Ministers of Welfare/Social Justice, 8 Sept 2009, Prime Minister Singh expressed 'shock' that the conviction rate of cases of atrocities against the SC/STs is less than 30% against the average of 42% for all cognisable offences under the Indian Penal Code. In rape cases the conviction rate is just 2%. In 2010, Karnataka has only eight Special courts, though 15 of 30 districts are declared 'atrocity prone'. Overall conviction rates remain at or below 5%. Even the few special courts seem to be biased. Of the 101 cases disposed of in the Tumkur special court, not one was convicted. Gulbarga, another atrocity prone district had a conviction rate of just 2%. 7 districts had a conviction rate of 0%.

In 2019, despite the sizable and increasing pendency, only 11 states have exclusive special courts (mandated for district with high pendency under Section 14). In total, there are just 194 exclusive special courts in the country. Andhra 1, Bihar 5, Gujarat 16, Himanchal 3, Karnataka 8, Madhya Pradesh 43, Maharashtra 3, Odisha 5, Rajasthan 31, Tamil Nadu 14, and Uttar Pradesh 65.

The very first union report on the implementation of the Act, placed before parliament on 14 December 1993 notes that at the conference of the welfare ministers of Andhra Pradesh, Karnataka, Kerala, Tamil Nadu, and Pondicherry held at Thiruvananthapuram on 28 and 29 August 1992 the first main recommendation was that *all atrocity cases should be decided by the courts in six months to one year*. Thirty years on, in 2022, it remains a dream. The second main recommendation was that *cases of acquittals and cases in which accused get minor punishment should be seriously examined.* Thirty years later, no action is seen.

Considering that there are 254,475 pending cases (96.1% pendency rate) in the court for scheduled castes as of 31 December 2021, and 40,640 pending cases (95.4% pendency rate) for the scheduled tribes, this is a substantial loss in relief since 25% of the relief is linked to completion of the case. Even assuming the lower end of the scale of relief (which varies from ₹ 85,000 to ₹ 825,000) the monetary loss alone due to wholly avoidable judicial delays is in the range of ₹ 15 billion, USD 200 million. As of 30 April 2022 at least one of these cases is in court since 1992 - i.e. 30 years.

Relief and Socio-economic Rehabilitation

Relief and socio-economic rehabilitation are dealt with under Section 15A Rights of Victims and Witnesses, Rule 12(4) Relief and Rehabilitation, and Rule 15(1) Contingency Plan (which deals with who is responsible and the time line).

Rationale

Atrocities often take place when persons belonging to the scheduled communities do not fulfill their 'caste functions' by doing ritually prescribed 'unclean' work or break the caste boundaries such as sitting in the bus or wearing a turban or footwear or sporting a mustache—often the preserve of the dominant castes. Atrocities are a form of 'collective' punishment for daring to have even some semblance of non-dependence which is termed as 'prosperous', and the atrocity is to bring them back into the situation of total dependence and servitude. The state therefore has the duty to help the community back on its feet.

As the minister for home affairs acknowledged:

- In fact, a part of the reason why atrocities are committed is economic activity. In my experience, I have seen that in some areas, the Scheduled Caste or the

> Scheduled Tribe person is prosperous. My knowledge is mostly about the Scheduled Caste, not about the Scheduled Tribe. It is because of the economic activity, because of the enterprise, there are areas where the Scheduled Caste people have also become prosperous. The Scheduled Caste people are able to build brick and stone houses. The Scheduled Caste people are able to acquire vehicles. The Scheduled Caste people are able to dress better, send their children to better schools. One of the reasons why atrocities take place in those places is to cripple them economically. Every riot, every arson case cripples them economically. Therefore, it is important that the State must immediately rush in social and economic measures for the rehabilitation of those who have suffered through these atrocities.

Relief

The Act has prescribed a schedule for relief and socio-economic rehabilitation under Rule 12(4) as Annexure 1 entitled Norms for Relief Amount which ranges from ₹ 85,000 to ₹ 825,000 depending on the crime. This is periodically updated. As is often the case, the 'minimum' becomes the maximum. In 2021, Tamil Nadu became the first state ever to increase the minimum amount to more than the guidance of the union government with a range from ₹ 100,000 to ₹ 1,200,000.

The relief is paid in parts depending on the stage of the case. Generally it is 25% on registering the FIR, 50% on filing the chargesheet, and 25% on conviction. However, there are exceptions and variations. For most crimes involving women, the final 25% is on completion of the trial irrespective of the verdict. For acid attack it is 50% on registering the FIR and 50% on getting the medical report, and for disability or murder it is 50% on getting the medical certificate or post mortem report and 50% when the chargesheet is sent to court. Additional relief of up to ₹ 500,000 is provided in the case of murder, rape, permanent disability, and arson by the Dr. Ambedkar National Relief to the SC/ST Victims of Atrocities Scheme administered by the Ambedkar Foundation, an autonomous institution under the union government. The survivors are also entitled to dietary expenses, travel allowance and maintenance expenses, and full cost of medical care (including hospitalisation) at government cost when injured. Attendants for those hospitalised, or for survivors and witnesses or their dependents who are children, women, or senior citizens, are also entitled to travel allowance and maintenance expenses for the duration. These need to be paid immediately, or at the latest within three days (Rule 11).

Socio-economic Rehabilitation

Socio-economic rehabilitation (including relocation if required) for the victim, the dependents, informants, or witnesses during investigation, inquiry, and trial is the responsibility of the Special Court or the Exclusive Special Court trying a case under this Act [Section 15A(6)].

In practice, administratively, it is often by the line departments of the government.

Individual

Individual rehabilitation is time-bound, and there is additional relief to victims of murder, death, massacre, rape, gang rape, permanent incapacitation, and dacoity. This is in addition to the cash relief and the relief provided by Ambedkar foundation (Rule 12(5)).

Rule 12(4) Schedule annexure-I Sr. No. 46 Additional relief to victims of murder death, massacre, rape, gang rape, permanent incapacitation and dacoity: In addition to relief amounts paid under above items, relief may be arranged within three months of date of atrocity as follows:-

- Basic pension of [1] 5,000 as applicable to a government servant with admissible dearness allowance (About [1] 10,000 per month in 2022).
- Employment to one member of the family of the deceased.
- Provision of agricultural land.
- House.
- Full cost of the maintenance and education up to graduation level of the children of the victims.
- Utensils, rice, wheat, dals, pulses, etc., for a period of three months.

Community

Common resources and services (such as wells and other water sources fouled, right of passage) are to be restored at government cost (Rule 12(4) Schedule annexure-I).

Helpdesk

The government has also set up a helpdesk to monitor implementation in 2021.

Implementation Record

- *Rule 8 Protection Cell and Rule 9 Nodal Officers:* 23 States have set up SC/ST Protection Cells. Nodal Officers have been appointed in 28 States.
- *Rule 13(2) Special police stations* have been set up only in five states - Bihar 40, Chhattisgarh 26, Jharkhand 22, Keralam 3, and Madhya Pradesh 51 (total 142) (Annual Report under Section 21(4) for the calendar year 2019). The pendency of cases in courts is increasing every year - from 174,931 in 2018 to 193,149 in 2019 to 223,017 in 2020, though the cases are supposed to be disposed off within two months of registering the FIR and there are supposed to be special courts and exclusive special courts for speedy disposal of cases. (Reply to question AU4152 in Parliament (lok sabha) on 29 March 2022).
- *Rule 15(1) Contingency plan:* Only 11 states (Bihar, Chhattisgarh, Goa, Gujarat, Haryana, Himachal Pradesh, Karnataka, Madhya Pradesh, Odisha, Punjab, and

Tamil Nadu) have prepared the mandatory contingency plan under Rule 15(1) as prescribed in Section 15A. (Reply to question AU1012 in parliament (lok sabha) on 8 February 2022).

Tamil Nadu has prepared the contingency plan both in English and in Tamil.

- *Rule 16(2) State Vigilance and Monitoring Committee meetings:* Despite being mandatory to conduct State Vigilance and Monitoring Committee (SVMC) meetings in January and July each year, 20 states did not conduct a single meeting in 2016, 2017, or 2018 - all pre-pandemic years. Assam conducted 1 (2018), Chhattisgarh 2 (2016=0, 2017=1, 2018=1), Gujarat 4 (0,1,3), Haryana 5 (1,2,2), Karnataka 2 (1,0,1), Kerala 1 (0,1,0), Maharashtra 1 (0,0,1), and West Bengal 4 (1,1,2). But for Puducherry (0,1,1) and Chandigarh (0,0,1), no union territory conducted a single meeting either. (Reply to question AS323 in Parliament (lok sabha) on 17 March 2020). Andhra has not constituted the SVMC ever since its bifurcation on 1 June 2014 (Annual Report under Section 21(4) for the calendar year 2019).
- *Section 21(1) and 21(2)* of Act stipulates that the State Government shall take all such measures as may be necessary for its effective implementation. As 'police' and 'public order' are state subjects, primary responsibility for prevention of atrocities and maintenance of law and order rests with the State Governments. A responsive police administration has always been recognized as an essential requirement in any society that seeks to take care of its citizens. Such responsive administration is essential for prevention of atrocities likely to be inflicted upon the scheduled communities by unscrupulous elements from other communities.

However, despite the Act and Rules, the situation has not changed much. The incidence of recorded atrocities is increasing, and the implementation of the law leaves much to be desired as this statement of the Union Minister for Home Affairs shows:

"Madam, I must concede that the statistics do not reflect any decline in the atrocities. On the contrary, the information compiled by the Crime Records Bureau shows that the number of cases registered of atrocities against the Scheduled Castes and the Scheduled Tribes is, in fact, on the rise. I have the numbers from 2006 to 2008, subsequent years are being compiled. Take for example the case of the Scheduled Castes. The number of cases of atrocities against the Scheduled Castes registered in 2006 was 26,665. That itself is an understatement. Many of the cases are simply not registered. In 2007, it was 29,825 and in 2008 it was 33,365. So, this clearly shows the rise in trend.

I can make one or two deductions from this.

- Firstly that there is no let up in the atrocities committed on the Scheduled Castes.
- The other inference one can make is, perhaps, because of the pressure that is

put on the State Governments by the Central Government, by public opinion and by NGOs, now the States are showing greater willingness to deal with the problem. Therefore, more cases are being registered.

We cannot be happy about the fact that approximately 33,000 cases are being registered as atrocities against Scheduled Castes in one year. What makes it even more disturbing is that while so many cases are registered, the conviction rate hovers around 30%. What makes it doubly painful is that there is rise in atrocities, but when you try to prosecute and convict, the conviction rate is only 30%. It was 28%, 31.4% and 32%. Not only are acquittals very high; pendency is about 80%.

I am afraid that the disposal of the cases is low; the rate of conviction is low. Therefore, it is fair to conclude that the feeling amongst the Scheduled Castes and the Schedule Tribes that all these laws and all these statements, all these pronouncements have really not brought any relief to them. That feeling is running high and I cannot but say that feeling is justified." (p143,144 of the printed text).

Though the Act and rules are stringent, it is not a deterrent, as the Minister for Home Affairs P Chidambaram admitted in the Lok Sabha, referring to the Central Committee monitoring the implementation of the Act:

A committee under the Chairmanship of the Minister of Social Justice was set up after the Act was passed. That Committee has met, so far, 10 times. The situation in 25 States and 4 Union Territories were reviewed. That committee has expressed that the most important areas of concern are the following five:

- firstly, the high rate of acquittal;
- secondly, the high rate of pendency of cases and very low rate of disposal;
- thirdly, inadequate use of the preventive provisions of the Act, while the punitive provisions are invoked and FIR is registered, preventive provisions are rarely invoked;
- fourthly, that the committees and other mechanisms provided in the Act have virtually not been put to use; and fifthly,
- the Act itself may not be deterrent, perhaps it is not being as deterrent as we thought it could be.

Misuse and Bias

Misuse

For some, the low conviction rates are evidence of misuse of the Act by the SCs and STs to threaten and blackmail other communities. The acquittal rates are abnormally high, as acknowledged by the prime minister and home minister (quoted above). There is also a high rate of FIRs rejected as being 'false' by the police, with 10% of the total cases investigated in 2016 being closed as 'false'. There has also been concern regarding misuse of the Act for settling of personal scores. 75% cases were found to be false in Madhya Pradesh in a survey. 81% cases under the Act were registered against persons from OBC section, 14% upper castes and 5 percent minorities sections. According to data available with Rajasthan police around 40% of cases filed under the Act are fake.

Justice Karnan, a High Court judge had used the provisions of this Act to pass orders against the then Chief Justice of India Jagdish Singh Khehar punishing him with 5 years rigorous imprisonment.

There has also been reports of a man committing suicide after being threatened with a case against him under the Act. A man in UP had to spend 20 years in prison after being implicated in a false case under the provisions of this act.

Administrative Bias

Perhaps the most important bias (re implementation of this Act) is that there is little done to prevent atrocities. Most of the reports are of what is done after an atrocity has been committed. Few states have preventive measures in place. The 'relief' provided is a pittance and the confidence of the community is seldom rebuilt.

While the legal text is explicit in seeking remedies, the implementation of the text appears to evade actual performance. Laws and legal processes are not self-executing; they depend on the administrative structure and the judiciary with the anticipation that the social attitudes are driven by notions of equity, social justice and fair play. However, the increasingly indifferent responses of those involved in the implementation of laws protecting the weak, the oppressed and the socially disadvantaged have persisted over the years and the system has failed to provide for self-correction. The problem is that the victims of atrocities suffer not only bodily and mental pain but also feelings of insecurity and social avoidance which is not present for the victims of other crimes. If the judge delegated to protect them shows indifference, it further aggravates their already vulnerable position.

Judicial Bias

Going through the Indian judicial system is degrading for any Dalit because of the still existing biases of the court judges. One example is the conduct of an Allahabad High Court judge who had his chambers "purified" with water from the 'ganga jal' because a Dalit judge had previously sat in that chamber before him.

Another example is the case of State of Karnataka v. Ingale. The State of Karnataka had charged five individuals with violating the Act. At trial, four witnesses testified that the defendants had threatened Dalits with a gun to stop them from taking water from a well. The defendants told the Dalits that they had no right to take water, because they were 'untouchables'. The trial judge convicted all of the defendants. On appeal, the Additional Sessions judge confirmed the conviction of three defendants but acquitted two. On further appeal to the High Court, the judge acquitted all the defendants after rejecting testimony of the four Dalit witnesses. The Dalits finally got relief from the Supreme Court. The High Court's reluctance to believe the Dalits was a "patent error," according to Justice Ramaswamy.

The issue of false cases and misuse of the Act found its way into the March 2018 decision of a two judge bench of Justices UU Lalit and AK Goel of the Supreme Court of India in *Subhash Kashinath Mahajan v. State of Maharashtra & Anr.* In addition to questioning Section 18 of the Act, which prohibits grant of anticipatory bail for offences committed under the Act, the court laid down guidelines, substantially diluting the provisions of the Act. The court granted additional powers to the investigating officer to conduct a preliminary inquiry before lodging a complaint. Further, written permission of the appointing authority for all public officials and of the District Superintendent of Police for other persons is required before a complaint is registered. - wilfully ignorant of the fact that all FIRs under this Act can only be filed after the District Magistrate and the Superintendent of Police visit the spot and conduct a preliminary enquiry (Rule 12(1)), and only then can the Superintendent of Police order an FIR to be filed (Rule 12(2)). Further, it also ignored the fact '*that the charges in this regard against the public servant shall be booked on the recommendation of an administrative enquiry* (Section 4(2)) - so the question of not conducting a preliminary inquiry does not arise. In fact, the law was clear that the FIR can be filed only after a spot visit and inquiry has been done by the senior-most police official in the district (in the case of civilians) [Rule 12(2)] and only after an administrative enquiry (in the case of public servants)[Section 4(2)].

If the steps for the investigation outlined above are followed, there is virtually no scope for 'false' or 'mistake of fact' cases. Instead of taking the officials to task for not doing what is a legally mandated part of their job, the judges of the supreme court held that the cases were false and a misuse of the Act, in effect blaming the victim.

Empowering Provisions

Rights of Victims and Witnesses

This is the first law in India to detail the rights of victims and witnesses [Chapter IVA, Section 15A]. It is the duty of the state to ensure these rights [Section 15A(1)]. The rights are comprehensive - from the right to be *treated with fairness, respect and dignity and with due regard to any special need that arises because of the victim's age or gender or educational disadvantage or poverty* [Section 15A(2)], to protection, to the right to be assisted at all times by a concerned individual, organisation, and an advocate [Section 15A(12)].

Relief and Rehabilitation

Relief and socio-economic rehabilitation is a duty of the government, and independent of recovery of the amount from the perpetrator [Section 15A, Rule 11, Rule 12(4), and Rule 12(4) Annexe Schedule I].

Legal Aid

Legal aid is available for all victims, dependents, and their families, regardless of financial status. This *includes state payment for a private advocate of choice, who will be paid more than the panel advocate and the special public prosecutor* [Rule 4(5)]. Normally, legal aid depends on the financial status, in India.

Civil Society Response

Monitoring Implementation

Many civil society organisations (CSOs) started using this Act to provide some relief to the victims almost immediately. The full monitoring of the Act by civil society is a later phenomenon.

The full monitoring of the Act is virtually a 'systems audit' that, in addition to the police and judicial process, includes the monthly, quarterly, half-yearly, and annual reports; compliance regarding prevention, rehabilitation, performance reviews, quarterly subdivisional (SdVMC) and district vigilance and monitoring committee (DVMC) meetings, and half yearly state vigilance and monitoring committee (SVMC) meetings.

Comprehensive tools were developed to monitor the implementation of the Act for each case, and at the district and state levels. A few Dalit and human rights organisations took to monitoring violence against the scheduled communities, documenting them, publicising them and also monitoring the use of the Act in dealing with these crimes. One of the first to monitor the implementation of this Act was Sakshi Human Rights Watch Andhra Pradesh (Sakshi-AP), under the leadership of Nanda Gopal Vudayagiri from 1998 itself, in (undivided) Andhra Pradesh (present Telangana and Andhra Pradesh).

Civil society monitoring has not matured in that civil society shadow reports under Section 21(4) on the implementation of the Act are yet to be done at the union level.

At the state level, some organisations monitor the implementation of the Act and bring out reports and factsheets.

- *Karnataka*: Monitoring by Committee Monitoring and Strengthening the POA in Karnataka (CMASK) led by the Karnataka Dalit Mahilla Vedike (KDMV). Annual reports by CMASK have been brought out for Karnataka since 2009 (in English and Kannada), (with monitoring tools), auditing the performance of the state, including the bureaucracy, judicial system, police and monitoring mechanisms (DVMCs and SVMC). Also available in Kannada is the monitoring calendar.
- *Tamil Nadu*: Citizens vigilance and monitoring committees (CVMC) monitor the Act in Tamil Nadu since 2016 and bring out annual status reports and report cards in English and Tamil since 2018, and earlier by SASY. The reports are available in Tamil and English. A thirty year scorecard in English and Tamil was released on the 30th anniversary of the Act on 11 September 2020.

However, recorded atrocities across the country continue to rise, and convictions still remain low, as the annual Crime In India reports of the National Crime Records Bureau show.

Filing PILs for Implementation

Some organisations used Public Interest Litigation (PIL) to demand better implementation of the Act at the High Courts and in the Supreme Court of India.

In Tamil Nadu, petitions were filed for judicial orders to conduct the State Vigilance and Monitoring Committee (SVMC) meetings in 2013 and 2020. The government complied days before the verdict in both cases.

In Karnataka, the Citizens Committee Monitoring and Strengthening the SCs and STs (PoA) Act in Karnataka, (CMASK) sued for compliance (Writ Petition No. 7990/2020) in June 2020.

The National Campaign on Dalit Human Rights (NCDHR) had earlier filed for compliance in the Supreme Court of India.

National Coalition for Strengthening SC&ST PoA Act

Just before the 20th anniversary of its enactment, CSOs came together from across the country to review its implementation and formed the National Coalition for Strengthening SC & ST Prevention of Atrocities Act. This coalition took stock of the implementation of the Act as of 2009 in a report card, analysed the lacunae and suggested a set of amendments for improving the implementation. State specific "fact sheets" were also made available for Madhya Pradesh and Bihar. This was followed up with a peoples reportcard in 2012. Many important areas such as social and economic boycotts, causing hurt, destruction of property, defining the SC communities to include those who profess a religion other than Hinduism, Sikhism, Buddhism, and better monitoring mechanisms identified earlier in the K B Saxena study commissioned by the National Human Rights Commission, NHRC, were revisited and a campaign was launched that culminated in the ordinance of 2014. The campaign continued its momentum till the Amendment Act was passed in 2015, and then had a brief revival in 2018 from the Supreme Court Judgement in March till the Amendment Act in August.

Parliamentary Privileges and Media

Parliamentary privilege is a legal immunity enjoyed by members of certain legislatures, in which legislators are granted protection against civil or criminal liability for actions done or statements made in the course of their legislative duties. It is common in countries whose constitutions are based on the Westminster system.

Origins

In the United Kingdom, it allows members of the House of Lords and House of

Commons to speak freely during ordinary parliamentary proceedings without fear of legal action on the grounds of slander, contempt of court or breaching the Official Secrets Act. It also means that members of Parliament cannot be arrested on civil matters for statements made or acts undertaken as an MP within the grounds of the Palace of Westminster, on the condition that such statements or acts occur as part of a *proceeding in Parliament*—for example, as a question to the Prime Minister in the House of Commons. This allows Members to raise questions or debate issues which could slander an individual, interfere with an ongoing court case or threaten to reveal state secrets, such as in the Zircon affair or several cases mentioned by the Labour MP Tam Dalyell.

There is no immunity from arrest on criminal grounds, nor does the civil privilege entirely extend to the devolved administrations in Scotland or Wales. A consequence of the privilege of free speech is that legislators in Westminster systems are forbidden by conventions of their House from uttering certain words, or implying that another member is lying. The rights and privileges of members are overseen by the powerful Committee on Standards and Privileges. If a member of the House is in breach of the rules then he/she can be suspended or even expelled from the House. Such past breaches have included giving false evidence before a committee of the House and the taking of bribes by members.

Similar rights apply in other Westminster system countries such as Canada and Australia. In the United States, the Speech or Debate Clause in Article One of the United States Constitution provides for a similar privilege, and many state constitutions provide similar clauses for their state legislatures.

Parliamentary privilege is controversial because of its potential for abuse; a member can use privilege to make damaging allegations that would ordinarily be discouraged by defamation laws, whether or not those allegations have a strong foundation. A member could, even more seriously, undermine national security and/or the safety of an ongoing military or covert operation or undermine relations with a foreign state by releasing sensitive military or diplomatic information.

India

The government of India, based largely on the Westminster model, grants limited immunity from legal proceedings to members of Parliament and State Legislature under Articles 105 and 194 respectively, of the Indian Constitution. Article 105(2) reads as follows:

No member of Parliament shall be liable to any proceedings in any court in respect of anything said or any vote given by him in Parliament or any committee thereof, and no person shall be so liable in respect of the publication by or under the authority of either House of Parliament of any report, paper, votes or proceedings.

Famous Cases Involving Journalists and News Media Organizations

- R. Rajagopal v. State of Tamil Nadu (1994): In this landmark case, the Supreme

Court of India ruled in favor of journalist R. Rajagopal, upholding the freedom of the press. The case involved a defamation suit filed against Rajagopal for an article he wrote about a criminal case. The court established that the right to privacy cannot be used to suppress the legitimate exercise of the freedom of the press.

- State of Maharashtra v. Raj Narain (1975): This case revolved around the publication of a report in the 'National Herald' newspaper, alleging that certain government officials in Maharashtra were involved in corrupt activities. The court held that publication of information on matters of public interest is protected by the right to freedom of speech and expression.
- Indian Express Newspapers (Bombay) Private Ltd. v. Union of India (1985): This case dealt with the constitutional validity of certain provisions of the Contempt of Courts Act, 1971. The Supreme Court held that criticism of judicial conduct or decisions does not necessarily amount to contempt, as long as it is fair, bona fide, and within reasonable limits.
- Arundhati Roy Contempt Case (2002): Author and activist Arundhati Roy faced contempt proceedings for her criticism of the Supreme Court's handling of a case related to the construction of the Narmada Dam. The court ultimately decided not to pursue the contempt charges, emphasizing the importance of free speech and criticism.
- Kapil Sibal v. Subramanian Swamy (2014): Subramanian Swamy, a politician and public figure, was sued for defamation by Kapil Sibal, a prominent lawyer and politician. Swamy had made allegations of corruption against Sibal. The case highlighted the balance between freedom of speech and the right to protect one's reputation.
- Priya Ramani vs. M.J. Akbar (2019): This defamation case garnered significant attention during the #MeToo movement in India. Journalist Priya Ramani accused former Minister of State for External Affairs M.J. Akbar of sexual harassment. Akbar filed a defamation suit against Ramani, which she defended on the grounds of truth and public interest.
- NDTV India Ban (2016): The government imposed a one-day ban on the Hindi news channel NDTV India for allegedly revealing sensitive information during its coverage of the Pathankot attack. The ban raised concerns about press freedom and government censorship.
- Teesta Setalvad's Defamation Cases (Various): Teesta Setalvad, a civil rights activist and journalist, has been involved in multiple defamation cases over the years due to her advocacy work. These cases highlight the legal challenges faced by activists and journalists who speak out against powerful interests.

6

Media and Intellectual Property Rights

Right to Information Act 2005

The Right to Information (RTI) is an act of the Parliament of India which sets out the rules and procedures regarding citizens' right to information. It replaced the former Freedom of Information Act, 2002. Under the provisions of RTI Act, any citizen of India may request information from a "public authority" (a body of Government or "instrumentality of State") which is required to reply expeditiously or within thirty days. In case of matter involving a petitioner's life and liberty, the information has to be provided within 48 hours. The Act also requires every public authority to computerize their records for wide dissemination and to proactively publish certain categories of information so that the citizens need minimum recourse to request for information formally.

The RTI Bill was passed by Parliament of India on 15 June 2005 and came into force with effect from 12 October 2005. Every day on an average, over 4800 RTI applications are filed. In the first ten years of the commencement of the act, over 17,500,000 applications had been filed.

Although Right to Information is not included as a Fundamental Right in the Constitution of India, it protects the fundamental rights to Freedom of Expression and Speech under Article 19(1)(a) and Right to Life and Personal Liberty under Article 21 guaranteed by the Constitution. The authorities under RTI Act 2005 are called public authorities. The Public Information Officer (PIO) or the First Appellate Authority in the public authorities perform quasi judicial function of deciding on the application and appeal respectively. This act was enacted in order to consolidate the fundamental right in the Indian constitution 'freedom of speech'. Since RTI is implicit in the Right to Freedom of Speech and Expression under Article 19 of the Indian Constitution, it is an implied fundamental right. Information disclosure in India had traditionally been restricted by the Official Secrets Act 1923 and various other special laws, which the new RTI Act overrides.

Right to Information codifies a fundamental right of the citizens of India. RTI has proven to be very useful, but is counteracted by the Whistle Blowers Protection Act, 2011. The Right to Information (Amendment) Bill, 2019, seeks to amend Sections 13, 16, and 27 of the RTI Act.

Section 13 of the original Act: It sets the term of the central Chief Information Commissioner and Information Commissioners at five years (or until the age of 65, whichever is earlier). Finally in Ashwanee K. Singh's case on 20 September 2020, it is stabilised that right to information is a fundamental right.

Scope

The Act extends to the whole of India. It covers all the constitutional authorities, including executive, legislature and judiciary; any institution or body established or constituted by an act of Parliament or a state legislature. It is also defined in the Act that bodies or authorities established or constituted by order or notification of appropriate government including bodies "owned, controlled or substantially financed" by government, or non-Government organizations "substantially financed, directly or indirectly by funds".

Private Bodies

Private bodies are not within the act's purview. In a decision of *Sarbjit Roy vs Delhi Electricity Regulatory Commission*, the Central Information Commission also reaffirmed that privatised public utility companies fall within the purview of RTI. As of 2014, private institutions and NGOs receiving over 95% of their infrastructure funds from the government come under the Act.

Political Parties

The Central Information Commission (CIC) held that the political parties are public authorities and are answerable to citizens under the RTI Act. The CIC said that eight national parties - Congress, BJP, NCP, CPI(M), CPI, BSP, NPP and AITC - has been substantially funded indirectly by the Central Government and have the character of public authorities under the RTI Act as they perform public functions. But in August 2013 the government introduced a Right To Information (Amendment) Bill which would remove political parties from the scope of the law. Currently no parties are under the RTI Act and a case has been filed for bringing all political parties under it.

Amendment

The Right to Information Act 2019 passed on July 25, 2019 modified the terms and conditions of service of the CIC and Information Commissioners at the centre and in states. It had been criticized as watering down the independence of the information commissions, namely by empowering the government to fix the term of service and salaries of information commissioners.

Supreme Court Judgement

Supreme Court of India on 13 November 2019, upheld the decision of the Delhi High Court bringing the office of Chief Justice of India under the purview of the Right to Information (RTI) Act.

Governance and Process

The Right to information in India is governed by two major bodies:

- Central Information Commission (CIC) – Chief Information commissioner who heads all the central departments and ministries- with their own public Information officers (PIO)s. CICs are directly under the President of India.
- State Information Commissions – State Public Information Officers or SPOs head over all the state department and ministries. The SPIO office is directly under the corresponding State Governor.

State Information Commissions are independent bodies and Central Information Commission has no jurisdiction over the State Information Commission.

Fees

A citizen who desires to seek some information from a public authority is required to send, along with the application (a Postal order or DD (Demand draft) or a bankers cheque) or a court stamp payable to the Accounts Officer of the public authority as fee prescribed for seeking information. If the person is from a disadvantaged community, he/she need not pay. The applicant may also be required to pay further fee towards the cost of providing the information, details of which shall be intimated to the applicant by the PIO (Public Information Officer) as prescribed by the RTI ACT.

Digital Right to Information Systems

A digital portal has been set up, *RTI Portal*, a gateway to the citizens for quick search of information on the details of first Appellate Authorities, PIOs etc. amongst others, besides access to RTI related information disclosures published on the web by various Public Authorities under the government of India as well as the State Governments. It is an initiative taken by Department of Personnel and Training, Ministry of Personnel, Public Grievances and Pensions.

Controversies

The Right to information in India has been mired with controversies ranging from their use in political battles, asking for educational degrees of political rivals, or cases of blatant refusals to provide information on high-profile projects to allegations of misuse by civil society. The backlash against RTI by the state hampered the citizen's right to know.

Attacks on RTI Activists and Protection Suggestions

Commonwealth Human Rights Initiative (CHRI) data points to over 310 cases across India where people were either attacked, physically or mentally harassed or had their property damaged because of the information they sought under RTI. The data throws up over 50 alleged murders and two suicides that were directly linked with RTI applications filed. R.T.I. Act 2005 applies to both central as well as state governments. It also covers the acts and functionaries of the public authorities.

There is a consensus felt that there is a need to amend the RTI Act to provide for the protection of those seeking information under the Act. The Asian Centre for Human Rights recommends that a separate chapter, "Protection of those seeking information under the (RTI) Act", be inserted into the Act.

Protection measures suggested include:

- Mandatory, immediate registration of complaints of threats or attacks against RTI activists on the First Information Report and placing such FIRs before the magistrate or judge of the area within 24 hours for issuance of directions for protection of those under threats and their family members, and periodic review of such protection measures
- Conducting inquiry into threats or attacks by a police officer not below the rank of Deputy Superintendent of Police/Assistant Commissioner of Police to be concluded within 90 days and we also use RTI and get its benefit.

Intellectual Property Rights

Many civil society members have recently alleged the subversion of the right to information Act by the invocation of Intellectual Property rights argument by the government agencies from time to time.

Most notable are:

- The Right to Information denied by RBI on Demonetization citing Intellectual Property Laws.
- The Right to Information Denied by Uttar Pradesh Irrigation Department after more than 8 months of a wait on under construction Gomti Riverfront Development Project. A group of researchers requested for environment Impact and Project Report on the project which is flagged for negative impacts, tax money wastage by environmental scientists and research reports.

Banned People from Filing RTI

Gujarat State Information Commission banned 10 people from filing RTI queries, citing that these people were "harassing government officials" by filing multiple queries with "malafide intentions". This was the first time in Gujarat that a ban on filing RTI inquiries took place, noted NGO Mahiti Adhikar Gujarat Pahel, also stating that no provision in the act allowed for the blacklisting of applicants.

Debates

Rejection of RTIs

Scholars argue that the Right to Information Act's original intent to make government transparent and accountable is faltering as RTI requests are rejected and the bureaucratic systems are bogged down by thousands of requests.

Many RTIs are rejected because the bureaucratic requirements (including the technocratic language used) of filing are too onerous and legalistic for ordinary citizens. Sixty percent of the RTI appeals made to Information Commissioners in Delhi are rejected for a variety of reasons, including that appeals are not typed or not written in English, or lack an index of the papers attached or a list of date. This bureaucratic barrier, worse for those without access to higher education or information, makes the right to information inaccessible. Many citizens have to seek out NGOs, RTI activists, or lawyers, to file their RTIs.

Benefits

Many activists view the Right to Information Act as a final liberation from British colonialism; they describe the RTI law as "a tool for empowering ordinary citizens and changing the culture of governance by making it transparent, less corrupt, participatory, and accountable". They also note that RTI requests provide strategy and substance for activists on a broad range of social issues, including "land and environmental rights, social security benefits, the working of financial institutions, political party financing reform, civic infrastructure, and even public-private partnerships".

Exempted Organisations

As per section 24 of the Act, intelligence and security organisations, both central and state, are exempted from the RTI Act except in cases of corruption or human rights violation. Such central organisations are listed in schedule 2 of the Act. The schedule has been amended four times, in September 2005, March 2008, October 2008 and May 2021.

1. Intelligence Bureau
2. Research and Analysis Wing including its technical wing, Aviation Research Centre
3. Directorate of Revenue Intelligence
4. Central Economic Intelligence Bureau
5. Directorate of Enforcement
6. Narcotics Control Bureau

7. Special Frontier Force
8. Border Security Force
9. Central Reserve Police Force
10. Indo-Tibetan Border Police
11. Central Industrial Security Force
12. National Security Guard
13. Assam Rifles
14. Sashastra Seema Bal
15. Directorate General of Income-tax (Investigation)
16. National Technical Research Organisation
17. Financial Intelligence Unit, India
18. Special Protection Group
19. Defence Research and Development Organisation
20. Border Roads Organisation
21. National Security Council Secretariat (secretariat of the National Security Council, in the Cabinet Secretariat)

Copyright Act 1957 and Intellectual Property Rights

Copyright Act 1957

The Copyright Act 1957 as amended governs the subject of copyright law in India. The Act is applicable from 21 January 1958. The history of copyright law in India can be traced back to its colonial era under the British Empire. The Copyright Act 1957 was the first post-independence copyright legislation in India and the law has been amended six times since 1957. The most recent amendment was in the year 2012, through the Copyright (Amendment) Act 2012.

India is a member of most of the important international conventions governing the area of copyright law, including the Berne Convention of 1886 (as modified at Paris in 1971), the Universal Copyright Convention of 1951, the Rome Convention of 1961 and the Agreement on Trade Related Aspects of Intellectual Property Rights (TRIPS). Initially, India was not a member of the WIPO Copyright Treaty (WCT) and the WIPO Performances and Phonograms Treaty (WPPT) but subsequently entered the treaty in 2013.

Applicable Copyright Act before 1958

Prior to 21 January 1958, the Indian Copyright Act, 1914, was applicable in India and still applicable for works created prior to 21 January 1958, when the new Act came into force. The Indian Copyright Act, 1914 was based on the Imperial Copyright Act of 1911 passed by the Parliament of the United Kingdom, but was slightly modified in terms of its application to Indian law. According to this Act, the period of copyright for photographs was 50 years from the time it was created (Act language is: "the term for which copyright shall subsist in photographs shall be fifty years from the making of the original negative from which the photograph was directly or indirectly derived, and the person who was owner of such negative at the time when such negative was made shall be deemed to be the author of the work, and, where such owner is a body corporate, the body corporate shall be deemed for the purposes of this Act to reside within the parts of His Majesty's dominions to which this Act extends if it has established a place of business within such parts.") For photographs published, before 21 January 1958 in India, the period of copyright is thus 50 years, as for them the old Act is applicable.

Definition of Copyright

Copyright is a bundle of rights given by the law to the creators of literary, dramatic, musical and artistic works and the producers of cinematograph films and sound recordings. The rights provided under Copyright law include the rights of reproduction of the work, communication of the work to the public, adaptation of the work and translation of the work. The scope and duration of protection provided under copyright law varies with the nature of the protected work.

In a 2016 copyright lawsuit, the Delhi High Court states that copyright is "not an inevitable, divine, or natural right that confers on authors the absolute ownership of their creations. It is designed rather to stimulate activity and progress in the arts for the intellectual enrichment of the public. Copyright is intended to increase and not to impede the harvest of knowledge. It is intended to motivate the creative activity of authors and inventors in order to benefit the public."

Types of Works Protected

The Indian copyright law protects literary works, dramatic works, musical works, artistic works, cinematograph films and sound recordings.

Foreign Works

Copyrights of works of the countries mentioned in the International Copyright Order are protected in India, as if such works are Indian works. The term of copyright in a work shall not exceed that which is enjoyed by it in its country of origin.

Ownership of Copyright under the Copyright Act 1957

The author of a work is generally considered as the first owner of the copyright under the Copyright Act 1957. However, for works made in the course of an author's employment under a "contract of service" or apprenticeship, the employer is considered as the first owner of copyright, in the absence of any agreement to the contrary. The concept of joint authorship is recognised in Section. 2(z) of the Act which provides that "*a work produced by the collaboration of two or more authors in which the contribution of one author is not distinct from the contribution of the other author or authors*" is a work of joint authorship. This concept has been elucidated in cases like Najma Heptulla v. Orient Longman Ltd. and Ors.

Section 19 of the Copyright Act 1957 lays down the modes of assignment of copyright in India. Assignment can only be in writing and must specify the work, the period of assignment and the territory for which assignment is made. If the period of assignment is not specified in the agreement, it shall be deemed to be 5 years and if the territorial extent of assignment is not specified, it shall be presumed to be limited to the territories of India. In a recent judgement (*Pine Labs Private Limited vs Gemalto Terminals India Limited*), a division bench of the Delhi High Court confirmed this position and held that in cases wherein the duration of assignment is not specified, the duration shall be deemed to be five years and the copyright shall revert to the author after five years.

Exceptions to Copyright Infringement in India

The Copyright Act 1957 exempts certain acts from the ambit of copyright infringement. While many people tend to use the term fair use to denote copyright exceptions in India, it is a factually wrong usage. While the US and certain other countries follow the broad fair use exception, India follows a different approach towards copyright exceptions. India follows a hybrid approach that allows :

- fair dealing with any copyrighted work for certain specifically mentioned purposes and
- certain specific activities enumerated in the statute.

While the fair use approach followed in the US can be applied for any kind of uses, the fair dealing approach followed in India is clearly limited towards the purposes of

1. private or personal use, including research, and education,
2. criticism or review,
3. reporting of current events and current affairs, including the reporting of a lecture delivered in public.

While the term fair dealing has not been defined anywhere in the Copyright Act 1957, the concept of 'fair dealing' has been discussed in different judgments, including the decision of the Supreme Court of India in Academy of General Education v. B. Malini Mallya (2009) and the decision of the High Court of Kerala in Civic Chandran v. Ammini Amma.

IBomma is a website which releases movies for free illegally. It copies movies of streaming services such as Prime Video, Netflix etc. Surprisingly no one has lodged a complaint against this torrent website which has been running for a long time. In September 2016, the Delhi High Court ruled in Delhi University's Rameshwari Photocopy Service shop case, which sold photocopies of chapters from academic textbooks was not infringing on their publisher's copyright, arguing that the use of copyright to "stimulate activity and progress in the arts for the intellectual enrichment of the public" outweighed its use by the publishers to maintain commercial control of their property. However, in December 2016, the ruling was reversed and taken back to court, citing that there were "triable issues" in the case.

Remedies Available against Copyright Infringement in India

The Copyright Act 1957 provides three kinds of remedies - administrative remedies, civil remedies and criminal remedies. The administrative remedies provided under the statute include detention of the infringing goods by the customs authorities. The civil remedies are provided under Chapter XII of the Copyright Act 1957 and the remedies provided include injunctions, damages and account of profits. The criminal remedies are provided under Chapter XIII of the statute and the remedies provided against copyright infringement include imprisonment (up to 3 years) along with a fine (up to 200,000 Rupees).

Jurisdiction [Place of Suing] Under Copyright Act, 1957 - in 2015 the jurisdiction law regarding copyright violation underwent significant change through the judgement of the Supreme Court in the 2015 case Indian Performing Rights Society Ltd. Vs. Sanjay Dalia – If cause of action has arisen wholly or in part in place where plaintiff resides or is doing business suit has to be filed at such place – Plaintiff cannot drag defendant to far off place under guise that he carries business there also. — Interpretation of statutes – Mischief Rule – Construction that suppresses even counter mischief has to be adopted.

Intellectual Property Rights

Intellectual property in India refers to the patents, copyrights and other intangible assets in India.

Government Policy

Indian government approved its first Intellectual Property Rights Policy in May 2016.

Laws

Copyrights

The copyright law of India is governed by the Copyright Act, 1957, which was enacted to protect the rights of creators and encourage the growth of creative industries. The Act was subsequently amended in 1983, 1984, 1992, 1994, 1999, 2002, 2012, and 2017 to align with international standards and address emerging challenges in the digital age.

Key provisions of the Copyright Act, 1957:

- Definition of Copyright: Copyright is the exclusive right given to the creator of original literary, dramatic, musical, and artistic works, as well as the producers of cinematograph films and sound recordings, to reproduce, distribute, and perform their works.
- Works Covered by Copyright: The Act protects a wide range of creative works, including literary, dramatic, musical, and artistic works, as well as cinematograph films and sound recordings.
- Exclusive Rights of Copyright Holders: Copyright holders have the exclusive rights to reproduce the work, communicate it to the public, issue copies, perform it in public, and make adaptations or translations of the work.
- Duration of Copyright: The duration of copyright protection varies depending on the type of work. Generally, copyright lasts for the lifetime of the creator plus an additional 60 years.
- Ownership of Copyright: The original creator of a work is typically the first owner of the copyright. However, there are provisions for works created in the course of employment, anonymous works, and works created under certain circumstances.
- Fair Use and Exceptions: The Act allows for certain exceptions to copyright, such as fair dealing for purposes of research, private use, criticism, review, news reporting, and education.
- Moral Rights: The Act recognizes the moral rights of authors, which include the right to attribution and the right to object to derogatory treatment of their work.
- Performers' Rights: The Act grants certain rights to performers, including the right to reproduce their performances, distribute copies, and communicate their performances to the public.
- Rights of Broadcasting Organizations: Broadcasting organizations have the right to communicate, perform, or broadcast their programs to the public.
- Copyright Societies: The Act allows for the establishment of copyright societies, which facilitate licensing and distribution of copyrighted works on behalf of copyright owners.
- Remedies and Enforcement: The Act provides for civil and criminal remedies in case of copyright infringement, including injunctions, damages, and seizure of infringing copies.
- Digital Rights Management (DRM): The Act addresses issues related to digital rights management, circumvention of technological protection measures, and liability of internet service providers.

Indian Trademark Law

Indian trademark law statutorily protects trademarks as per the Trademark Act, 1999 and also under the common law remedy of passing off. Statutory protection of trademark is administered by the Controller General of Patents, Designs and Trade Marks, a government agency that reports to the Department of Industrial Policy and Promotion (DIPP), under the Ministry of Commerce and Industry.

The law of trademark deals with the mechanism of registration, protection of trademark and prevention of fraudulent trademark. The law also provides for the rights acquired by registration of trademark, modes of transfer and assignment of the rights, nature of infringements, penalties for such infringement and remedies available to the owner in case of such infringement.

History

The law of trademark in India before 1940 was based on the common law principles of passing off and equity as followed in England before the enactment of the first Registration Act, 1875. The first statutory law related to trademark in India was the Trade Marks Act, 1940 which had similar provision to the UK Trade Marks Act, 1938. In 1958, the Trade and Merchandise Marks Act, 1958 was enacted which consolidated the provisions related to trademarks contained in other statutes like, the Indian Penal Code, Criminal Procedure Code and the Sea Customs Act. The Trade and Merchandise Marks Act, 1958 was repealed by the Trade Marks Act, 1999 and is the current governing law related to registered trademarks. The 1999 Act was enacted to comply with the provisions of the TRIPS. Though some aspects of the unregistered trade marks have been enacted into the 1999 Act, but they are primarily governed by the common law rules based on the principles evolved out of the judgments of the Courts. Where the law is ambiguous, the principles evolved and interpretation made by the Courts in England have been applied in India taking into consideration the context of the legal procedure, laws and realities of India.

Trademark

Trademark defined under Section 2 (zb) of the Trade Marks Act, 1999 as, "trade mark means a mark capable of being represented graphically and which is capable of distinguishing the goods or services of one person from those of others and may include shape of goods, their packaging and combination of colours." A mark can include a device, brand, heading, label, ticket, name, signature, word, letter, numeral, shape of goods, packaging or combination of colors or any such combinations. The trademark prevents unauthorized use of an individual's or company's product or service without their permission.

Trademark Rules

With effect from 6 March 2017, the new trademark rules came into existence. The intention is to simplify the whole trademark registration process and make it hassle-free and quick. Some of the features of the new rules are sound marks are made registrable; 3D marks are made registrable; e-filing is promoted; provisions pertaining to the well-known mark; separate fees structure for an individual/startup/small enterprise and others; expedited processing of application; hearing via video conferencing; and the number of forms has been cut down to 8 from the existing around 75 forms.

Trademark Classes

Trademark law 2002, suggests that trademark can be registered in India under the following classes:

- Class 1: Chemical used in industry, science, photography, agriculture, horticulture and forestry; unprocessed artificial resins, unprocessed plastics; manures; fire extinguishing compositions; tempering and soldering preparations; chemical substances for preserving foodstuffs; tanning substances; adhesive used in industry
- Class 2: Paints, varnishes, lacquers; preservatives against rust and against deterioration of wood; colorants; mordents; raw natural resins; metals in foil and powder form for painters; decorators; printers and artists
- Class 3: Bleaching preparations and other substances for laundry use; cleaning; polishing; scouring and abrasive preparations; soaps; perfumery, essential oils, cosmetics, hair lotions, dentifrices
- Class 4: Industrial oils and greases; lubricants; dust absorbing, wetting and binding compositions; fuels(including motor spirit) and illuminants; candles, wicks
- Class 5: Pharmaceutical, veterinary and sanitary preparations; dietetic substances adapted for medical use, food for babies; plasters, materials for dressings; materials for stopping teeth, dental wax; disinfectants; preparation for destroying vermin; fungicides, herbicides
- Class 6: Common metals and their alloys; metal building materials; transportable buildings of metal; materials of metal for railway tracks; non-electric cables and wires of common metal; ironmongery, small items of metal hardware; pipes and tubes of metal; safes; goods of common metal not included in other classes; ores
- Class 7: Machines and machine tools; motors and engines (except for land vehicles); machine coupling and transmission components (except for land vehicles); agricultural implements other than hand-operated; incubators for eggs
- Class 8: Hand tools and implements (hand-operated); cutlery; side arms; razors
- Class 9: Scientific, nautical, surveying, electric, photographic, cinematographic, optical, weighing, measuring, signalling, checking (supervision), life saving and

teaching apparatus and instruments; apparatus for recording, transmission or reproduction of sound or images; magnetic data carriers, recording discs; automatic vending machines and mechanisms for coin-operated apparatus; cash registers, calculating machines, data processing equipment and computers; fire extinguishing apparatus

- Class 10: Surgical, medical, dental and veterinary apparatus and instruments, artificial limbs, eyes and teeth; orthopaedic articles; suture materials
- Class 11: Apparatus for lighting, heating, steam generating, cooking, refrigerating, drying ventilating, water supply and sanitary purposes
- Class 12: Vehicles; apparatus for locomotion by land, air or water
- Class 13: Firearms; ammunition and projectiles; explosives; fire works
- Class 14: Precious metals and their alloys and goods in precious metals or coated therewith, not included in other classes; jewellery, precious stones; horological and other chronometric instruments
- Class 15: Musical instruments
- Class 16: Paper, cardboard and goods made from these materials, not included in other classes; printed matter; bookbinding material; photographs; stationery; adhesives for stationery or household purposes; artists' materials; paint brushes; typewriters and office requisites (except furniture); instructional and teaching material (except apparatus); plastic materials for packaging (not included in other classes); playing cards; printers' type; printing blocks
- Class 17: Rubber, gutta percha, gum, asbestos, mica and goods made from these materials and not included in other classes; plastics in extruded form for use in manufacture; packing, stopping and insulating materials; flexible pipes, not of metal
- Class 18: Leather and imitations of leather, and goods made of these materials and not included in other classes; animal skins, hides, trunks and travelling bags; umbrellas, parasols and walking sticks; whips, harness and saddlery
- Class 19: Building materials, (non-metallic), non-metallic rigid pipes for building; asphalt, pitch and bitumen; non-metallic transportable buildings; monuments, not of metal.
- Class 20: Furniture, mirrors, picture frames; goods(not included in other classes) of wood, cork, reed, cane, wicker, horn, bone, ivory, whalebone, shell, amber, mother- of-pearl, meerschaum and substitutes for all these materials, or of plastics
- Class 21: Household or kitchen utensils and containers(not of precious metal or coated therewith); combs and sponges; brushes(except paints brushes); brush making materials; articles for cleaning purposes; steelwool; unworked or semi-

worked glass (except glass used in building); glassware, porcelain and earthenware not included in other classes

- Class 22: Ropes, string, nets, tents, awnings, tarpaulins, sails, sacks and bags (not included in other classes) padding and stuffing materials(except of rubber or plastics); raw fibrous textile materials
- Class 23: Yarns and threads, for textile use
- Class 24: Textiles and textile goods, not included in other classes; bed and table covers.
- Class 25: Clothing, footwear, headgear
- Class 26: Lace and embroidery, ribbons and braid; buttons, hooks and eyes, pins and needles; artificial flowers
- Class 27: Carpets, rugs, mats and matting, linoleum and other materials for covering existing floors; wall hangings(non-textile)
- Class 28: Games and playthings, gymnastic and sporting articles not included in other classes; decorations for Christmas trees
- Class 29: Meat, fish, poultry and game; meat extracts; preserved, dried and cooked fruits and vegetables; jellies, jams, fruit sauces; eggs, milk and milk products; edible oils and fats
- Class 30: Coffee, tea, cocoa, sugar, rice, tapioca, sago, artificial coffee; flour and preparations made from cereals, bread, pastry and confectionery, ices; honey, treacle; yeast, baking powder; salt, mustard; vinegar, sauces, (condiments); spices; ice
- Class 31: Agricultural, horticultural and forestry products and grains not included in other classes; live animals; fresh fruits and vegetables; seeds, natural plants and flowers; foodstuffs for animals, malt
- Class 32: Beers, mineral and aerated waters, and other non-alcoholic drinks; fruit drinks and fruit juices; syrups and other preparations for making beverages
- Class 33: Alcoholic beverages(except beers)
- Class 34: Tobacco, smokers' articles, matches
- Class 35: Advertising, business management, business administration, office functions.
- Class 36: Insurance, financial affairs; monetary affairs; real estate affairs.
- Class 37: Building construction; repair; installation services.
- Class 38: Telecommunications.
- Class 39: Transport; packaging and storage of goods; travel arrangement.

- Class 40: Treatment of materials.
- Class 41: Education; providing of training; entertainment; sporting and cultural activities.
- Class 42: Scientific and technological services and research and design relating thereto; industrial analysis and research services; design and development of computer hardware and software.
- Class 43: Services for providing food and drink; temporary accommodation.
- Class 44: Medical services, veterinary services, hygienic and beauty care for human beings or animals; agriculture, horticulture and forestry services.
- Class 45: Legal services; security services for the protection of property and individuals; personal and social services rendered by others to meet the needs of individuals.

Indian Patent Office

The Office of the Controller General of Patents, Designs and Trade Marks (CGPDTM) generally known as the Indian Patent Office, is an agency under the Department for Promotion of Industry and Internal Trade which administers the Indian law of Patents, Designs and Trade Marks.

Foundation

On 28 February 1856, the Government of India promulgated legislation to grant what was then termed as "exclusive privileges for the encouragement of inventions of new manufactures". On 3 March 1856, a civil engineer, George Alfred DePenning of 7, Grant's Lane, Calcutta petitioned the Government of India for grant of exclusive privileges for his invention — "An Efficient Punkah Pulling Machine". On 2 September, DePenning, submitted the Specifications for his invention along with drawings to illustrate its working. These were accepted and the invention was granted the first ever Intellectual Property protection in India.

Amendments to the Patents Act & Rules

Amendments (in 1999, 2002, 2005) were necessitated by India's obligations under TRIPS, allowing product patents in drugs and chemicals. A pre-grant representation in addition to the existing post-grant opposition has been re-introduced. A provision of later amendments was on software patent-ability, which was later withdrawn in another amendment in 2005. The amendment in 2012 focused on change in marks of Patent Agent Examination.

Indian Patent Rules were amended in 2003, 2005, 2006, 2012, 2013, 2014, 2016, 2018, 2019 and 2020. The 2006 amendment of rules introduced reduced time lines and a fee structure based on specification size and number of claims, in addition to a basic fee.

Indian Patent amendment rules 2012 was for amendments in criteria for patent agent exam qualification. Gazette Notification of Patent (Amendments) Rules 2013 has made necessary provisions for recognising Patent office as Examining authority and Searching authority on international level for filing, searching and examination of patent along with necessary fees. Patent amendment rules 2014 introduced a third category of applicant for small entities and revised the basic fee for filing a patent application. Patent amendment rule 2016 implemented on 16 May 2016, and introduced such as electronic communication to applicant/agent, and applicant can withdrawn their application using Form-29, and majorly introduced for the expedited examination for startup companies, and the timeline to put the grant of applicant has been reduced from 12 months to 6 months. In addition, video conference has been introduced for hearing the patent matters. Patent amendment rules 2019 introduced a patent agent shall submit all documents only by electronic transmission duly authenticated. Further, fee reductions for small entity, and fast track examination for specific applicants including female were introduced in 2019.

Patent Administration

The CGPDTM reports to the Department for Promotion of Industry and Internal Trade (DPIIT) under the Ministry of Commerce and Industry and has five main administrative sections:

- Patent Office
- Designs Registry
- Trademarks Registry
- Geographical indications Registry
- Rajiv Gandhi National Institute of Intellectual Property Management (NIIPM)
- Patent Information System

The patent office is headquartered at Kolkata with branches in Chennai, New Delhi and Mumbai, but the office of the CGPDTM is in Mumbai. The office of the Patent Information System and National Institute for Intellectual Property Management is at Nagpur. The Controller General (CG), who supervises the administration of the Patents Act, the Designs Act, and the Trade Marks Act, also advises the Government on matters relating to these subjects. Shri. Unnat P. Pandit is the current CG and took charge on April 2022. Under the office of CGPDTM, a Geographical Indications Registry has been established in Chennai to administer the Geographical Indications of Goods (Registration and Protection) Act, 1999.

The Indian Patent Office has 526 Patent Examiners, 97 Assistant Controllers, 42 Deputy Controllers, 1 Joint Controller, and 1 Senior Joint Controller, all of whom operate from four branches. Although the designations of the Controllers differ, all of them (with the exception of the Controller General) have equal authority in administering the Patents Act. An Indian Patent Examiner is mandated to search for prior art and for objections under any other ground as provided in the Patent's Act, then to report to the Controller, who has the power to either accept or reject Examiners' reports. Unlike the system at the USPTO /EPO/JPO, Examiners at IPO have only recommending power and the controllers are empowered by statute either to accept or refuse their recommendations. Examiners' reports to the Controller are not open to the public unless courts allow it (section 144 of the Patents Act). A Parliamentary committee has recommended repealing S144.

Patent Duration

Term of every patent in India is 20 years from the date of filing of patent application, irrespective of whether it is filed with provisional or complete specification. However, in case of applications filed under PCT the term of 20 years begins from the International filing date accorded under PCT.

Since the rights granted by an Indian Patent Office extends only throughout the territory of the India and ceases to have effect in a foreign country, an inventor who wishes patent protection in another country must apply for a patent in a specific country (according to its law) either through :PCT route or through conventional filing of application.

Patent Renewal and Restoration of Lapsed Patent

In order to keep the patent rights for the entire period, India's Patent Act has made it mandatory for the patent holders to pay a renewal fee. Once the patent is granted the patentee does not need to pay a renewal or maintenance fee for the first two years. The first renewal fee will be payable from the third year onwards. The patentee is also given a choice to pay the whole fees at a time or they can pay it every year. If in case the patent is not renewed by the company or individual, the patent ceases to exist and will be moved to the public domain. Once the subject matter that has been patented enters the public domain it is no longer protected and can be used by anyone without facing any suit or consequences of patent infringement.

Restoration of a lapsed patent is relatively time taking and a complex procedure. According to Section 60 of The Patents Act, 1970, an application for the restoration of the patent can be made by the patentee or their legal representative and the petition should be applied to the controller at the Indian Patent Office (IPO) within eighteen months from the date at which the patent ceases to have an effect. However, the application should contain a statement which states the reason behind the failure in paying the renewal fees and evidence which can be in the form of a letter, copy of documents or a deed. The applicant should also be ready to submit additional evidence regarding the same if asked by the controller. After examining all the information provided by the applicant, if the controller feels that the reason and the evidence provided by the applicant imply towards unintentional failure to pay the renewal fees then he/ she would publish the application and any person can oppose the restoration application within the prescribed period by filling form 14 and paying a fee. If in case the opposition gives a notice during the prescribed period then the controller would notify the applicant about the same and would give an opportunity to both the applicant and the controller to present their respective arguments before deciding the case. If no notice is given by the opposition or if the decision of the controller is in favor of the applicant if in case of the opposition, then upon payment of any unpaid additional and renewal fee the patent is restored.

Geographical Indications

India, as a member of the World Trade Organization (WTO), enacted the Geographical Indications of Goods (Registration & Protection) Act, 1999 has come into force with effect from 15 September 2003. GIs have been defined under Article 22(1) of the WTO Agreement on Trade-Related Aspects of Intellectual Property Rights (TRIPS) Agreement as: "Indications which identify a good as originating in the territory of a member, or a region or a locality in that territory, where a given quality, reputation or characteristic of the good is essentially attributable to its geographic origin."

The GI tag ensures that none other than those registered as authorised users (or at least those residing inside the geographic territory) are allowed to use the popular product name. In 2004–05, Darjeeling tea became the first GI tagged product in India and since then by July 2012, 178 had been added to the list.

Modernisation

The Indian Patent Office has implemented a modernisation program according to an Indian govt website. And according to this website "Efforts have been made to improve the working of the Patent Offices within the resources available and that the problem of backlog is also being attacked through 50% higher monthly target for disposal of patent applications per Examiner". E- Filing of Patents & Trademarks is made possible and according to an Indian Minister the first phase of the modernisation comes to an end and the Indian Patent office wishes to be an International search Authority. The second phase of modernisation has been proposed with the aim of achieving US patent examination efficiency among others. Patent filings during the year 2007–08 were 35218.

Criticism

As per an Indian patent attorney, patents which were beyond the Act were granted by the office. The Indian Patent office had an unusually high grant rate for the year 2005–06 in respect of numbers of refused patent applications compared to other major patent offices. The monthly target for Indian examiners is 30 new and amended applications per month and the Indian Patent Office strictly has only 12 months to grant/refuse the application as compared to foreign patent offices where applicants can extend the final date indefinitely. Knowledge commission, an Indian Government appointed body has recommended measures regarding the functioning of the office.

The controversial promotion of examiners as assistant controllers has led to an imbalance in the set-up with more controllers than examiners. Controller General had promised time-bound promotions to officers and recruitment of new examiners to mitigate the crisis of lack of officers and the problem of attrition due to low pay and lack of promotion. Cases of corruption have been reported. In 2012, only 137 out of the announced 257 candidates expressed interest to join. The monthly target for examiners are 15 new cases(FERs) and 25 disposals which has led to officers working under tremendous pressure to show output thereby affecting the quality of grant of patents. Indian patent examiners have the higher workload and the pay is amongst the lowest. While a patent examiner in the European Patent Office would handle less than seven patent applications per month and a USPTO examiner would handle eight applications per month, an Indian examiner reportedly handles at least 40 applications a month. However an Indian examiner's monthly salary is less than a third of his/her counterparts in other foreign patent offices. The issue of attrition due to lack of promotion to examiners was acknowledged by the Minister of Commerce and Industry Nirmala Sitharaman during IP day celebrations. A concerned government official recommended outsourcing of search in view of increased work load and the IPO has started to outsource prior-art searches violating the stipulations of the prevailing Patents Act. However, because of quality and legal issues with outsourcing, the outsourcing contracts were cancelled. The Department of Industrial Policy & Promotion under the Ministry of commerce, Government of India has come out with a discussion paper in order to address the issues plaguing the Indian Patent Office such as granting financial and administrative autonomy, separation of Patent and Trademark offices, setting up of additional offices are some of the issues put forth for input from stakeholders.

Accessibility

The IP Office's systems and processes in India have been under scrutiny for their lack of accessibility. They currently do not fully comply with the GIGW 3.0 guidelines and the BIS Standard (IS 17802). Persons with disabilities using screen readers encounter challenges when attempting to access the IP office online systems.

On 29th November 2021, Dr. Kalyan C. Kankanala, a Patent & Trademark Attorney with Blindness, initiated legal action against this issue by filing a Writ petition in the Karnataka High Court. His petition emphasized the need for the IP office's systems to be made accessible to persons with disabilities, ensuring that documents and emails are available in formats compatible with screen readers. The case has been registered as W.P. No. 21978/2021.

In response to the concerns raised by Dr. Kalyan and the legal proceedings, the Office of Controller General of Patents, Designs & Trademarks (O/o CGPDTM) issued the Guidelines for Accessibility and Reasonable Accommodations for Persons with Disabilities on 4th March, 2022. These guidelines underscore their dedication to enhancing accessibility and providing reasonable accommodations for Persons with Disabilities practicing and interacting with IP Offices under O/o CGPDTM.

Authority

The Intellectual Property India is administered by the Office of the Controller General of Patents, Designs & Trade Marks (CGPDTM). This is a subordinate office of the Government of India and administers the Indian law of Patents, Designs, Trade Marks and Geographical Indications.

Cable Television Network (Regulation) Act 1995

Object of the Act

The object of the Act was to regulate the 'haphazard mushrooming of cable television networks'. Due to the lack of licensing mechanism for cable operators; this resulted in large number of cable operators, broadcasting programmes without any regulation. The Act aimed at regulating content and operation of cable networks. This was due to the availability of signals from foreign television networks via satellite communication. The access to foreign television networks was considered to be a "cultural invasion" as these channels portrayed western culture. It also wanted to lay down the "responsibilities and obligations in respect of the quality of service both technically as well content wise, use of materials protected under the copyright law, exhibition of uncertified films, and protection of subscribers from anti-national broadcasts from sources inimical to national interests".

There were three amendments made to the Act. The Act is divided into five chapters. The first chapter discusses the scope and extent of the Act and meaning of the terms used in the Act. The second chapter deals with "Regulation of Cable Television Network". The third chapter relates to "Seizure and Confiscation of certain Equipments". The fourth chapter focuses on "Offences and Penalties". The fifth chapter covers other miscellaneous provisions.

Regulation of Cable Television Network

The regulation of cable television network under the Act is ensured through a two step process. In order to keep track of cable operators, it has mandate a compulsory registration for cable operators. It also lays down provisions to regulate content to be broadcasted by the cable operator.

Registration of Cable Operators

In order to regulate cable television networks, it was made mandatory for cable television network operators to be registered. Procedure for registration is laid down is section 5 of the Act. Any person who is operating or desires to operate a cable network may apply for registration to the registering authority.

An application for registration of cable operator has to be made under Form 1 along with the payment of fees of Rs.50 to the head post master within whose territorial jurisdiction the office of cable operator is situated. The registration certificate which is issued by the registering authority after inspection is valid for 12 months and can be renewed.

The registering authority may also refuse the registration of a cable operator. The reason for such refusal has to be recorded in writing and communicated to the applicant.

Section 4A was inserted into the Act by the TRAI (Amendment) Act, 2002. Section 4A deals with "transmission of programmes through addressable system". [Refer to section on "2003- Amendment to the Cable Television Networks (Regulation) Act, 1995 (Amendment Act)"].

Content Regulation

The Central Government, in public interest can put an obligation on every cable operator to transmit or retransmit a programme of any pay channel through addressable system. In public interest the central government may also 'specify one or more free-to-air channels to be included in the package of channels' (basic service tier). The Central Government may also, in public interest specify the maximum amount which can be charged by the operator to the subscriber for receiving the programmes transmitted in the basic service tier provided by such cable operators. The cable operators have to publicize to subscribers the subscription rates of each pay channel at regular intervals.

Sections 5 and 6 of the Act deal with advertisement code and programme code. All cable services should be in conformity with the codes. Under section 7, cable operators have to maintain a register as to the content transmitted or retransmitted. All cable operators shall compulsorily re-transmit Doordarshan channels.

Section 9 of the Act mandates 'use of standard equipment in cable television network'. It is the duty of the cable operator to make sure that the cable television networks do not interfere with authorized telecommunication systems.

Offences and Penalties

Section 11 gives power to the authorized government authority to seize any cable operator's equipment, if such officer has reason to believe that the cable operator is using the equipment without proper registration.

Sections 16, 17 and 18 of the Act deal with offences under the Act. They lay down punishments for any act which is in contravention with the provisions of the Act.

Section 16:

- Ingredients of the Offence: Anyone who is held to be in violation of the provisions of this Act
- Penalty/ Fine: For the first offence: Imprisonment for a term which may extend to 2 years or with fine which may extend to Rs. 1000 or with both. For every subsequent offence: Imprisonment for a term which may extend to 5 years and with fine which may extend to Rs. 5000.

Section 17 deals with when an offence under this Act is committed by a company; in this case the person in charge will be liable. The Act also gives power to the authorized officer[4] to prohibit the transmission of certain programmes in public interest under section 19 of the Act.

Under section 20 of the Act, the Central Government in public interest may prohibit the operation cable television network. The Central Government may make such an order in the interest of the (i) sovereignty and integrity of India; or (ii) security of India; or (iii) friendly relations of India with any foreign state; or (iv) public order, decency or morality.

2003- Amendment to the Cable Television Networks (Regulation) Act, 1995 (Amendment Act)

Numerous complaints were received by the Government stating that there has been unreasonable price hike in cable television by the cable operators. Moreover, the cable operator were not paying appropriate revenue by concealing there income and under-reporting their income. The cable operators defended themselves by stating that the broadcasting industry is unregulated and they are forced to increase the price for proving cable television services as the broadcasting companies can increase the charges as per their wish. In order to address these problems, the government appointed a specialized task force.

Special task force in its study noted that the consumers do not have the choice to select the premium channels they wanted to watch rather it is provided to them in a bundle irrespective of the fact they want to subscribe to such channel or not. In order to give choice to the consumer it recommended the introduction of conditional access systems (CAS). This would require the consumers to set up set-top boxes which will allow the consumers to view all the free to air channel and he can choose to watch any of the premier channels for a charge.

This recommendation of the task force was introduced through the 2003 amendment to the Act. The main objective of the Amendment Act was to address to the frequent and arbitrary increase in cable charges. This was introduced section 4A which allowed operators to transmit pay channels through an addressable system apart from basic package of free-to-air channels.

There was a lot controversy with respect to implementation of the CAS. In order to explain the controversy, it is important to understand the structure of the cable market. The cable market is divided into three categories. Broadcasters, who are at the top of the pyramid, the Multi-System Operators are in the middle and the local cable operators are at the bottom of the pyramid.

The 2003 Amendment introduced to CAS was welcomed by the broadcasters and the MSOs. But the consumer and the local cable service providers were unhappy with this decision because the consumers feared that they have to pay special rates for pay channels whereas the local operators were outraged because they believed that CAS would affect their revenue. Due to the adverse reaction from the consumers and the local cable operator, the government delayed the implementation of CAS indefinitely. This finally culminated in a case before the Delhi High Court.

The Delhi High Court decided that implementation of CAS cannot be delayed. Subsequently to this, the government announced in 2004 that Telecom Regulatory Authority of India (TRAI) will be handling the problems regarding CAS and make recommendations on the same. TRAI recommended that CAS should be denotified and it can be re-introduced later when there is adequate regulation to properly implement it.

The government on the recommendation of TRAI withdrew the implementation of CAS. However, this decision was faced with a new challenge and this time the single judge bench of the Delhi High Court held that the Government does not have any ground to suspend the CAS and it has disregarded the previous decision of the Delhi High Court in *Jay Polychem* case. Finally, the government re-introduced CAS but after issuing rules as to its working and implementation.

Information Technology Act 2000 and Cyber Laws

Information Technology Act 2000

The Information Technology Act, 2000 (also known as ITA-2000, or the IT Act) is an Act of the Indian Parliament (No 21 of 2000) notified on 17 October 2000. It is the primary law in India dealing with cybercrime and electronic commerce. Secondary or subordinate legislation to the IT Act includes the Intermediary Guidelines Rules 2011 and the Information Technology (Intermediary Guidelines and Digital Media Ethics Code) Rules, 2021.

Background

The bill was passed in the budget session of 2000 and signed by President K. R. Narayanan on 9 May 2000. The bill was finalised by a group of officials headed by the Minister of Information Technology Pramod Mahajan.

Summary

The original Act contained 94 sections, divided into 13 chapters and 4 schedules out of which the third schedule and fourth schedule are omitted.The laws apply to the whole of India. If a crime involves a computer or network located in India, persons of other nationalities can also be indicted under the law, .

The Act provides a legal framework for electronic governance by giving recognition to electronic records and digital signatures. It also defines cyber crimes and prescribes penalties for them. The Act directed the formation of a Controller of Certifying Authorities to regulate the issuance of digital signatures. It also established a Cyber Appellate Tribunal to resolve disputes rising from this new law. The Act also amended various sections of the Indian Penal Code, 1860, the Indian Evidence Act, 1872, the Banker's Book Evidence

Act, 1891, and the Reserve Bank of India Act, 1934 to make them compliant with new technologies.

Amendments

A major amendment was made in 2008. It introduced Section 66A which penalized sending "offensive messages". It also introduced Section 69, which gave authorities the power of "interception or monitoring or decryption of any information through any computer resource".

Additionally, it introduced provisions addressing - pornography, child porn, cyber terrorism and voyeurism. The amendment was passed on 22 December 2008 without any debate in Lok Sabha. The next day it was passed by the Rajya Sabha. It was signed into law by President Pratibha Patil, on 5 February 2009.

Offences

List of offences and the corresponding penalties:

Section 65:

- Tampering with computer source documents
- Imprisonment up to three years, or/and with fine up to ₹ 2,00,000

Section 66:

- Hacking with computer system
- Imprisonment up to three years, or/and with fine up to ₹ 5,00,000

Section 66B:

- Receiving stolen computer or communication device
- Imprisonment up to three years, or/and with fine up to ₹ 1,00,000

Section 66C:

- Using password of another person
- Imprisonment up to three years, or/and with fine up to ₹ 1,00,000

Section 66D :

- Cheating using computer resource
- Imprisonment up to three years, or/and with fine up to ₹ 1,00,000

Section 66E :

- Publishing private images of others
- Imprisonment up to three years, or/and with fine up to ₹ 2,00,000

Section 66F :

- Acts of cyberterrorism
- Imprisonment up to life.

Section 67 :

- Publishing information which is obscene in electronic form.
- Imprisonment up to five years, or/and with fine up to [1] 10,00,000

Section 67A :

- Publishing images containing sexual acts
- Imprisonment up to seven years, or/and with fine up to [1] 10,00,000

Section 67C :

- Failure to maintain records
- Imprisonment up to three years, or/and with fine.

Section 68 :

- Failure/refusal to comply with orders
- Imprisonment up to 2 years, or/and with fine up to [1] 1,00,000

Section 69 :

- Failure/refusal to decrypt data
- Imprisonment up to seven years and possible fine.

Section 70 :

- Securing access or attempting to secure access to a protected system
- Imprisonment up to ten years, or/and with fine.

Section 71 :

- Misrepresentation
- Imprisonment up to 2 years, or/and with fine up to [1] 1,00,000

Section 72 :

- Breach of confidentiality and privacy
- Imprisonment up to 2 years, or/and with fine up to [1] 1,00,000

Section 72A :

- Disclosure of information in breach of lawful contract
- Imprisonment up to 3 years, or/and with fine up to [1] 5,00,000

Section 73 :

- Publishing electronic signature certificate false in certain particulars
- Imprisonment up to 2 years, or/and with fine up to [1] 1,00,000

Section 74 :

- Publication for fraudulent purpose
- Imprisonment up to 2 years, or/and with fine up to [1] 1,00,000

Notable Cases

Section 66

- In February 2001, in one of the first cases, the Delhi police arrested two men running a web-hosting company. The company had shut down a website over non-payment of dues. The owner of the site had claimed that he had already paid and complained to the police. The Delhi police had charged the men for hacking under Section 66 of the IT Act and breach of trust under Section 408 of the Indian Penal Code. The two men had to spend 6 days in Tihar jail waiting for bail.
- In February 2017, A Delhi based Ecommerce Portal made a Complaint with Hauz Khas Police Station against some hackers from different cities accusing them for IT Act / Theft / Cheating / Misappropriation / Criminal Conspiracy / Criminal Breach of Trust / Cyber Crime of Hacking / Snooping / Tampering with Computer source documents and the Web Site and extending the threats of dire consequences to employees, as a result four hackers were arrested by South Delhi Police for Digital Shoplifting.

Section 66A

- In September 2012, a freelance cartoonist Aseem Trivedi was arrested under the Section 66A of the IT Act, Section 2 of Prevention of Insults to National Honour Act, 1971 and for sedition under the Section 124 of the Indian Penal Code. His cartoons depicting widespread corruption in India were considered offensive.
- On 12 April 2012, a Chemistry professor from Jadavpur University, Ambikesh Mahapatra, was arrested for sharing a cartoon of West Bengal Chief Minister Mamata Banerjee and then Railway Minister Mukul Roy. The email was sent from the email address of a housing society. Subrata Sengupta, the secretary of the housing society, was also arrested. They were charged under Section 66A and B of the IT Act, for defamation under Sections 500, for obscene gesture to a woman under Section 509, and abetting a crime under Section 114 of the Indian Penal Code.

- On 30 October 2012, a Puducherry businessman Ravi Srinivasan was arrested under Section 66A. He had sent tweet accusing Karti Chidambaram, son of then Finance Minister P. Chidambaram, of corruption. Karti Chidambaram had complained to the police.
- On 19 November 2012, a 21-year-old girl was arrested from Palghar for posting a message on Facebook criticising the shutdown in Mumbai for the funeral of Bal Thackeray. Another 20-year-old girl was arrested for "liking" the post. They were initially charged under Section 295A of the Indian Penal Code (hurting religious sentiments) and Section 66A of the IT Act. Later, Section 295A was replaced by Section 505(2) (promoting enmity between classes). A group of Shiv Sena workers vandalised a hospital run by the uncle of one of girls. On 31 January 2013, a local court dropped all charges against the girls.
- On 18 March 2015, a teenaged boy was arrested from Bareilly, Uttar Pradesh, for making a post on Facebook insulting politician Azam Khan. The post allegedly contained hate speech against a community and was falsely attributed to Azam Khan by the boy. He was charged under Section 66A of the IT Act, and Sections 153A (promoting enmity between different religions), 504 (intentional insult with intent to provoke breach of peace) and 505 (public mischief) of Indian Penal Code. After the Section 66A was repealed on 24 March, the state government said that they would continue the prosecution under the remaining charges.

Section 69A

- On 29 June 2020, the Indian Government banned 59 Chinese mobile apps, most notably TikTok, supported by Section 69A and citing national security interests.
- On 24 November 2020, another 43 Chinese mobile apps were banned supported by the same reasoning, most notably AliExpress.
- 54 more apps including popular video game Garena Free Fire were banned on 14 February 2022 under the same section.

Future Changes

On 2 April 2015, the Chief Minister of Maharashtra, Devendra Fadnavis revealed to the state assembly that a new law was being framed to replace the repealed Section 66A. Fadnavis was replying to a query Shiv Sena leader Neelam Gorhe. Gorhe had said that repeal of the law would encourage online miscreants and asked whether the state government would frame a law to this regard. Fadnavis said that the previous law had resulted in no convictions, so the law would be framed such that it would be strong and result in convictions. On 13 April 2015, it announced that the Ministry of Home Affairs would form a committee of officials from the Intelligence Bureau, Central Bureau of

Investigation, National Investigation Agency, Delhi Police and ministry itself to produce a new legal framework. This step was reportedly taken after complaints from intelligence agencies that, they were no longer able to counter online posts that involved national security matter or incite people to commit an offence, such as online recruitment for ISIS. Former Minister of State with the Ministry of Information Technology, Milind Deora has supported a new "unambiguous section to replace 66A".

In 2022, it was reported of a proposal to replace the Information Technology Act with a more comprehensive and updated Digital India Act, which would cover a wider range of information technology issues and concerns. This law could ostensibly have focal areas around privacy, social media regulation, regulation of over-the-top platforms, internet intermediaries, introducing additional contraventions or offences and governance of new technologies.

Importance of the Information Technology Act

The Indian government closely connects data to citizens' privacy and this is demonstrated when Shiv Shankar Singh states, "Each person must be able to exercise a substantial degree of control over that data and its use. Data protection is legal safeguard to prevent misuse of information about individual person on a medium including computers."

Secondary Legislation

The Information Technology (Intermediary Guidelines and Digital Media Ethics Code) Rules, 2021 suppresses India's Intermediary Guidelines Rules 2011.

Cyber Laws

Cyber laws in India encompass a range of legal provisions and regulations that govern activities conducted in the digital realm. These laws are designed to address various aspects of cybercrime, data protection, electronic transactions, and online behavior. Here are some of the key cyber laws in India:

- Information Technology Act, 2000 (IT Act): The IT Act is the primary legislation governing electronic transactions and digital communication in India. It provides legal recognition to electronic records and digital signatures and establishes mechanisms to regulate electronic commerce and online activities.
- Amendments to the IT Act (2008, 2017): The IT Act has undergone amendments to strengthen provisions related to data protection, privacy, and cybersecurity. Notable amendments include the introduction of Section 66A (later struck down by the Supreme Court), Section 66B (punishment for dishonestly receiving stolen computer resources or communication devices), and Section 66C (punishment for identity theft).
- Information Technology (Intermediary Guidelines and Digital Media Ethics

Code) Rules, 2021: These rules provide a framework for the regulation of digital intermediaries, social media platforms, and digital content publishers. They require platforms to implement measures for content removal, user verification, and grievance redressal, among other obligations.

- Indian Cyber Crime Coordination Centre (I4C): The I4C was established to act as a central agency for coordinating efforts to combat cybercrime in India. It plays a crucial role in the prevention, detection, and investigation of cybercrimes.
- National Critical Information Infrastructure Protection Centre (NCIIPC): The NCIIPC is responsible for protecting critical information infrastructure in India. It formulates and enforces policies and procedures to secure critical information systems.
- Data Protection Laws (Draft Personal Data Protection Bill, 2019): Though not yet enacted, the Personal Data Protection Bill aims to regulate the processing and handling of personal data in India. It includes provisions related to consent, data localization, and rights of data subjects.
- Cybercrime Investigation Cells: Various states in India have established specialized cells and units within law enforcement agencies to investigate cybercrimes. These units work in tandem with central agencies to combat cyber threats.
- Cyber Appellate Tribunal (CAT): The CAT was established to adjudicate disputes related to cyber laws and provide a forum for hearing appeals against orders issued by adjudicating officers under the IT Act. However, it was dissolved in 2017, and appeals now go directly to the respective High Courts.
- Cyber Security and Incident Response Teams (CSIRTs): CSIRTs are specialized teams tasked with monitoring, detecting, and responding to cyber threats. They play a crucial role in maintaining cybersecurity within the country.
- International Cooperation and Treaties: India actively participates in international efforts to combat cybercrime and has entered into bilateral and multilateral agreements for cooperation in cyber investigations and cybersecurity.

Cinematograph Act 1952 and Film Censorship

Cinematograph Act 1952

The Central Board of Film Certification (CBFC) is a statutory film-certification body in the Ministry of Information and Broadcasting of the Government of India. It is tasked with "regulating the public exhibition of films under the provisions of the Cinematograph Act 1952." The Cinematograph Act 1952 outlines a strict certification process for commercial films shown in public venues. Films screened in cinemas and on television may only be publicly exhibited in India after certification by the board and edited.

Certificates and Guidelines

The board currently issues four certificates. Originally, there were two: U (unrestricted public exhibition with family-friendly movies) and A (restricted to adult audiences but any kind of nudity not allowed). Two more were added in June U/A (unrestricted public exhibition, with parental guidance for children under 12) and S (restricted to specialised audiences, such as doctors or scientists). The board may refuse to certify a film. Additionally, V/U, V/UA, V/A are used for video releases with U, U/A and A carrying the same meaning as above.

U Certificate

Films with the U certification are fit for unrestricted public exhibition and are family-friendly. These films can contain universal themes like education, family, drama, romance, sci-fi, action etc. These films can also contain some mild violence, but it cannot be prolonged. It may also contain very mild sexual scenes (without any traces of nudity or sexual detail).

U/A Certificate

Films with the U/A certification can contain moderate adult themes that are not strong in nature and are not considered appropriate to be watched by a child below 12 years of age with parental guidance. These films may contain moderate to strong violence, moderate sexual scenes (traces of nudity and moderate sexual detail can be found), frightening scenes, blood flow, or muted abusive language. Sometimes such films are re-certified with V/U for video viewing.

A Certificate

Films with the A certification are available for public exhibition, but with restriction to adults (aged 18+). These films can contain violence, explicit and strong sexual scenes, abusive language, but words which insult or degrade women or any social group and nudity are not allowed. Some controversial and adult themes are considered unsuitable for young viewers. Such films are often re-certified with V/U and V/UA for TV and video viewing, which does not happen in case of U and U/A certified movies.

S Certificate

Films with S certification cannot be viewed by the public. Only people associated with it (doctors, scientists, etc.), are permitted to view these films.

History

The Indian Cinematograph Act came into effect in 1920, seven years after the production of India's first film: Dadasaheb Phalke's *Raja Harishchandra*. Censorship boards were originally independent bodies under the police chiefs of the cities of Madras (now Chennai), Bombay (now Mumbai), Calcutta (now Kolkata), Lahore (now in Pakistan), and Rangoon (now Yangon in Myanmar) it was amended again on 1st august 2023 with the introduction of cinematography amendment bill. the bill awaits presidential assent

After the 1947 independence of India, autonomous regional censors were absorbed into the Bombay Board of Film Censors. The Cinematograph Act of 1952 reorganised the Bombay board into the Central Board of Film Censors. With the 1983 revision of cinematography rules, the body was renamed the Central Board of Film Certification.

In 2021 the Film Certification Appellate Tribunal (FCAT) was scrapped by the Indian government.

Principles

The board's guiding principles are to ensure healthy public entertainment and education and, using modern technology, to make the certification process and board activities transparent to filmmakers, the media and the public also every video have to undergo CBFC certification for telecasting or distributing over any platform in India and suggestible same standards for anywhere in the world.

Refusal to Certify

In addition to the certifications above, there is also the possibility of the board refusing to certify the film at all. The board's guidelines are:

- Anti-social activities (such as violence) may not be glorified
- Criminal acts may not be depicted
- The following is prohibited:

oInvolvement of children in violent acts or abuse

oAbuse or ridicule of the physically or mentally handicapped

oUnnecessary depictions of cruelty to animals

- Gratuitous violence, cruelty, or horror
- No scenes encouraging alcohol consumption, drug addiction or smoking
- No vulgarity, obscenity, depravity, double entendres or scenes degrading women, including sexual violence (as much as possible)
- No denigration by race, religion or other social group
- No promotion of sectarian, obscurantist, anti-scientific and anti-national attitudes
- Relations with foreign countries should not be affected.
- No national symbols or emblems, except in accordance with the Emblems and Names (Prevention of Improper Use) Act, 1950 (12 of 1950)

Enforcement

Since 2004, censorship has been rigorously enforced. An incident was reported in which exhibitor staff – a clerk who sold the ticket, the usher who allowed minors to sit, a theatre manager and the partners of the theatre complex – were arrested for non-compliance with certification rules.

Composition and Leadership

The board consists of a chairperson and 23 members, all of whom are appointed by the central government. Prasoon Joshi chairs the board; Joshi became its 28th chairperson on 11 August 2017, after Pahlaj Nihalani was fired. Nihalani had succeeded Leela Samson after Samson quit in protest of an appellate tribunal's overturning of a board decision to refuse certification for *MSG: The Messenger*. Samson had succeeded Sharmila Tagore.

The board, headquartered in Mumbai, has nine regional offices:

- Bangalore
- Chennai
- Cuttack
- Guwahati
- Hyderabad
- Kolkata
- Mumbai
- New Delhi
- Trivandrum

Controversies

The board has been associated with a number of scandals. Film producers reportedly bribe the CBFC to obtain a UA certificate, which entitles them to a 30-percent reduction in entertainment tax.

In 2002, *War and Peace* (a documentary film by Anand Patwardhan which depicted nuclear weapons testing and the September 11 attacks) was edited 21 times before the film was approved for release. According to Patwardhan, "The cuts that [the Board] asked for are so ridiculous that they won't hold up in court. But if these cuts do make it, it will be the end of freedom of expression in the Indian media." A court ruled that the cut requirement was unconstitutional, and the film was shown uncensored.

That year, Indian filmmaker and CBFC chair Vijay Anand proposed legalising the exhibition of X-rated films in selected cinemas. Anand said, "Porn is shown everywhere in India clandestinely ... and the best way to fight this onslaught of blue movies is to show them openly in theatres with legally authorised licences". Anand resigned less than a year after becoming chairperson in the wake of his proposal.

The board refused to certify *Gulabi Aaina* (a film about Indian transsexuals produced and directed by Sridhar Rangayan) in 2003; Rangayan unsuccessfully appealed the decision twice. Although the film is banned in India, it has been screened in the UK.

Final Solution, a 2004 documentary examining religious riots between Hindus and Muslims in Gujarat which killed over 1,000 people, was also banned. According to the board, the film was "highly provocative and may trigger off unrest and communal violence". After a sustained campaign, the ban was lifted in October of that year.

The CBFC demanded five cuts from the 2011 American film, *The Girl with the Dragon Tattoo*, because of nudity and rape scenes. The producers and the director, David Fincher, eventually decided not to release the film in India.

CEO Rakesh Kumar was arrested in August 2014 for accepting bribes to expedite the issuance of certificates. The board demanded four cuts (three visual and one audio) from the 2015 Malayalam film, *Chaayam Poosiya Veedu*) (directed by brothers Santosh Babusenan and Satish Babusenan), because of nude scenes. The directors refused to make the changes, and the film was not certified.

CBFC chair Leela Samson resigned in protest of political interference in the board's work in 2015 after its decision to refuse certification of the film, *MSG: The Messenger*, was overturned by an appellate tribunal. Samson was replaced by Pahlaj Nihalani, whose Bharatiya Janata Party affiliation triggered a wave of additional board resignations. The board was criticised for ordering the screen time of two kissing scenes in the James Bond film *Spectre* (2015) to be cut by half for release.

Udta Punjab (2016), co-produced by Anurag Kashyap and Ekta Kapoor, inspired a list of 94 cuts and 13 pointers (including an order to remove Punjabi city names). The film was approved for release with one cut and disclaimers by the Bombay High Court. A copy of the film was leaked online, with evidence indicating possible CBFC involvement. Kashyap posted on Facebook that although he did not object to free downloads, he hoped that viewers would pay for the film. In August 2017, days after his removal as CBFC chair, Nihalani said in an interview that he had received instructions from the Ministry of Information and Broadcasting to block the release of this film and at least one other.

Lipstick Under My Burkha (2017), directed by Alankrita Shrivastava and produced by Prakash Jha, was originally denied certification. The film, which had been screened at international film festivals, was eligible for the Golden Globe Awards. The filmmakers appealed to the board's Film Certification Appellate Tribunal (FCAT), which authorised its release. The FCAT requested some cuts (primarily to sex scenes), and the film was released with an A certificate. Shrivastava said, "Of course I would have loved no cuts, but the FCAT has been very fair and clear. I feel that we will be able to release the film without hampering the narrative or diluting its essence."

Film Censorship

Film censorship in India is governed by the Cinematograph Act of 1952, which provides the legal framework for the certification and regulation of films exhibited in India. The Central Board of Film Certification (CBFC) is the statutory body responsible for certifying films for public exhibition.

Key aspects of film censorship in India include:

- Certification Categories:The CBFC classifies films into various categories based on their content and suitability for different audiences. The categories are:
  - U (Universal) - Suitable for all age groups.
  - UA (Parental Guidance) - Suitable for children above 12 years, or with parental guidance.
  - A (Adult) - Restricted to adult audiences (18 years and above).
  - S (Special) - Restricted to specialized audiences, such as doctors or scientists.
- Film Certification Process: Producers are required to submit their films to the CBFC for certification before public exhibition. A panel of members appointed by the government evaluates the film and assigns an appropriate certification.
- Censorship Guidelines: The CBFC follows guidelines laid down in the Cinematograph Act to assess the content of films. These guidelines cover various aspects, including scenes of violence, sexual content, nudity, language, and other sensitive themes.
- Cuts and Modifications: The CBFC has the authority to suggest or mandate cuts or modifications to a film if it deems certain scenes or content to be inappropriate or in violation of guidelines.
- Reasons for Certification: The CBFC provides a certification along with a list of specific reasons justifying the certification. These reasons may include references to violence, sexual content, language, or any other potentially objectionable content.
- Revisiting Certifications: Filmmakers have the option to appeal to the Film Certification Appellate Tribunal (FCAT) if they are dissatisfied with the certification given by the CBFC. However, as of 2021, the FCAT has been abolished, and appeals are made directly to the courts.
- Controversies and Challenges: Film censorship in India has been a subject of controversy and debate. Filmmakers often raise concerns about creative freedom and artistic expression, while certain sections of society advocate for stricter censorship in line with cultural or moral values.

- Online Streaming Platforms: With the rise of digital platforms, there have been discussions about the regulation and certification of content released on platforms like Netflix, Amazon Prime, and others. As of now, there is no specific regulatory framework for digital content, but discussions on this topic continue.
- Regional Censor Boards: In addition to the Central Board of Film Certification, there are regional censor boards in states and union territories of India. These boards certify films in their respective regions, and their decisions may be subject to review by the CBFC.

Advertising Standards and Regulatory Bodies

In India, advertising standards and regulatory bodies play a crucial role in ensuring that advertisements are truthful, fair, and do not mislead or harm consumers. The primary regulatory body overseeing advertising in India is the Advertising Standards Council of India (ASCI). Here are some key aspects of advertising standards and the regulatory framework in India:

- Advertising Standards Council of India (ASCI): ASCI is a self-regulatory body established in 1985. It is a non-profit organization that aims to maintain and enhance the public's confidence in advertising. ASCI sets and enforces advertising standards through a voluntary code of self-regulation.
- ASCI Code for Self-Regulation in Advertising: The ASCI Code outlines the fundamental principles that advertisements must adhere to. It covers areas such as truthfulness and honesty, fairness, non-exploitation, and social responsibility. Advertisers and agencies are encouraged to voluntarily comply with the ASCI Code.
- Role of ASCI: ASCI evaluates complaints against advertisements received from consumers, industry, and other stakeholders. If an advertisement is found to be in violation of the ASCI Code, the advertiser is advised to modify or withdraw the advertisement.
- Advisory on Misleading Advertisements: ASCI issues advisory notes on various advertising practices to provide guidance to advertisers and agencies. These advisories cover topics like celebrity endorsements, comparative advertising, and use of disclaimers.
- ASCI National Advertising Monitoring Service (NAMS): NAMS is a service provided by ASCI to monitor and track advertisements across various media channels. It helps in identifying potential violations of advertising standards.
- Consumer Complaints Against Advertisements: Consumers can file complaints against advertisements they find objectionable or misleading. ASCI reviews these complaints and takes appropriate action, which may include advising the advertiser to modify or withdraw the advertisement.

- Collaboration with Government Bodies: ASCI collaborates with government bodies, such as the Ministry of Information and Broadcasting, to promote responsible advertising practices. It also participates in discussions related to advertising standards and regulations.
- Collaboration with Industry Stakeholders: ASCI works with industry associations, advertisers, advertising agencies, media houses, and other stakeholders to promote responsible advertising practices and uphold ethical standards.
- Compliance Reports and Monitoring: Advertisers are encouraged to submit compliance reports to ASCI after making modifications to their advertisements based on ASCI's recommendations. This helps in tracking and ensuring compliance with advertising standards.
- Public Awareness and Education: ASCI conducts workshops, seminars, and awareness campaigns to educate stakeholders, including advertisers, agencies, and consumers, about responsible advertising practices and the ASCI Code.

7

Regulatory Bodies and Guidelines

Press Council Act and Press Council of India

The Press Council Act, 1978 is an Act of the Parliament of India that established the Press Council of India (PCI), a statutory quasi-judicial body to serve as a watchdog of the press in India. The Act was enacted to preserve the freedom of the press and to maintain and improve the standards of newspapers and news agencies in India.

Objectives of the Press Council of India

The objectives of the Press Council of India, as stated in Section 13 of the Press Council Act, 1978, are to:

- Preserve the freedom of the press.
- Maintain and improve the standards of newspapers and news agencies in India.
- Develop a code of conduct for newspapers and news agencies.
- Ensure that the press remains an instrument of public service.

Functions of the Press Council of India

The Press Council of India has a wide range of functions, including:

- Hearing complaints against the press from individuals, organizations, or the government.
- Investigating cases of misconduct by the press.
- Advising the government on matters relating to the press.
- Promoting research and training in journalism.

- Organizing seminars and conferences on press-related issues.
- Publishing an annual report on the state of the press in India.

Composition of the Press Council of India

The Press Council of India consists of a chairman and 28 other members. The chairman is appointed by the President of India on the recommendation of a committee consisting of the Prime Minister, the Speaker of the Lok Sabha, and the Chief Justice of India. The other members are appointed by the chairman from among journalists, editors, publishers, and other persons with knowledge and experience in the field of journalism or mass communication.

Powers of the Press Council of India

The Press Council of India has the power to:

- Summon and examine witnesses.
- Compel the production of documents.
- Issue warnings or reprimands to newspapers and news agencies.
- Hold newspapers and news agencies in contempt.
- Recommend to the government the withdrawal of government advertising from newspapers and news agencies that repeatedly violate the code of conduct.

Impact of the Press Council of India

The Press Council of India has played a significant role in upholding the freedom of the press and maintaining the standards of journalism in India. It has investigated numerous cases of misconduct by the press and has issued warnings and reprimands to newspapers and news agencies. It has also played a role in promoting self-regulation within the press.

Ministry of Information and Broadcasting Guidelines

The Ministry of Information and Broadcasting (MIB) in India is responsible for formulating and implementing policies, guidelines, and regulations related to media, broadcasting, film, advertising, and communication. These guidelines are designed to ensure that content disseminated through various media platforms adheres to specific standards and aligns with the values and interests of the nation. Here are some of the key guidelines issued by the Ministry of Information and Broadcasting in India:

- Content Regulation on Television: The MIB issues guidelines for television broadcasters to regulate the content aired on television channels. These guidelines cover aspects such as program content, advertising standards, telecast of sensitive material, and adherence to the Cable Television Networks (Regulation) Act.

- Content Regulation on Radio: The MIB regulates the content broadcasted on radio channels, including FM and AM stations. It issues guidelines to ensure that radio programs adhere to cultural, ethical, and legal standards. These guidelines cover areas such as program content, advertising, and compliance with the All India Radio (Broadcasting Code).
- Film Certification: The Central Board of Film Certification (CBFC), under the jurisdiction of the MIB, certifies films for public exhibition. The MIB issues guidelines and regulations to govern the certification process, including categorization of films (U, UA, A, S), advisory notes, and modifications/cuts if necessary.
- Advertising Standards: The MIB collaborates with the Advertising Standards Council of India (ASCI) and issues guidelines to promote ethical advertising practices. These guidelines aim to ensure that advertisements do not mislead or harm consumers and adhere to the principles of truthfulness and fairness.
- Online Content Regulation: The MIB has begun addressing the regulation of online streaming platforms and digital content. It has proposed guidelines for digital media platforms to establish mechanisms for self-regulation, including provisions related to content classification, parental controls, and grievance redressal.
- Policy on FDI in Broadcasting Sector: The MIB issues guidelines and policies related to Foreign Direct Investment (FDI) in the broadcasting sector. These guidelines dictate the limits and conditions under which foreign investment is allowed in various segments of the broadcasting industry.
- Community Radio Guidelines: The MIB issues guidelines for the establishment and operation of community radio stations. These guidelines are designed to promote local content, community engagement, and ensure that the stations operate within the framework of societal and cultural norms.
- Guidelines for Government Advertising: The MIB issues guidelines for the allocation and expenditure of government funds for advertising and publicity campaigns. These guidelines aim to ensure transparency, accountability, and ethical practices in government-sponsored advertisements.
- Guidelines for Accreditation of Journalists: The MIB has issued guidelines for the accreditation of journalists, which include eligibility criteria, rights and privileges of accredited journalists, and the process for obtaining and renewing accreditation.

Role of Professional Organizations in Media Ethics

Professional organizations play a crucial role in upholding media ethics and ensuring responsible journalism practices. They establish and enforce ethical standards, provide guidance to media professionals, and advocate for ethical practices within the industry.

- Establishing Ethical Standards: Professional organizations develop and promulgate codes of ethics that outline the principles and guidelines that media professionals should adhere to. These codes typically address issues such as accuracy, fairness, objectivity, respect for privacy, and avoidance of conflict of interest. They serve as a benchmark for ethical conduct and provide a framework for decision-making in various journalistic situations.
- Enforcing Ethical Standards: Professional organizations have mechanisms to investigate complaints against media professionals and hold them accountable for violations of ethical standards. They may issue reprimands, suspensions, or even expulsion from the organization for serious transgressions. This enforcement process helps to maintain the credibility and integrity of the media industry.
- Providing Guidance and Education: Professional organizations offer training programs, workshops, and seminars to educate media professionals on ethical issues and best practices. They also provide resources and support to help journalists navigate complex ethical dilemmas. This ongoing education helps to enhance the ethical awareness and decision-making skills of media practitioners.
- Promoting Ethical Practices: Professional organizations advocate for ethical practices within the media industry and promote public understanding of the importance of ethical journalism. They may engage with media outlets, government bodies, and civil society groups to raise awareness of ethical issues and promote reforms. This advocacy helps to create an environment that supports and encourages ethical journalism.
- Encouraging Self-Regulation: Professional organizations encourage self-regulation within the media industry, recognizing the importance of maintaining journalistic independence while upholding ethical standards. They support initiatives that foster self-reflection and peer review within media organizations, promoting a culture of ethical responsibility among journalists.
- Promoting Diversity and Inclusion: Professional organizations advocate for diversity and inclusion in media coverage and representation. They encourage media professionals to be mindful of cultural sensitivities, avoid stereotypes and biases, and ensure that diverse voices are heard in the media. This promotes fairness and representation in media content.
- Protecting Press Freedom: Professional organizations defend press freedom and advocate for journalists' rights to gather and disseminate information without undue interference. They challenge attempts to restrict press freedom and protect journalists from harassment, intimidation, or violence. This safeguards the essential role of the press in informing the public and holding power to account.

- Promoting Transparency and Accountability: Professional organizations encourage transparency and accountability within the media industry. They advocate for open communication between journalists and their audiences, and they support mechanisms for journalists to address complaints and correct errors. This transparency fosters trust and credibility in the media.
- Encouraging Public Engagement: Professional organizations encourage public engagement in discussions about media ethics and standards. They promote media literacy initiatives and foster dialogue between journalists and the public to enhance understanding and trust in the media. This public engagement helps to strengthen the relationship between the media and the communities they serve.
- Adapting to Evolving Technologies: Professional organizations recognize the impact of new technologies on media practices and ethical considerations. They adapt their codes of ethics and guidance to address emerging issues such as online privacy, artificial intelligence, and social media manipulation. This adaptability helps to ensure that ethical principles remain relevant and applicable in the ever-changing media landscape.

Adversarial Role of Media and Human Rights Considerations

The adversarial role of media in relation to human rights is a complex and nuanced topic. On one hand, a robust and independent media is essential for safeguarding human rights, as it acts as a watchdog, exposes abuses, and holds those in power accountable. On the other hand, there can be instances where the media's pursuit of a story may conflict with certain human rights considerations, such as privacy, dignity, and protection of vulnerable individuals.

- Freedom of Expression and Information: Freedom of expression and access to information are fundamental human rights. A free and independent media plays a crucial role in upholding these rights by providing a platform for diverse voices, enabling the dissemination of information, and facilitating public discourse.
- Accountability and Transparency: The media serves as a check on power by scrutinizing the actions of governments, institutions, and individuals. Investigative journalism can expose corruption, human rights abuses, and other wrongdoings, leading to increased accountability.
- Right to Privacy and Dignity: There can be instances where the media's pursuit of a story may infringe upon an individual's right to privacy and dignity. Balancing the public interest in a story with the need to protect an individual's personal information is a crucial ethical consideration.
- Sensitivity to Vulnerable Groups: Media outlets should exercise care and sensitivity when reporting on issues involving vulnerable groups such as

children, victims of sexual assault, refugees, and marginalized communities. Upholding their dignity and protecting them from further harm is a paramount concern.

- Avoiding Sensationalism and Stereotyping: Media organizations should strive to avoid sensationalizing stories or perpetuating harmful stereotypes. Responsible reporting requires a commitment to accuracy, fairness, and balanced representation.
- Ethical Considerations in Reporting: Adhering to a code of ethics, such as the Society of Professional Journalists' Code of Ethics, is crucial. This includes verifying information, minimizing harm, and acting independently and transparently.
- Legal Framework and Press Freedom: A robust legal framework that protects press freedom is essential. Laws and regulations should be crafted to balance the need for free expression with the protection of human rights, ensuring that media organizations can operate independently and without undue interference.
- Self-Regulation and Accountability: Media organizations should engage in self-regulation and hold themselves accountable for the content they produce. This can be facilitated through internal editorial standards, ombudsman offices, or adherence to industry codes of conduct.
- Social Responsibility of Media: The media has a social responsibility to act in the public interest, promote diversity of voices, and contribute to a well-informed citizenry. This involves a commitment to accuracy, fairness, and responsible reporting.

Conclusion

The media plays a pivotal role in shaping public discourse, influencing societal norms, and holding power accountable. In India, the media operates within a complex legal and ethical framework that aims to balance the fundamental right to freedom of expression with the need to protect individual rights, maintain public order, and uphold ethical standards. Understanding this framework is crucial for media professionals, legal practitioners, and informed citizens alike.

Legal Framework: A Balancing Act between Rights and Responsibilities

The Indian Constitution, the supreme law of the land, enshrines freedom of speech and expression as a fundamental right under Article 19(1)(a). This right extends to the press, enabling it to function independently and inform the public without undue government interference.

However, this right is not absolute. Reasonable restrictions can be imposed in the interest of public order, morality, decency, or to protect the reputation or rights of others. These restrictions are enshrined in various laws, including:

- The Press Council Act, 1978: Establishes the Press Council of India, a quasi-judicial body that oversees the press and promotes ethical standards.
- The Indian Penal Code, 1860: Defines and penalizes offenses such as defamation, sedition, and inciting violence, which may arise in the context of media coverage.
- The Information Technology Act, 2000: Regulates online content and intermediaries, addressing issues such as cybercrime, obscenity, and hate speech.
- The Cable Television Networks (Regulation) Act, 1995: Regulates the content and operation of cable television networks.

Ethical Framework: Upholding Standards and Building Trust

In addition to legal constraints, media professionals are also bound by ethical principles that guide their conduct and ensure responsible journalism practices. These principles are often codified in the codes of ethics of various media organizations and professional bodies.

Key ethical principles include:

- Accuracy: Reporting facts truthfully and avoiding misinformation or disinformation.
- Fairness: Presenting all sides of an issue impartially and avoiding bias or prejudice.
- Objectivity: Striving for neutrality and avoiding personal opinions or agendas.
- Respect for Privacy: Protecting the privacy of individuals, especially in sensitive matters.
- Avoiding Conflict of Interest: Disclosing any personal or financial interests that may influence reporting.
- Accountability: Taking responsibility for errors and correcting them promptly.

Challenges and Opportunities in the Digital Age

The advent of the digital age has brought about significant challenges and opportunities for media laws and ethics in India. The rapid growth of online media, social media, and mobile platforms has expanded the reach of information and transformed the way news is consumed. However, this has also blurred traditional boundaries between media and non-media actors, amplified the spread of misinformation, and raised concerns about privacy and data protection.

In response to these challenges, there is a growing need for:

- Clarity in Online Content Regulation: Clearer guidelines and regulations for online content intermediaries to effectively address issues such as hate speech, fake news, and online harassment.
- Data Protection and Privacy: Strengthening data protection laws and enhancing user privacy protections in the digital realm.
- Media Literacy and Ethical Education: Promoting media literacy among the public to enable critical evaluation of information sources and fostering ethical awareness among media professionals.
- Self-Regulation and Collaboration: Encouraging self-regulation within the media industry and fostering collaboration between media organizations, civil society groups, and the government to address emerging ethical challenges in the digital age.

Final Thought: A Continuous Process of Evolution

The interplay of media laws and ethics in India is a dynamic and evolving field, constantly adapting to new technologies, societal changes, and legal developments. Understanding this framework is essential for media professionals to operate responsibly, for legal practitioners to provide sound counsel, and for informed citizens to engage critically with the media landscape. By upholding ethical principles, adhering to legal boundaries, and adapting to the changing media environment, we can ensure that the media fulfills its crucial role in informing, empowering, and holding power accountable in a democratic society.

Importance of Media Laws and Ethics in a Democratic Society

Media laws and ethics form the cornerstone of a healthy, functioning democracy. They provide the framework within which the media operates, ensuring that it serves the public interest, upholds democratic values, and respects individual rights. In a democratic society, where the free flow of information is crucial, media laws and ethics play a pivotal role in safeguarding the rights of both journalists and the public. This stage will delve into the multifaceted importance of media laws and ethics, exploring how they foster accountability, protect fundamental rights, and contribute to a robust democratic environment.

Safeguarding Freedom of Expression

One of the fundamental tenets of a democratic society is the right to freedom of expression. Media laws provide the legal framework that protects this right, allowing journalists to report, investigate, and disseminate information without fear of censorship or reprisal. This freedom is essential for holding those in power accountable, as it enables journalists to act as watchdogs, uncovering wrongdoing and exposing corruption. Without robust media laws, the ability of journalists to act as the Fourth Estate, scrutinizing the actions of the government and other powerful entities, would be compromised.

Ensuring Transparency and Accountability

Media laws establish mechanisms for transparency and accountability in the media industry. They outline ethical guidelines and standards that journalists and media organizations must adhere to, preventing the dissemination of false or misleading information. These laws also provide avenues for redress in cases of defamation, libel, or other forms of harm caused by irresponsible journalism. By holding media outlets accountable for their reporting, media laws maintain public trust in the information disseminated and reinforce the credibility of the media as a whole.

Protecting Individual Rights and Dignity

While freedom of expression is paramount, it is not absolute. Media laws strike a delicate balance between the right to express and the protection of individual rights and dignity. They establish boundaries that prevent the media from infringing on an individual's privacy, engaging in character assassination, or sensationalizing sensitive issues. This protection is particularly crucial for vulnerable groups, ensuring that they are not unfairly targeted or marginalized by media coverage.

Fostering Diversity of Voices

A democratic society thrives on the diversity of voices and perspectives. Media laws work to prevent monopolization of the media industry, promoting a pluralistic media landscape where a range of opinions and viewpoints can be heard. They may include regulations that prevent undue concentration of media ownership or provisions that promote access to media platforms for marginalized or underrepresented communities. This diversity is essential for a vibrant democracy, as it ensures that a wide array of perspectives is available to the public.

Enhancing Public Discourse and Informed Citizenship

In a democratic society, an informed citizenry is crucial for meaningful participation in the democratic process. Media laws and ethics contribute to this by ensuring that information presented to the public is accurate, unbiased, and relevant. They discourage the spread of misinformation or propaganda, enabling citizens to make informed decisions about their government, society, and community. A well-informed public is better equipped to engage in constructive public discourse and hold their representatives accountable.

Final Thought

Media laws and ethics are indispensable pillars of a thriving democratic society. They protect the freedom of expression, ensure accountability, safeguard individual rights, and promote a diverse and inclusive media landscape. By upholding these principles, media laws contribute to an informed and engaged citizenry, fostering a robust democratic environment. It is imperative that societies continue to uphold and strengthen these laws to preserve the integrity and vitality of their democratic institutions.

Glossary

- Censorship: The suppression or restriction of information, media content, or speech by a government, authority, or regulatory body. It can infringe on freedom of expression and is a subject of ethical and legal debate.
- Conflict of Interest: A situation in which a person or organization has competing interests or loyalties that could potentially compromise their professional judgment or decision-making. In journalism, it refers to situations where a journalist's personal interests may influence their reporting.
- Copyright Law: The legal framework that grants creators exclusive rights to their original works, allowing them to control the reproduction, distribution, and public display of their content. It applies to various forms of media, including written works, music, art, and audiovisual productions.
- Defamation: The communication of false statements that harm the reputation of an individual or entity. It includes both libel (written or printed defamation) and slander (spoken defamation).
- Fair Use: A legal doctrine that allows limited use of copyrighted material without permission from the copyright holder. It is typically applicable for purposes such as criticism, comment, news reporting, teaching, scholarship, and research.
- Freedom of Expression: The right to express one's opinions, ideas, and information freely without government interference or censorship. It is a fundamental human right and a cornerstone of democratic societies.
- Intellectual Property: Creations of the mind, such as inventions, literary and artistic works, designs, symbols, names, and images, that are protected by intellectual property rights, including copyrights, trademarks, and patents.
- Media Ethics: The moral principles and values that guide the conduct of media

professionals and organizations. It includes considerations of truthfulness, accuracy, fairness, objectivity, and accountability in reporting.

- Media Law: The body of laws and regulations that govern the functioning, rights, and responsibilities of media organizations, journalists, and content creators. It encompasses areas such as freedom of expression, defamation, privacy, copyright, and regulation of media industries.
- Media Literacy: The ability to access, critically evaluate, and create media content. It includes understanding media's role in society, discerning reliable sources, and being aware of ethical considerations in media consumption.
- Plagiarism: The act of using someone else's work, ideas, or intellectual property without proper attribution or permission, presenting it as one's own. It is considered unethical and can lead to legal consequences.
- Press Council: An independent regulatory body or council established to oversee and uphold ethical standards in journalism. It may have the authority to receive complaints, investigate issues, and adjudicate disputes related to media practices.
- Privacy Law: The legal framework that protects an individual's right to privacy from intrusion, disclosure of private information, and other forms of unwarranted surveillance or interference.
- Public Interest: The general welfare and well-being of the public, often considered as a justification for government intervention, policies, or actions. In media, it refers to reporting that serves the greater good and informs the public about matters of importance.
- Source Confidentiality: The ethical principle that protects the identity of sources who provide information to journalists under a promise of anonymity. It is crucial for fostering trust and ensuring the free flow of information.

References

- Communication Law: Practical Applications in the Digital Age by Dom Caristi and William R. Davie (Publisher: Routledge, Year: 2019)
- Communications Law: Liberties, Restraints, and the Modern Media by John D. Zelezny (Publisher: Cengage Learning, Year: 2019)
- Comparative Media Law and Ethics edited by Tim Crook (Publisher: Routledge, Year: 2018)
- Ethics for Journalists by Richard Keeble and Sharon Wheeler (Publisher: Routledge, Year: 2018)
- Free Expression, Globalism, and the New Strategic Communication edited by Monroe E. Price and Susan Dente Ross (Publisher: Cambridge University Press, Year: 2020)
- Global Journalism Ethics: Widening the Conceptual Base edited by Stephen J. A. Ward and Herman Wasserman (Publisher: Routledge, Year: 2018)
- Global Media Ethics: Problems and Perspectives edited by Stephen J. A. Ward (Publisher: Wiley-Blackwell, Year: 2013)
- Handbook of Research on Media Literacy in Higher Education Environments edited by Serpil Meri-Yilan (Publisher: IGI Global, Year: 2019)
- Handbook of Research on Media Literacy Research and Applications Across Disciplines edited by Serpil Meri-Yilan (Publisher: IGI Global, Year: 2020)
- Journalism Ethics at the Crossroads: Democracy or Disarray? edited by Patrick Lee Plaisance (Publisher: Routledge, Year: 2018)
- Law and Ethics for Today's Journalist: A Concise Guide by Joe Mathewson (Publisher: Routledge, Year: 2018)

References

- Mass Media Law by Don Pember and Clay Calvert (Publisher: McGraw-Hill Education, Year: 2020)
- Media and Law Enforcement: A View from the Street by Raymond Surette (Publisher: SAGE Publications Inc, Year: 2020)
- Media Ethics and Accountability Systems by Charles Brown (Publisher: Routledge, Year: 2020)
- Media Ethics Goes to the Movies: Journalism and Journalism Education in a Pop Culture World by Howard Good (Publisher: Routledge, Year: 2018)
- Media Ethics: Cases and Issues by Philip Patterson and Lee Wilkins (Publisher: McGraw-Hill Education, Year: 2020)
- Media Ethics: Cases and Moral Reasoning by Clifford G. Christians, Mark Fackler, Kathy Brittain Richardson, Peggy J. Kreshel (Publisher: Routledge, Year: 2018)
- Media Law and Ethics by Roy L. Moore (Publisher: Routledge, Year: 2020)
- Media Law and Ethics in the 21st Century: Protecting Free Expression and Curbing Abuses by Julian A. Parrott (Publisher: Wiley-Blackwell, Year: 2019)
- Media Law and Ethics in the Digital Age: Protecting Free Expression and Curbing Abuses by Gideon Balogun (Publisher: Routledge, Year: 2020)
- Media Law and Policy in the Internet Age by Doreen Weisenhaus and Simon N. M. Young (Publisher: Hart Publishing, Year: 2017)
- Media Law for Canadian Journalists by Dean Jobb (Publisher: Emond Publishing, Year: 2020)
- Media Law for Canadian Journalists by Dean Jobb (Publisher: Emond Publishing, Year: 2019)
- Media Law for Journalists by Ursula Smartt (Publisher: SAGE Publications Ltd, Year: 2020)
- Media Law in New Zealand edited by Ursula Cheer (Publisher: LexisNexis New Zealand, Year: 2020)
- Media Law: A Practical Guide by Ashley Hurst and Kuhan Milroy (Publisher: Oxford University Press, Year: 2019)
- Media Law: A User's Guide for Film and Programme Makers by Ashley Hurst and Lucy Adams (Publisher: Bloomsbury Professional, Year: 2020)
- Privacy in the Digital Age: 21st-Century Challenges to the Fourth Amendment by Jon M. Garon (Publisher: ABC-CLIO, Year: 2019)
- Social Media and Journalism: Developments, Interactions and Enrichments edited by Shuang Liu and David H. Weaver (Publisher: Routledge, Year: 2020)

- The Handbook of Global Media and Communication Policy edited by Robin Mansell and Marc Raboy (Publisher: Wiley-Blackwell, Year: 2011)
- The Oxford Handbook of International Human Rights Law edited by Dinah Shelton (Publisher: Oxford University Press, Year: 2013)

Index

R

U